ASSESSMENT AND TREATMENT OF DEPRESSION IN CHILDREN AND ADOLESCENTS

ASSESSMENT AND TREATMENT OF DEPRESSION IN CHILDREN AND ADOLESCENTS
(Second Edition)

Harvey F. Clarizio
Michigan State University

CLINICAL PSYCHOLOGY PUBLISHING CO., INC.
4 CONANT SQUARE
BRANDON, VT 05733

Copyright © 1989, 1994 by Clinical Psychology Publishing Company, Inc., Brandon, Vermont. Second edition 1994.

All rights reserved. No portion of this book may be reproduced in any form, by photostat, microfilm, retrieval system, or by any means now known or later devised, without prior written permission of the publisher. Permission is not necessary for brief passages embodied in critical reviews and articles.

Library of Congress Catalog Card Number: 93-71833
ISBN: 0-88422-103-2

   4 Conant Square
Brandon, Vermont 05733

Cover design: Sue Thomas

Printed in the United States of America.

TABLE OF CONTENTS

Preface ix
1. Introduction 1
    Definitional Issues: Five Schools of Thought 2
    Differentiation from Normality 7
    Differentiation from Related Diagnoses 8
    Classification Systems 16
    Prevalence 28
    Etiology 31
    Summary 39
2. A Developmental Approach 49
    Normal Development and Childhood Depression 50
    Developmental Trends in Depressive Symptomatology 54
    Age Trends in Prevalence Figures 58
    Gender Differences 60
    Continuity 63
    Summary 78
3. Diagnosis and Assessment 85
    Levels of Diagnosis 85
    Assessment Techniques 87
    Multistage Model 117
    Additional Diagnostic Concerns 119
    Guidelines for Assessment 125
    Summary 127

4. Treatment of Childhood Depression 135
   Psychoanalytic Approaches 137
   Behavioral and Social Skills Approaches 138
   Cognitive Approaches 150
   Drug Therapy 170
   Family Therapy 176
   Multimodal Therapy 179
   Implications for Practice 181
   Summary 184
5. Suicide in School-Aged Youth 195
   Prevalence 197
   Identification and Prediction of Youth at Risk 200
   Assessing the Suicidal Adolescent 211
   Treatment 213
   Strategies for Prevention 223
   Summary 239

LIST OF TABLES

1.1	Differentiation of Childhood Depression from Related Conditions	9
1.2	Differentiating Features of Anxiety and Depression	14
1.3	*DSM-III-R* Classification of Mood Disorder	17
1.4	*DSM-III-R* Criteria for Major Depressive Episode	18
1.5	*DSM-III-R* Criteria for Dysthymia	20
1.6	Weinberg Criteria for Childhood Depression	24
2.1	Developmental Changes in Depressive Symptomatology	59
2.2	Advantages and Disadvantages of Research Designs Used in Continuity Studies	65
3.1	CBCL-NUR Items	98
3.2	Symptoms Checklist for Major Depressive Disorders	105
3.3	Characteristics and Content of Interviews	112
4.1	The Children's Reinforcement Survey Schedule: Sample Items	141
4.2	Adolescent Activities Checklist: Sample Items	142
4.3	Sequencing of Treatment Program	147
4.4	The Cognitive Triad Inventory for Children	153
4.5	Using RET with Depressed Children	161
4.6	Self-Control Therapy	168
4.7	Common Psychopharmacologic Medications Used with Depressed Children or Adolescents	172
4.8	Strategies for Dealing with Depressive Behaviors	185

LIST OF TABLES

5.1	Indicators of Suicidal Risk	201
5.2	Selected Characteristics of Suicide Completers Versus Attempters	202
5.3	Interview Questions for Children and Parents	214
5.4	Ground Rules for Family Meetings	216
5.5	Phases, Goals, and Selected Interventions in Individual Psychotherapy with Suicidal Youth	218
5.6	Components of Crisis Intervention for Suicide Attempters	220
5.7	No-Suicide Contract	222
5.8	Preventive Steps	229

PREFACE

The topic of childhood depression has undergone rapid and significant changes in the course of a few decades. Mental health specialists initially overlooked this condition, later argued against its existence, then recommended universal acceptance of it as a separate clinical entity very similar in nature to adult depression. Most recently they have expressed concern over the impact of the child's cognitive, linguistic, and socioemotional development capabilities on depressive symptomatology and treatment. Despite signs of increasing agreement among mental health professionals, controversy continues unabated over developmental, diagnostic, and intervention issues. Although the research base is indeed sketchy, the number of empirical studies is expanding appreciably, and answers to many of the currently perplexing questions should be forthcoming in the next decade.

This introductory text is written for practitioners as well as for advanced undergraduates or graduate students who are preparing to become psychologists, social workers, counselors, or special education teachers working with affectively disturbed children and youth. No attempt has been made to present a consistent theoretical framework. Instead, major attention has been devoted to those promising viewpoints currently popular among mental health specialists. Although examining the interactional contributions of biological and social forces to affective disorders, the focus is clearly on psychological factors thought to be operative in depression and suicide among young people. The most distinctive features of the book are its research base, its developmental orientation, and its practitioner emphasis.

Many people have contributed in various ways to the development of the book. I would like to thank Marjory Hoffman for her skillful preparation and careful proofreading of the manuscript. I am especially grateful to the anonymous reviewers for their thorough and insightful reviews of the manuscript.

INTRODUCTION

Harold: Major Depression

Harold was referred for clinical evaluation at age 8 following a year of behavioral difficulties. He disliked school, was very shy, and had few buddies. He was afraid of new situations and was frequently moody and quiet. The mother's side of the family had a strong history of depression including four suicides and two other members with periodic depressions. Between 8 and 12 years of age, Harold did better in his social functioning and school accomplishments. At age 12, however, he again became depressed, and his dislike of school became more intense. It was difficult to pinpoint the duration of his acute symptoms, but they probably did not exceed several months. At age 17, he was well mannered and shy and rarely smiled. He reported that he could slip into an unhappy mood for no apparent reason. On these occasions, he would be irritable and fatigued and would avoid people. His mother stated, "He is not happy, but he is easy to live with." He was afflicted with recurrent depressions throughout the later adolescent years. At age 22, he still appeared quiet, serious, and thoughtful. He saw himself as vulnerable to stress and social conflicts, particularly with women. He had three disappointing love affairs and was unsure of himself sexually. Although he earned some money mopping floors, his mother provided most of his support. He likes to practice music most of the day. He describes his existence as going from slow deadness to acute crises. At one time, he wished to die, slept excessively, and was very withdrawn socially. His dysphoria, loss of interest in usual activities, fatigue, feeling of worthlessness, and diminished ability to think and concentrate, qualify him for the diagnosis of major depression.

Note. From "Depression in Childhood and Adolescence" by S. Chess, A. Thomas, and M. Hassibi, 1983, *The Journal of Nervous and Mental Disease, 171,* pp. 411-420.

This chapter covers a number of significant concerns in the field of childhood and adolescent depression. First, controversies surrounding the definition of this condition are examined. Then, adult and child-oriented classification systems are examined. Next, figures are presented regarding the prevalence of depressive problems showing the demographic factors that place one at risk for this disorder. Finally, theories of causation are presented within an interactional framework.

DEFINITIONAL ISSUES: FIVE SCHOOLS OF THOUGHT

In a relatively short time, childhood depression has gone from being essentially overlooked, to having its existence challenged and denied, to being accepted as a distinct clinical syndrome whose defining characteristics are isomorphic with its adult counterpart (Carlson & Garber, 1986). Case studies on childhood depression appeared early in the 20th century (e.g., Bleuler, 1934; de Saussure, 1947). Pioneering works called attention to the role of separation and attachment disorders in depressive symptomatology in children (Bowlby, 1973; Freud & Burlingham, 1944; Spitz, 1946), but it was not until the journal *The Nervous Child* devoted a special issue to manic-depressive illness in 1952 that depression among pre-adolescents attracted much professional attention. Despite this widespread interest, even today, childhood depression is not listed in the "childhood" section in the third revision of the *Diagnostic and Statistical Manual of Mental Disorders* (American Psychiatric Association, 1987), although special criteria for children are included in its discussion of mood disorders.

As with any syndrome, the first task is to identify the core clinical picture. This has not proved to be an easy task. Rather, there is considerable disagreement and controversy surrounding essential versus associated features. Five schools of thought are identifiable in the literature, some of which are more current than others.

Advocates of the first school of thought question whether a clinical syndrome of depression exists in children. *Psychoanalytically oriented theorists* held that major depression as we know it in adults cannot exist in prepubertal youngsters because they lacked a well-developed, internalized superego at that stage of development. Although clinical observation contradicted psychoanalytic theory, this notion continued to dominate psychodynamic perspectives on childhood mood disorders (Garfinkel, 1986). Other nonpsychoanalytic psychologists have cited epidemiological data as a basis for rejecting the notion of depression as a clinical entity in children. For example, epidemiological research shows that many normal children exhibited depressive symptoms and that many of these were transitory in nature (Lefkowitz & Burton, 1978). Accordingly, depressive manifestations were not regarded as deviant in either a statistical or psychopathological sense. Costello (1980) subsequently questioned the assumptions underlying Lefkowitz and Burton's critique of the concept of childhood depression and questioned the limits of a statistical criterion of abnormality.

The second viewpoint, which was popular in the 1960s and 1970s, asserted that depression in children is *"masked"* or expressed in *"depressive equivalents."* The basic assumption of this perspective is that children do not show the signs and symptoms of depression in the same ways that adults do. Instead, depression in children is expressed through other behaviors and disturbances. "Depressive equivalents" are numerous, but those receiving the most attention include acting-out or delinquent behavior, school avoidance or failure, and psychosomatic or hypochondriacal symptoms. Thus, even though the child does not present commonly seen overt symptoms such as depressed mood or loss of interest in most pursuits, he or she could be diagnosed as depressed on the basis of "depressive equivalents." Regrettably, proponents of this view do not provide operational criteria whereby, for example, conduct disorders that are a mask for depression can be differentiated from conduct disorders with no underlying depression. Indeed, Kovacs, Paulauskos, Gatsonis and Richards (1988) concluded that depression in children with conduct disorder did not differ in symptoms or course compared with depression in children without conduct disorder. Moreover, the research literature indicates that the correlates of major depression may well differ in young persons with and without conduct disorder with respect to age of onset, family history and longitudinal course into adulthood (Zoccolillo, 1992). For those who develop antisocial personality disorder, the average age of the first symptom was between 8 and 9 (Robins & Price, 1991), whereas in studies of adults in the general population the age of onset of major depression was 26. Even in the youngest cohort, it was 18 (Weissman, Bruce, Leaf, Florio, & Holzer, 1991). In delinquents with and without depression, the depressed subjects are more likely to have higher rates of major depression in their first-degree family members (Puig-Antich et al., 1989). Finally, children with conduct disorder and depression were much less likely to be depressed as adults than children with depression alone (Harrington, Fudge, Rutter, Pickles, & Hill, 1991).

The relationship between "depressive equivalents" and a presumed underlying depression remains to be cogently explicated. Given the frequency of symptoms such as attentional disorders, hyperactivity, aggressive behavior, truancy, delinquency, temper tantrums, decreased school performance, psychosomatic problems, and boredom in the childhood population, one wonders if any youngster would be exempt from a diagnosis of "masked depression" at one time or another over the course of development. It is most unlikely that childhood depression underlies all such problems.

There is also the problem of cause–effect relationships. The rationale underlying the notion of masked depression is that depressed feelings are replaced by behavior problems. Thus, a child who is convinced that he or she is bad or unacceptable begins to act in an antisocial manner consistent with his or her belief system. It could well be, however, that symptoms such as aggressiveness, delinquency, and hyperactivity *result* in consequences such as rejection, criticism, and incarceration that leave children feeling unhappy, helpless, and worthless. That is, these symptoms may *cause* depression rather than reflect a defense against it. Longitudinal studies will be needed to ferret out cause–effect relations.

Multiple problems can also coexist without one having caused another. Children can and do sometimes meet the diagnostic criteria for depression as well as other disorders. Using cluster analysis, Edelbrock and Achenbach (1980) found that some youngsters in the 6- to 11-year-old group showed evidence of depression in addition to other types of behavioral disturbances. For instance, one group of boys in this age group was identified as having elevated scores on depression, social withdrawal, and aggression. Rutter, Tizard, and Whitmore (1970/1981) found depression was equally distributed across their three clinical groups—neurotic, antisocial, and mixed diagnoses. In a similar vein, Teri (1982), in a study of 568 high school students, noted that subjects reporting more depression also reported more difficulties in other areas of their lives as well. These findings suggest that what is labeled depression in children and adolescents occurs across all diagnostic groups and does not represent a separate, discrete pathological condition. As is true in adult abnormalities, depressive behaviors may be superimposed on a variety of disabilities without representing a distinctive syndrome. The question remains as to whether there is a syndrome of childhood depression that differentiates one subgroup of troubled children from those whose dysphoria is but one aspect of other syndromes. These data question whether the concept of masked depression is parsimonious or necessary. Due to the ambiguity surrounding this concept and the ubiquity of behaviors allegedly overshadowing depression in children, the heuristic and clinical value of "masked depression" remains questionable. It may well be that many of the symptoms specified as overshadowing depression are essentially nothing more than presenting complaints. Clinical practice with adults informs us that patients often manifest nonspecific somatic complaints (Kovacs & Beck, 1977), yet we do not consider them as "masking" depression. Why we do so with children is not yet clear.

Albert: Masked Depression

Albert, a 12-year-old boy who had been referred because of his disruptive behavior in school, was aggressive and hyperactive. His grades were poor and his social adjustment marginal. A look at the home situation suggested two major probable causes: The mother held a full-time job, was usually unavailable to her children, and had once been investigated for child abuse; the father was an alcoholic who assumed no responsibility for the family and who frequently beat Albert. In sum, the child, like many others with a similar condition, had experienced both rejection and depreciation.

Throughout the interview, Albert was apathetic and sad. "He described himself as dumb, as the laughing stock of his schoolmates, and expressed the belief that everyone was picking on him." He saw himself as inadequate and helpless. "On the fantasy level the boy showed a strong preoccupation with themes of annihilation, violence, explosions, and death, invariably with a bad outcome for the main figures."

Albert did not improve. In fact, 1½ years later he was sent to a residential school for delinquent boys.

The investigators suggest that the boy's delinquency and aggressiveness were attempts to escape from a basic depression. They admit that such a defense is self-destructive, but "it helps ward off the unbearable feeling of despair" and, on the basis of the newest evidence, seems to be far commoner than most of us think. In other words, many children who have a behavior problem may be basically depressed.

Note. From *Causes, Detection and Treatment of Childhood Depression* (p. 2), National Institute of Mental Health, DHEW Publication No. 78-612, Washington, DC: Government Printing Office.

Against this background of disagreement and confusion, a third and very current school of thought has emerged around *DSM-III-R criteria,* the most widely used system for classifying psychopathological disorders in North America. Published by the American Psychiatric Association, the system is used in the United States as the "official" one for reporting of mental disorders to government health agencies and for categorizing the mentally ill in various official reports. It has now become widely accepted in the United States as embodying the common language of mental health clinicians and researchers. Proponents of this perspective (which was designed to enhance standardization and uniformity) have recommended universal acceptance and use of the *DSM-III-R* criteria as the foundation for diagnosing major affective disorders in children. For those advocates (Cytryn, McKnew, & Bunney, 1980; Puig-Antich, Blau, Marx, Greenhill, & Chambers, 1978) there is a one-to-one correspondence between the signs and symptoms of adult depressive disorders and those of children. Following the recommendation to use *DSM-III-R* criteria would have the advantage of allowing for comparison of research findings across studies but the disadvantage of overlooking important developmentally based differences in childhood affective disorders.

Advocates of the fourth school of thought describe childhood depression as encompassing the core clinical features that characterize the adult disorder (sadness, anhedonia, low self-esteem, and various somatic symptoms). Also included, however, are certain *symptoms exhibited only by children and/or adolescents,* such as social withdrawal, anxiety, aggression, negativism, conduct disorders, and school refusal. Thus, according to this perspective, childhood depression includes the essential characteristics of adult depression as well as associated characteristics specific to age and developmental level (Cantwell & Baker, 1991). It is not clear at this time whether these other symptoms are essential features or secondary to childhood depression (Rutter, 1986). We urgently need comprehensive studies that examine the symptomatology of depressive disorders across childhood, adolescence, and adulthood.

Most recently, a fifth school of thought, *the organizational-developmental approach,* has arisen from the writings of developmental psychopathologists (Cicchetti & Schneider-Rosen, 1986; Sroufe & Rutter, 1984) who charge that it is unreasonable to expect behavioral isomorphism between the signs and symptoms of adults and of children suffering from affective disorders. Significant differences in the developmental sequencing of cognitive, linguistic, and socioemotional capabilities preclude direct, one-to-one behavioral correspondence between depressed children and adults. According to this viewpoint, the simple categorization of symptoms and behaviors is not adequate. One must also attend to the broader notions or patterns of adaptation and competence. Behaviors are viewed as becoming hierarchically organized into more complex patterns within developmental systems. The developmental approach stresses the interaction between cognitive, social, emotional, and neuropsychological systems, together with the consequences of lags or advances within one system for the functioning of other systems. For instance, with the advent of concrete operational thought, the child becomes able to conceptualize multiple emotions simultaneously as they relate to self-cognitions. This ability to maintain simultaneously multiple emotions with the self as object may represent a significant factor in one's vulnerability to, or protection against, depression. Because the transition to concrete operations also makes possible self-attributions that are stable, enduring, and global, elementary school children can make negative, stable attributions of self that promote a sense of learned helplessness. At the same time, they can simultaneously make opposite positive, stable self-attributions that counteract the negative self-evaluation. The organizational-developmental approach highlights the need to develop a classification system of childhood psychopathology that addresses not only the static notion of signs and symptoms, but the various types of healthy and abnormal functioning, together with a cataloging of the most salient age-appropriate tasks for each developmental phase. The latter task might prove challenging, in that responsiveness to stress might well be nonspecific (Carlson & Garber, 1986).

DIFFERENTIATION FROM NORMALITY

Distinguishing depressive disorders from normality might seem a relatively straightforward task given the availability of operational criteria such as those found in *DSM-III-R*. Diagnostic confusion arises, however, from three sources, namely, discriminating depression from demoralization, from grief or stress reactions, and from reactions to physical illness (Rutter, 1986). The *demoralization* syndrome (Klein, Gittelman, Quitkin, & Rifkin, 1980) is common among normal children and very common among youngsters with problems other than depression. For example, demoralization occurs among the majority of learning disabled students who are disheartened in school. Yet, just as we do not diagnose all children who have academic difficulty in school as learning disabled, so we must not diagnose all unhappy, ineffective, discouraged students as clinically depressed even though they look depressed. Rating scales generally will not differentiate between these two states. Fortunately, from a diagnostic standpoint, demoralized youth differ from clinically depressed youth in at least two ways. They lack the pervasive anhedonia (loss of interest or pleasure in all, or almost all, activities) characteristic of the seriously depressed. For instance, their pleasure appetite increases when they are offered the chance to visit their favorite vacation spot or meet their favorite sports hero. Clinically depressed youngsters fail to show a sense of *anticipatory pleasure* under those circumstances. Also, demoralized individuals do not respond to antidepressant medication. As clinicians, we must guard against medicating demoralized patients who are not in need of it.

The differentiation between depression and *"normal grief"* or stress reactions involves rather different issues. Many grief reactions fulfill the diagnostic criteria for major depressive disorders, yet it is argued that they should be viewed as normal phenomena rather than as a psychopathological condition because they are both common and understandable (Clayton, 1982). Although seemingly cogent at first glance, this argument, by edict, essentially rules out psychosocial factors as causes of psychopathological conditions. We do not follow this same logic with physical conditions. For instance, influenza is both common and understandable, but it is not regarded as normal. Rutter believes that the best tactic is to determine whether the depressive disorders that follow bereavement or other acute stress differ from other depressive disorders in their correlates, natural course, or response to treatment (Rutter, 1986). The evidence to date is contradictory and inconclusive (Brown & Harris, 1978; Parker, 1983). It seems reasonable to conclude that life events may precipitate the onset of a variety of depressive disorders as well as mania. Whatever differences there are in the type of depression due to psychosocial causation are likely to be matters of degree or frequency rather than of kind. Stress or adjustment reactions that do not meet the full criteria for a depressive disorder often have a substantially better outlook (Kovacs, Feinberg, Crouse-Novak, Paulauskas, & Finkelstein, 1984), but the more favorable prognosis is probably a function of their mildness and acuteness rather than their mode of causation.

Similar logic can be applied to affective disorders that arise from the context of a *physical illness,* for it is not uncommon for individuals to become despondent and depressed following a severe physical illness and/or hospitalization.

DIFFERENTIATION FROM RELATED DIAGNOSES

Once depressive disorders have been distinguished from normality, it is necessary to differentiate depressive disorders from related psychopathological conditions that are similar to and sometimes overlap the depressive prob-

Table 1.1
Differentiation of Childhood Depression from Related Conditions

Learning disability
  Severe discrepancy between ability and achievement
  Often limited to reading
  Anhedonia limited to school
  Relatively early onset
  Boys at risk
  Chronic
  Absence of somatic symptoms
Attention-deficit hyperactivity disorder
  Chronic
  Early onset
Conduct disorders
  Others hurt more by their behavior
  Chronic
Anxiety disorders
  Anxiety dominant over dysphoria and anhedonia
Anorexia nervosa
  Chronic symptoms
  Preoccupation with food and size
  Absence of family history for affective disorders
Adolescent schizophrenia
  Severe social isolation
  Disordered thought process
Alcohol and substance abuse
  Salient affective features at onset

Note. Adapted from Garfinkel (1986).

lems. There are seven major conditions that are often confused with major affective disorders in young people. (See Table 1.1.) These include learning disabilities, attention-deficit hyperactivity disorder, conduct disorders, anxiety disorders, eating disorders, substance abuse, and the beginning stages of schizophrenia.

Learning Disabilities

Students who cannot concentrate, who do poorly in class, and are unpopular with their peers are often confused with learning disabled youth. Although a high percentage of learning disabled (LD) youth may also be suffering from some degree of depression, according to studies from Texas

(Wright-Strowderman & Watson, 1992) and Minnesota (Barry Garfinkel quoted in Swartz, 1987) there are several differentiating features between the two related conditions.

1. Whereas anhedonia is a pervasive characteristic of childhood depression, it is usually limited to school matters and does not detract from the child's out-of-school pursuits and enjoyment of interests and activities among LD youth. Depressed teenagers may describe their feeling of anhedonia as a general feeling of boredom or "vegging out." Routinely, they come home from school, eat dinner, watch television, then go to their room and listen to music.

2. LD students, by definition, show a *severe* discrepancy between ability and achievement. Although there is an inverse relationship between childhood depression measures and school achievement as measured by standardized achievement tests or school grades, the magnitude of the relationship is low (Reynolds, 1985; Vincenzi, 1987) to moderate at best (Edelsohn, Ialongo, Werthamer-Larsson, Crockett, & Kellam, 1992). For instance, in a study of regular school children, Lefkowitz and Tesiny (1985) reported correlations of -.11 for boys and -.27 for girls between peer nomination scores for depression and standardized reading scores with a sample of 3,020 3rd-, 4th-, and 5th-grade classes in New York City. Moreover, Stanford Achievement Test scores in reading and math failed to differentiate students identified by their teachers as depressed and a comparison group matched for age, sex, race, and standardized reading scores (Seagull & Weinshank, 1984). Likewise, Brumbach, Jackoway, and Weinberg (1980) failed to find differences on the Wide Range Achievement Test between depressed and nondepressed groups.

3. Whereas in LD the disability tends to be specific, most commonly in the area of reading, the disability in depression in young people tends to be one of general academic deterioration with numerous subject matters adversely affected.

4. The onset of LD occurs relatively early, with more than half of LD youth identified by the end of 2nd grade (Clarizio & Phillips, 1989; Cone, Wilson, Bradley, & Reese, 1985), whereas the onset of depression in youth typically occurs in the postpubescent years.

5. Gender is a risk factor for LD both before and after puberty (Buchanan & Wolf, 1986; Clarizio & Phillips, 1986), with boys outnumbering girls by a 2 or 3 to 1 margin. In the case of depressive disorders, gender is not a risk factor until after puberty (Lefkowitz & Tesiny, 1985), when girls outnumber boys by a significant margin.

6. Depressive disorders are characterized by somatic complaints such as experiencing changes in appetite or weight, being tired, and having aches. These vegetative problems are not typical of LD youngsters, however.

7. Childhood depression tends to be episodic (Kovacs et al., 1984), whereas LD tends to be chronic (Clarizio & McCoy, 1983). Although the differences between depression and learning disability have been stressed, it should be noted that a particular subtype of learning disability, namely, nonverbal learning disability, predisposes the child to risk for depression and suicide (Rourke, Young, & Leenaars, 1989).

Attention-Deficit Hyperactivity Disorder

Youngsters with attention-deficit hyperactivity disorder (ADHD) may resemble depressed children because they exhibit difficulty concentrating, mood lability, and some vegetative symptoms (notably sleep disturbance) and often have a high rate of depressive spectrum conditions within their families. Because of the chronic nature of ADHD, students so afflicted resemble children with dysthymia, a chronic but mild mood disturbance involving depressed or irritable mood. The primary differentiating feature of major affective disorder is its episodic nature with normal affect and symptom-free periods occurring between episodes. Also, ADHD typically has its onset in the preschool years. Finally, the low self-esteem seen in the ADHD syndrome is secondary to school failure and is not a primary feature of cognitively based self-perceptions as in childhood depression.

The high activity of children with ADHD also needs to be differentiated from states of frenetic energy and exhilaration exhibited by children in a manic episode. The "hyperactive" child's behavior is chronic and responds to Ritalin®. Moreover, this child is free from hallucinations and family history is negative for affective disorders. In contrast, the manic individual's behavior is not infrequently characterized by hallucinations and is episodic in nature. The family history is often positive for affective disorders. This condition responds to lithium (Carlson, 1990).

Conduct Disorder

It is also not uncommon for conduct disorders to co-occur in young people with major affective disorders far more often than might be expected by chance (Zoccolillo, 1992). Indeed, Carlson and Cantwell (1980) showed that one third of all youth with conduct disorder satisfy the criteria for major affective disorder. For males with conduct disorder, the highest prevalence of depression is in preadolescence and decreases into adulthood. Conversely, for females with conduct disorder, there is an increasing prevalence of emotional disorder as they pass from preadolescence to adolescence and then adulthood (Robins & Price, 1991). Thus both age and gender affect the rates of co-occurrence (Zoccolillo, 1992). Children with affective disorder who display disturbing behavior tend to hurt themselves more with their behavior than others toward whom the antisocial behavior is directed. Moreover, delinquent-like youth without major affective disorder show a chronic, continuous progression of more serious misbehavior, and disregard for property and the rights of others. As was true with LD, there is a significant number of troubled youth who are dually diagnosed as conduct disordered and depressed. Again, the practitioner must be alert to the co-existence of these two disorders as well as to the diagnostic differences between them.

Anxiety Disorders

Arguably the most difficult differentiation revolves around the relationship between anxiety and depression. Indeed, the conceptual and empirical association between these two broad-spectrum conditions remains a matter of concern and controversy. Because the two constructs may not be clinically distinct, some workers prefer the broadband term *negative affectivity* to refer to a pervasive personality trait that is independent of situation-specific anxiety (Finch, Lipovsky, & Casat, 1989). Anxiety and depression do co-occur (Bernstein, 1991). Anxiety is noted in 25% to 35% of depressed children (Kovacs et al., 1984) and symptoms of depression are found in as many as 50% of school-phobic youth (Bernstein & Garfinkel, 1986). Depressed children are more likely to report anxiety. Anxiety and depression may exist along a continuum, with anxiety preceding depression (Dobson, 1985).

Four points regarding the commonalities of anxiety and depression have been noted (Kendall & Watson, 1989). First, empirical evidence based on diverse samples demonstrates a high relationship between the two conditions. Clinicians, teachers, parents, and children themselves have considerable difficulty distinguishing between these two constructs (Finch et al., 1989). As noted above, many patients receive both diagnoses. Second, in the present conceptualization, these two constructs share several symptom criteria. For instance, *DSM-III-R* symptoms such as restlessness, fatigability, loss of energy, difficulty concentrating, and insomnia are criteria for both disorders. This overlap is not necessarily inappropriate, if these are valid symptoms for both anxiety and depression. Commonly used assessment scales, most of which were developed before the concern about overlap arose, lack discriminant validity. It remains for future research to improve the discriminant validity of existing measures by developing more specific and differentiated scales of anxiety and depression. Focusing on the critical differentiating features of these two constructs could serve as a basis for improved discrimination. Third, methodological problems are not the sole reason for the co-occurrence of anxiety and depression. A more fundamental reason is that both conditions involve substantial levels of subjective distress; there appears to be a strong general factor which pervades this subjective distress. Thus, various negative emotions such as fear, anger, guilt, and sadness tend to co-occur. Last, several precipitating and/or concomitant factors are common to both disorders. For instance, they share several dysfunctional cognitive *processes* such as negative automatic thoughts, maladaptive beliefs, and misinterpretation of events. *Stressful life events* are also a common precursor. Although certain life stressors are highly related to one condition or other, many stressful life events have nonspecific effects with respect to anxiety and depression. Finally, there might well be a common *constitutional predisposition* which underlies at least some forms of anxiety and depression. For instance, the evidence linking panic disorder and major depression is strong. Moreover, various twin studies suggest that depression and anxiety share a common genetic basis (Kendler, Neale, Kessler, Heath, & Eaves, 1992).

Despite the commonalities of these two conditions and the importance placed on the notion of a general distress factor, most mental health specialists recognize differentiating features between the two syndromes (see Table 1.2) and argue for their separateness. Negative affectivity is too diffuse a measure of psychological distress and malfunctioning to differentiate specific types of psychopathological disorders from one another. It is critical that greater detail be given to how co-occurring symptoms are interpreted if the findings on comorbidity are to be resolved (Klein & Last, 1989). For instance, school phobic children who miss school in part due to somatic complaints commonly avoid social interaction with classmates. Their avoidance of contact spares them the embarrassment of having to explain their inappropriate behavior. Yet, this decrease in the amount of social exchange might be regarded as a loss of social interest and listed as a depressive symptom. Changes in sleep patterns (e.g., insomnia) and eating patterns (e.g., skipping breakfast) arising from anxiety might also be counted as depressive symptoms. Disruptions in normal sleeping and eating patterns can, in turn, be interpreted as an inability to concentrate and counted as another indication of depression. The ensuing pessimism and demoralization associated with school failure can also be seen as part of the depressive syndrome. All of the above features are consistent with criteria for a major depressive disorder, even though they may stem from a basic anxiety disorder. It is not clear that studies on comorbidity of anxiety and depression have taken the care necessary to clarify the nature of clinical complaints so that we know whether they truly reflect affective dysfunction, anxiety, or both.

Table 1.2
Differentiating Features of Anxiety and Depression

	Anxiety	Depression
Cognitive Content	Future oriented. Anticipation of threat or danger.	Past oriented; focus on loss, failure, or degradation.
Self-views	Negative self-view	Even lower self-esteem. Perceived worthlessness, rejection, and ineffectuality more central in depression.
Life Stress	Negative events involving threat or danger.	Negative events more centrally related to depression; negative events involving perceived or actual loss.
Pleasurable Affects and Events	High negative affect.	High negative affect plus loss of pleasurable life events and a deficit in positive emotional experiences.
Behavioral Differences	Increased levels of maladaptive responding (e.g., phobic avoidance).	Reduced level of activity.
Temporal Patterning	No strong or consistent temporal patterning.	Vary in frequency over the course of the year (e.g., winter onset) and in intensity over the course of the day (e.g., worse in the morning in melancholia).
Treatment Focus	Reducing or eliminating maladaptive responses.	Increasing level of adaptive behavior.

Note. Adapted from *Anxiety and Depression: Distinctive and Overlapping Features* by P. Kendall & D. Watson, 1989, New York: Academic Press.

Using Bayesian item statistics to identify the most efficient diagnostic inclusionary and exclusionary criteria, investigators studied 34 depressed youngsters, 30 anxious students, and 70 who received neither diagnosis (Laurent, Landau, & Stark, 1993). All subjects were in grades four through seven and participants in a research project concerning childhood depression. Results showed that four symptoms—feeling unloved, anhedonia, excessive guilt and depressed mood—were the best *inclusion* items for a diagnosis of depression. Denial of depressed mood and excessive guilt were the best exclusionary items. That is, their denial strongly indicated that a diagnosis of depression was unlikely. These findings are similar to those of Clark and Watson's work (1991) with adults with respect to symptoms necessary for depression. Reports of being worried were most efficient at differentiating between children with anxiety disorders and youngsters with depressive disturbances. Anxious students did not report physiological symptoms that are associated with anxiety disorders in adults. The Bayesian perspective with its conditional probabilities has considerable merit in postulating inclusionary and exclusionary criteria for various conditions of childhood psychopathology. Yet it too has significant limitations, which the investigators note. Findings cannot be expected to generalize across subjects, informants, settings, and severity. The inclusionary and exclusionary criteria might well vary across students and inpatients, teachers, parents and children, public school settings and residential settings, and mild, moderate, and severe degrees of disturbance. Further, different methods for ascertaining symptoms might well yield different results (e.g., clinical interviews versus peer ratings). Last, because the K-SADS interview was used to determine both the children's diagnoses and the conditional probabilities of the symptoms, the results of this study yield data on internal consistency (reliability) of the symptoms rather than their actual validity. It remains for future research to determine whether distinguishing between these two constructs is useful, necessary, or possible (Finch et al., 1989).

Indeed, Carlson and Cantwell (1980) showed that one third of all youth with conduct disorder satisfy the criteria for major affective disorder. For males with conduct disorder, the highest prevalence of depression is in preadolescence and decreases into adulthood. Conversely, for females with conduct disorder, there is an increasing prevalence of emotional disorder as they pass from preadolescence to adolescence and then adulthood (Robins & Price, 1991). Thus both age and gender affect the rates of co-occurrence (Zoccolillo, 1992). Children with affective disorder who display disturbing behavior, however, tend to hurt themselves more with their behavior than others toward whom the antisocial behavior is directed. Moreover, delinquent-like youth without major affective disorder show a chronic, continuous progression of more serious misbehavior and a disregard for property and the rights of others. As was true with LD youth, there are a significant number of troubled youth who are dually diagnosed as conduct disordered and depressed. Again, the practitioner must be alert to the co-existence of these two disorders as well as to the diagnostic differences between them.

Anorexia Nervosa

Youth with anorexia nervosa may also have a major affective disorder and the anorexia symptoms may be simply vegetative symptoms of the depression (Cantwell, Sturzenberger, Burroughs, Salkin, & Green, 1977). Suggestive support for this notion comes from clinical observations that treatment with medications such as tricyclic antidepressants and monoamine oxidase inhibitors has been effective in some patients with eating disturbances. Differential diagnosis is based on three factors: chronic symptoms of eating disorders rather than episodic symptoms, the absence of a family history for affective disorders, and preoccupation with food and size predominating over affective symptoms.

Adolescent Schizophrenia

Dysphoria and other essential symptoms have long been observed as early features of the onset of schizophrenia in adolescents, but the early adolescent schizophrenic differs from the young depressive with respect to two characteristics: severe social isolation and a disorder of thought processes. Alcoholism and substance abuse have also been found among depressed adolescents. Street drugs and/or alcohol may be used to self-treat their depression, eventually leading to drug dependency. The salient affective symptoms at the time of onset of alcohol and/or drug abuse provide the best way to differentiate between these two disorders.

CLASSIFICATION SYSTEMS

DSM-III-R

Given the diversity of professional opinions expressed in the five schools of thought discussed above, the question naturally arises as to what the operational criteria should be for the diagnosis of childhood depression. Each of the schools of thought would require different yardsticks by which to measure childhood depression. The first school of thought has no associated taxonomy. Advocates of masked depression also have no classification system, perhaps because of the wide diversity of symptoms subsumed under this ru-

Table 1.3
DSM-III-R Classification of Mood Disorder

Bipolar disorders
  Manic episodes
  Cyclothymia
Depressive disorders
  Major depressive episodes
  Dysthymia

Note. Adapted from *Diagnostic and Statistical Manual of Mental Disorders* (Third Edition Revised), American Psychiatric Association, 1987, Washington, DC: Author.

bric. The third school of thought would use *DSM-III-R* as its taxonomy. As is shown in Table 1.3, this classification system, which was designed for use by researchers and practitioners, subdivides mood disorders into two broad areas: bipolar disorders and depressive disorders. The essential aspect of bipolar disorders is the presence of one or more manic or hypomanic episodes, typically with a history of major depressive episodes. The essential feature of depressive disorders is one or more periods of depression without a history of manic or hypomanic episodes. The bipolar disorders are subdivided into bipolar disorder (characterized by one or more manic episodes, generally with one or more major depressive episodes) and cyclothymia (characterized by several hypomanic episodes and numerous periods with depressive symptoms). The *DSM-III-R* criteria for mania include elevated, expansive, or irritable mood; increased activity level; increased talkativeness; inflated self-esteem and grandiosity; flight of ideas; decreased need for sleep; distractibility and a symptom duration of at least 1 week (American Psychiatric Association, 1987).

It is widely believed that manic disorders occur infrequently before puberty. Some authorities argue that episodes of mania tend to be underdiagnosed or misdiagnosed in childhood and early adolescence for four basic reasons (Bowring & Kovacs, 1992). First, the very low base rate of this disorder, estimated at a .6% lifetime prevalence (Carlson, 1990), keeps clinicians from forming a mental "template" of the diagnostic prototype. Second, its variable clinical presentation and fuzzy diagnostic boundaries render clinical descriptions confusing. Third, its symptomatic overlap with more common disorders (e.g., attention-deficit hyperactivity disorder, conduct disorder) leads to its being overlooked. For example, the sudden emergence of poor judgment and disinhibition in a 10-year-old boy who cheats in school, picks fights with teachers, runs away from home, dresses flamboyantly, and

Table 1.4
DSM-III-R Criteria for Major Depressive Episode

Note: A "Major Depressive Syndrome" is defined as criterion A below.

A. At least five of the following symptoms have been present during the same 2-week period and represent a change from previous functioning; at least one of the symptoms is either (1) depressed mood, or (2) loss of interest or pleasure. (Do not include symptoms that are clearly due to a physical condition, mood-incongruent delusions or hallucinations, incoherence, or marked loosening of associations.)
    (1) depressed mood (or can be irritable mood in children and adolescents) most of the day, nearly every day, as indicated either by subjective account or observation by others
    (2) markedly diminished interest or pleasure in all, or almost all, activities most of the day, nearly every day (as indicated either by subjective account or observation by others of apathy most of the time)
    (3) significant weight loss or weight gain when not dieting (e.g., more than 5% of body weight in a month), or decrease or increase in appetite nearly every day (in children, consider failure to make expected weight gains)
    (4) insomnia or hypersomnia nearly every day
    (5) psychomotor agitation or retardation nearly every day (observable by others, not merely subjective feelings of restlessness or being slowed down)
    (6) fatigue or loss of energy nearly every day
    (7) feelings of worthlessness or excessive or inappropriate guilt (which may be delusional) nearly every day (not merely self-reproach or guilt about being sick)
    (8) diminished ability to think or concentrate, or indecisiveness, nearly every day (either by subjective account or as observed by others)
    (9) recurrent thoughts of death (not just fear of dying), recurrent suicidal ideation without a specific plan, or a suicide attempt or a specific plan for committing suicide.
B. (1) It cannot be established that an organic factor initiated and maintained the disturbance.
    (2) The disturbance is not a normal reaction to the death of a loved one (Uncomplicated Bereavement).
        Note: Morbid preoccupation with worthlessness, suicidal ideation, marked functional impairment or psychomotor retardation, or prolonged duration suggest bereavement complicated by Major Depression.

Table 1.4
(Continued)

C. At no time during the disturbance have there been delusions or hallucinations for as long as 2 weeks in the absence of prominent mood symptoms (i.e., before the mood symptoms developed or after they have remitted).

D. Not superimposed on Schizophrenia, Schizophreniform Disorder, Delusional Disorder, or Psychotic Disorder NOS.

Note. From *Diagnostic and Statistical Manual of Mental Disorders* (Third Edition Revised, pp. 222-223), American Psychiatric Association, 1987, Washington, DC: Author.

intrusively touches the private parts of peers is likely to be seen as conduct-disordered behavior rather than manic. Fourth, existing diagnostic systems (e.g., *DSM-III-R*) do not adequately include systematic and standardized descriptions of how symptom expression changes with age.

The cause(s) of bipolar disorder is unknown, but family genetic factors assume a major role (Carlson, 1990). The mean age at onset is in the late 20s or early 30s; however, it is clear that the disorder most likely begins in adolescence and young adulthood. In children with onset before the age of 9, the initial presentation of symptomology reflects irritability across both depressive and manic episodes, less discrete episodes of profound depression or elated mania, and chronic rather than episodic disorders. In youngsters with onsets closer to puberty, the symptoms of bipolarity tend to be more "classic" in their initial manic or depressive manifestations.

Cyclothymia is a mood disorder similar to bipolar disorder in its symptomatology. It differs from bipolar in two ways, however. The symptoms are less severe in nature and must be present for 1 year with periods of up to 2 months in which the individual is without symptoms. A comprehensive study of 9 cyclothymic children found that age of onset was 12.4 with a range from 7 to 15 years (Klein, Depue, & Slater, 1985). Hypomanic episodes, a milder variant of mania without delusions, lasted slightly less than 2 days and depressive episodes lasted over 2 days. The distribution of episodes was bimodal with 20% experiencing less than 6 depressive episodes and 80% experiencing 12 or more episodes per year.

Depressive disorders are divided into major depression, characterized by one or more major depressive episodes (Table 1.4), and dysthymia, characterized by depressed mood more days than not for at least 1 year for children and adolescents (Table 1.5). Dysthymia and major depressive episodes have similar symptomatology and differ only in *duration* and *severity*. The boundaries between these two conditions are unclear, particularly in children and adolescents (American Psychiatric Association, 1987).

Richard: Dysthymic Disorder (Depressive neurosis)

Richard exhibited severe temper tantrums in nursery school and 1st grade. At age 5, he was diagnosed as adjustment disorder, severe. The family history was relatively free from mental illness.

Transfer to another school that encouraged his persistent intensive interest in academic work was helpful in alleviating his tantrums. By the 4th grade, however, his selective, persistent, intense interests were thwarted, leading to explosive, violent outbursts on his part. By age 10, hopelessness and helplessness were evident. He accepted his parents', teachers', and peers' repeated disapproval of his explosive tantrums as valid. He thought of himself as a "bad boy" and felt doomed to a life of irrational explosions and ensuing unhappy consequences. An appreciable depressive element appeared in his symptomatology, and a diagnosis of dysthymic disorder seemed warranted. The diagnosis was reaffirmed at age 14, when his behavior and schoolwork deteriorated as a result of a severe conflict with one of his teachers.

Note. From "Depression in Childhood and Adolescence" by S. Chess, A. Thomas, and M. Hassibi, 1983, *The Journal of Nervous and Mental Disease, 171,* pp. 415-416.

Table 1.5
DSM-III-R Criteria for Dysthymia

A. Depressed mood (or can be irritable mood in children and adolescents) for most of the day, more days than not, as indicated either by subjective account or observation by others, for at least 2 years (1 year for children and adolescents)
B. Presence, while depressed, of at least two of the following:
   (1) poor appetite or overeating
   (2) insomnia or hypersomnia
   (3) low energy or fatigue
   (4) low self-esteem
   (5) poor concentration or difficulty making decisions
   (6) feelings of hopelessness

Table 1.5
(Continued)

C. During a 2-year period (1-year for children and adolescents) of the disturbance, never without the symptoms in A for more than 2 months at a time.

Note. From *Diagnostic and Statistical Manual of Mental Disorders* (Third Edition Revised, p. 232), American Psychiatric Association, 1987, Washington, DC: Author.

Bert: Adjustment Disorder with Depressed Mood

Bert was a temperamentally difficult child, but the parents were patient and flexible so that a pathogenic parent–child interaction did not develop. There was no family history of mental disorder. At age 12, Bert's parents divorced, a parting that was acutely painful for him. He opted to stay with his father despite frequent conflicts and verbal fights between them. He became hostile and distant in his relationship with his mother. At the same time, he became aware of his homosexual orientation. Given his temperamental characteristics of negative reactions to the new and slow adaptability to change, Bert began to show signs of depression. He had difficulty getting up in the morning, could not make friends, and became a heavy abuser of marijuana. By age 15, he was also an alcohol abuser. Psychotherapeutic efforts failed twice due to his resistance. He was given a diagnosis of adjustment disorder with depressed mood.

Bert went to a special boarding school that provided Gestalt therapy. His functioning gradually improved and his alcohol and drug use diminished. By age 18, Bert showed no signs of depression, but his disturbed functioning warranted the diagnosis of personality disorder.

Note. From "Depression in Childhood and Adolescence" by S. Chess, A. Thomas, and M. Hassibi, 1983, *The Journal of Nervous and Mental Disease, 171,* p. 418.

To date, not all of the adult forms of affective disorder have been systematically documented in children. The vast majority fall into the categories of major depressive disorder, dysthymia, bipolar disorder, and adjustment disorder with depressive mood. At present, it is not known whether the schizoaffective and cyclothymic disorders will be systematically and empirically verified in children (Garfinkel, 1986). Even bipolar affective disorder, which is well recognized in children and adolescents (Strober & Carlson, 1982), is more difficult to document in children than adults because the primary manic features of elation and grandiosity are less readily observable. The primary characteristic of mania in children is increased psychomotor activity and is sometimes confused with hyperactivity.

Endogenous-Reactive Classification

In addition to official classifications, there are unofficial classifications that have been used by clinicians working with adult depressives and that seem to have validity as reflected in family history, natural course of the condition, responsiveness to treatment, and laboratory studies. One of the oldest and best known classifications is the endogenous-reactive dichotomy. (It should be noted that the endogenous subtype is still used in the Research Diagnostic Criteria [RDC] classification system, Spitzer, Endicott, & Robins, 1978. This system was developed for research purposes and is similar to *DSM-III-R* criteria but stricter.)

The term *endogenous* implies a biological origin, whereas the term *reactive* connotes a reaction to environmental stress. The terms also have another meaning, with endogenous connoting "psychosis" and reactive connoting "neurotic." Endogenous depressions are characterized by a distinct autonomous quality of severely depressed mood, psychomotor retardation, weight loss and early waking, depression worse in the morning, loss of interest in usually pleasurable events, and difficulty in concentration. Reactive depressions also have a characteristic set of symptoms, including a precipitator factor, sudden onset, irritability, mood responsiveness to the environment, self-pity, histrionics, and immaturity.

The validity of this dichotomy is reflected in certain laboratory studies, in studies of the natural course of the condition, and in its responsiveness to certain therapeutic regimens. For instance, endogenous depressions have a more favorable prognosis and respond more favorably to antidepressants and electroconvulsive shock treatment. The frequency of this condition in prepubertal children remains to be established. One study of 58 prepubertal depressed children indicated that about half met Research Diagnostic Criteria for the endogenous subtype (Chambers, Puig-Antich, Tabrizi, & Davies, 1982). *DSM-III-R* now refers to endogenous depression "with melancholia" but might well delete it in subsequent revisions. These researchers believe that properly phrased interview questions enable children to verbalize the features characteristic of endogenous depression. Other workers' clinical experience indicates that the frequency of the endogenous depression syndrome in children is lower and exceedingly uncommon in youngsters under the age of 9 (Carlson & Garber, 1986). Interviewing young depressed children can be challenging, and it is often not clear whether they have experienced the symptoms of endogenous depression, or if they do not understand it, or if we have not phrased questions in a way that is intelligible to them. We do know that endogenous depression is not a rarity in prepubertal children with major depressive disorders, but data indicating whether its prevalence among prepubescents is lower than that of adult depressives are inconclusive.

Classifications for Young People

Of the various operational criteria modified for childhood depression (Ling, Oftedal, & Weinberg, 1970; Petti, 1978), Weinberg's criteria have been the most influential (Weinberg, Rutman, Sullivan, Penick, & Dietz, 1973). Weinberg's criteria were originally based on a modification of Feighner's operational criteria for adult psychiatric research, which eventually stimulated modifications culminating in *DSM-III-R*. There is a close correspondence between *DSM-III-R* and Weinberg's criteria. Yet, Weinberg's criteria changed the essential features, rather than the associated ones, required for the diagnosis of adult depression. There are similarities, differences, and noncorrespondences between *DSM-III-R* and Weinberg's system. Whereas *DSM-III-R* requires either dysphoric mood or anhedonia, Weinberg's system requires both dysphoric mood and self-deprecatory ideation. Another difference centers around the number of symptoms required—only two of eight symptoms for Weinberg (see Table 1.6), but four of eight for *DSM-III-R*. Weinberg's requirement for symptom duration is 1 month as opposed to 2 weeks for *DSM-III-R*. Weinberg does not posit any exclusionary criteria. Because many of the required symptoms listed by Weinberg are very common among disruptive children, such as conduct disorder and attention-deficit disorder, Weinberg's system identifies more children as depressed than does *DSM-III-R*. About 5 of 6 children who meet *DSM-III-R* criteria for depression will also satisfy Weinberg's criteria. But, about 4 in 10 children who satisfy Weinberg criteria fail to meet *DSM-III-R* criteria (Cantwell, 1983). These findings do not indicate that one set of criteria is "correct" or more "valid." Only future studies that explore how various sets of criteria correspond to family history, natural course of the condition, and responsiveness to treatment will provide the information necessary to make that judgment. We should be aware, however, that research findings based on different sets of

Table 1.6
Weinberg Criteria for Childhood Depression

1. Dysphoric mood (melancholy)
   a. Statements or appearance of sadness, loneliness, unhappiness, hopelessness, and/or pessimism
   b. Mood swings, moodiness
   c. Irritable, easily annoyed
   d. Hypersensitive, cries easily
   e. Negative, difficult to please
2. Self-deprecatory ideation
   a. Feeling of being worthless, useless, dumb, stupid, ugly, guilty (negative self-concept)
   b. Belief of persecution
   c. Death wishes
   d. Desire to run away or leave home
   e. Suicidal thoughts
   f. Suicidal attempts

Two or more of the following eight:

3. Aggressive behavior (agitation)
   a. Difficult to get along with
   b. Quarrelsome
   c. Disrespectful of authority
   d. Belligerent, hostile, agitated
   e. Excessive fighting or sudden anger
4. Sleep disturbance
   a. Initial insomnia
   b. Restless sleep
   c. Terminal insomnia
   d. Difficulty waking in morning
5. Change in school performance
   a. Frequent complaints from teachers re: daydreaming, poor concentration, poor memory
   b. Loss of usual work effort in school subjects
   c. Loss of usual interest in nonacademic school activities
6. Diminished socialization
   a. Decreased group participation
   b. Less friendly, less outgoing
   c. Socially withdrawing
   d. Loss of usual social interests
7. Change in attitude toward school
   a. Does not enjoy school activities
   b. Does not want or refuses to attend school

Table 1.6
(Continued)

8. Somatic complaints
   a. Nonmigraine headaches
   b. Abdominal pain
   c. Muscle aches or pains
   d. Other somatic concerns or complaints
9. Loss of usual energy
   a. Loss of usual personal interests or pursuits other than school; e.g., hobbies
   b. Decreased energy; mental and/or physical fatigue
10. Unusual change in appetite and/or weight

Note. From "Depression in Children Referred to an Educational Diagnostic Center: Diagnosis and Treatment" by W. Weinberg, J. Rutman, L. Sullivan, E. Penick, and S. Dietz, 1973, *Journal of Pediatrics, 83*, p. 1066.

diagnostic criteria can lead to different conclusions regarding various groups of depressed children.

Organizational-Developmental Approach

Proponents of the organizational-developmental approach stress the need to revise current diagnostic criteria to reflect developmental advances in cognitive structures and functioning because these influence the ways in which youngsters experience, interpret, and express depressive feelings at different ages. Rather than giving equal weight to all symptoms as in *DSM-III-R*, a developmental perspective might use a three-tiered process. The first tier would consist of those signs and symptoms that, independent of age, occur with the same frequency among depressives. As in *DSM-III-R*, a set number of these symptoms would be required for the diagnosis of depression. The second tier would include those symptoms less frequently found in children (e.g., guilt, suicidal ideation) that would be included in the number of required symptoms but would not change the diagnosis if they were absent. Finally, a possible third tier might entail indicators highly specific to depression in children (e.g, social withdrawal) but not explicitly listed among adult criteria. If present, those would also be counted toward the mandatory number of symptoms. In this scheme, symptoms would be assigned differential weightings in the list of required criteria, in keeping with their different base rates at various ages. It is conceivable that future research will demonstrate the need to reconsider the number of symptoms required for a diagnosis of depression for different age groups because the base rates for symptoms might vary with age. The establishment of a developmentally oriented taxonomy of child psychopathology necessitates a clear understanding of normal developmental tasks in the cognitive, affective, and social realms before deviations from normality can be most meaningfully assessed. In short, the developmental perspective would move beyond static notions of symptomatology and identify the level and patterns of adaptation and competence relative to developmental periods. It should be a valuable addition to the diagnosis of depression in young people once operational criteria are available.

Subtypes of Childhood Depression

Very little work has been done in the search for subtypes of affective disorders in childhood along *DSM-III-R* lines. It is not clear whether *DSM-III-R* subtypes exist in childhood and, if so, whether they have the same meaning with respect to natural history, family pattern of illness, and responsiveness to treatment (Cantwell & Carlson, 1983).

Do subtypes of depression exist? If so, is there common agreement as to what they are? Many mental health specialists believe that there are subtypes of childhood depression (Maag & Forness, 1991). General agreement as to their nature is by no means a fait accompli, however. Malmquist's (1971) system, which mixes etiological and theoretical frameworks, postulated the existence of five major subgroups. The two etiological subtypes were associated with organic disease or impoverished, nonrewarding environments. The other three subtypes were based on developmental level, namely, those associated with difficulty in individuation, latency, or adolescence. McConville, Boag, and Purohit (1973) discussed three subvarieties: the affectual, which was believed more common in youngsters aged 6 to 8 and characterized by sadness, helplessness, hopelessness; self-esteem, which was believed to become more common after the age of 8 and to be characterized by "thought feelings" about depression; and the guilt type, which was believed to occur in a small number of children only after the age of 11. McConville and Boag (1973) subsequently asserted that these were not three subtypes but three successive stages influenced by the interaction of cognitive and affective factors in children at different stages of development. They found that the groups tended to differ in certain regards. A family history of depression was lowest in the negative self-esteem group (38%) but highest in the guilt-miscellaneous group (100%). The affective and the affective-negative self-esteem combination were more common in females, whereas the guilt-miscellany group was more frequent in males. Although the effects of treatment were not studied systematically, the negative self-esteem group showed the least therapeutic change. Despite methodological limitation, this study suggested that the course of therapy may differ for some of the subtypes described by McConville.

Frommer (1968) conducted one of the few studies to assess systematically symptomatology, family history, responsiveness to treatment, and prognosis with respect to three subtypes: enuretic depressives, pure depressives, and phobic depressives. All three subtypes were compared with 74 "neurotic," nondepressed children. Of the depressive subtypes, the phobic depressive group had the most markedly different sex ratio, with 22 boys and 40 girls. Somatic complaints were common, with the onset of the condition occurring by age 7 in nearly half of the group. Parental mental illness was appreciably lower in this subtype. The use of monoamine oxidase (MAO) inhibitors alone or with tranquilizers was considered the therapy of choice. Prognosis was good for cases with recent onset but was poor for the more chronic cases. Enuretic depressives often had serious difficulties in school and serious learning problems. Immaturity, social withdrawal, and antisocial behavior were common. Family discord, parental mental illness, and parental rejection were highest in this group. Amitriptyline was seen as the first therapy of choice unless there was an obvious precipitating factor, in which case MAO inhibitors would be indicated. Group therapy and removal from the home were considered highly effective in some cases. The pure depressive group subjects were characterized by irritability, weepiness, temper outbursts, difficulty in sleeping, nightmares, and sleepwalking. Members of this group accounted for almost all instances of suicidal ideation and attempts. Anxiety and a lack of confidence were not noticeable features in this group. About half were seen as gregarious with numerous friends, and about one fourth were seen as antisocial. MAO inhibitors were preferred except for those showing a pattern of early morning rising, in which case tricyclics might be preferred. Unfortunately, several blatant shortcomings (lack of operational criteria for defining subgroups, nonblind assessment of family history, absence of tests to determine statistical significance, nonsystematic evaluation of treatment programs) detracted from one of few attempts to assess subgroup differences.

A promising distinction has been made between primary and secondary depression (Carlson & Cantwell, 1979). Of those in the primary group, 90% had significant school problems in contrast to just 13% for those in the secondary group. Moreover, 90% of primary group depressives were still symptomatic at the time of untreated follow-up in comparison to only 38% of the secondary group. Much remains to be learned about dividing childhood depression into subtypes, but the limited data available suggest that useful distinctions can be made.

Other possible depressive subtypes deserving further study involve youngsters with attention-deficit hyperactivity disorder (ADHD) and anorexics. Various investigators have noted the frequency of depressive symptomatology among ADHD children once they reach adolescence (Mendelson, Johnson, & Stewart, 1971; Weiss, Minde, Werry, Douglas, & Nemeth, 1971).Carlson and Cantwell (1979), in their study of 102 children referred for psychiatric evaluation, found that 30% of ADHD children had a superimposed affective disorder and that 30% of depressed youngsters had a preexisting history of ADHD. It is conceivable that the ADHD child who fails in school, has poor visual-motor coordination, and poor peer relations may develop a depressive disorder as a reaction to the core symptoms of ADHD. There is also evidence showing that over half of the patients meeting *DSM-III-R* criteria for anorexia nervosa also met the criteria for a major depressive disorder (Hendren, 1983). It is not clear whether depressive syndromes have the same meaning when they occur in conjunction with other psychopathological disorders.

In sum, the various childhood schemes seem to center around three subtypes. The first group consists of the acute or pure depressions. These appear to meet the criteria for adult depression and have a relatively good prognosis. The second subtype is that of masked depression. Anxiety symptoms (phobias, separation anxiety, psychosomatic depression) or acting-out symptoms are prominent. The third subtype entails the chronic depressions characterized by long-term deprivation and learning problems or other difficulties (e.g., enuresis). These subtypes are somewhat different from adult subcategories and might well reflect some major differences in how depressions are expressed in children and adults. Certainly caution is to be recommended in the search for adult subtypes in children, especially the categories of endogenous, psychotic, bipolar, and episodic versus chronic (Carlson & Garber, 1986).

PREVALENCE

Given the lack of a firmly agreed-on description of the characteristics of childhood depression and reliable assessment, it is not surprising to find widely varying prevalence figures. Variation in definition and the absence of well-validated scales limit the amount of confidence that can be placed in prevalence figures. Let us first examine the figures for depression in *childhood psychiatric populations.* At one extreme Brumbach et al. (1980) found 62 of 100 consecutive referrals to an educational and diagnostic center to manifest signs of depression. Another investigation (Weinberg et al., 1973) found that 57% of 6- to 17-year-olds referred to an educational diagnostic clinic met their criteria for childhood depression. Achenbach and Edelbrock (1981) report that 43% of referred 4- to 5-year-old boys and 86% of referred 12- to 13-year-old girls were rated as depressed by their parents. Carlson and Cantwell (1980) interviewed 102 children seen at the UCLA Neuropsychiatric Institute and reported that 60% had depressive symptoms, 49% displayed evidence of depression on the Children's Depression Inventory, and 28% met the *DSM-III-R* criteria for depressive disorders. Kashani, Lababidi, and Jones (1982) reported a 13% incidence rate of major depressive disorders in children admitted to an inpatient community health center. Poznanski and Zrull (1970) found, however, that only 14 of 1,758 children referred to a psychiatric clinic showed clear signs of depression. Data based on 138,000 admissions to state and county mental hospital inpatient services in the United States in 1980 indicated that 9.5% of patients diagnosed as having affective disorders were under the age of 18 (U.S. Department of Health and Human Services, 1986).

Studies based on the *general childhood population* also show considerable variability in incidence estimates depending on the criteria and assessment devices used. For instance, Kashani and Simonds (1979) reported on the basis of their interviews with 103 children aged 7 to 11 that only 1.9% displayed clear evidence of depression, whereas Albert and Beck (1975) reported that 33% of 63 subjects aged 11 to 13 showed evidence of depression based on the Beck Depression Inventory. Rutter et al. (1970/1981) reported only 1 to 2 cases per 1,000 10- to 11-year-old children in their Isle of Wight study. Depressive symptomatology appears to be more common among adolescents.

Among a random sample of 2,303 14- and 15-year-olds living on the Isle of Wight, 21% of the boys and 23% of the girls reported frequent feelings of misery or depression on a "malaise inventory" (Rutter, Graham, Chadwick, & Yule, 1976). Far fewer of those adolescents who expressed experiencing such feelings in psychiatric interviews appeared sad and miserable to the clinician. Further, the mothers rated their children as depressed considerably less often than did the teenagers themselves. Finally, although depressive symptomatology may be rather common among normal adolescents, it rarely assumes clinical significance. In the Isle of Wight study mentioned above, only 0.4% of 14- and 15-year-olds were diagnosed as depressed, with an additional 1.1% showing a mixture of depression and anxiety (Rutter et al., 1976).

In a similar study, parents of 450 American 12- to 16-year-olds described no more than 13% of the youngsters at any age as "unhappy, sad or depressed" (Achenbach & Edelbrock, 1981). It might be that parents are better at describing objective, observable depressive symptoms, whereas they tend to be less aware of the subjective or inner feelings of their youngsters.

Data gathered on *school-based general education students* through peer nomination of 3,020 normal, middle-class, elementary school children with a mean age of almost 10 years suggested that 5.2% were depressed. Given that (a) only 71% of parents gave their children permission to participate and that nonresponders in epidemiological studies are likely to have more deviant scores (Graham, 1979) and (b) the relationship between socioeconomic status and measures of depression is inverse (Lefkowitz, Tesiny, & Gordon, 1980), the 5% figure might be an underestimate.

Studies of high school students yield higher prevalence rates. For instance, an epidemiological study of 2,875 high school students drawn from urban and suburban settings found that roughly one in six subjects (18%) was either moderately or severely depressed as measured by a slightly modified version of the Beck Depression Inventory (Reynolds, 1985). In a study of 8,206 high school students in New York State, 35% of adolescents were categorized as highly depressed as measured by Likert-type items (Kandel & Davies, 1982).

As expected, studies of *school-based special education* studies report higher rates of depression than do studies of general education samples. For example, Maag and Behrens (1989) found that 21% of learning disabled and seriously emotionally disturbed adolescents were depressed. Behaviorally disordered students in self-contained special education classrooms are more depressed than those behaviorally disordered students who are mainstreamed (Allen-Meares, 1991).

In sum, it is difficult to reach any sound conclusions regarding the prevalence of depression among children and adolescents. The estimates vary according to (a) the definitional criteria used (symptom, syndrome, disorder, disease; *DSM-III-R,* Weinberg criteria, Public Law 94-142 criteria; demoralization vs. depression; subtypes), (b) the population studied (preschool, middle childhood, adolescents; males vs. females; general population vs. clinical samples; general education vs. special education), (c) type of diagnostic method (self-report, interview), and (d) data source (child, parent, peers).

Despite methodological limitations (Fleming & Offord, 1990) and the unreliability of psychiatric diagnoses, certain conclusions appear warranted. (1) Relatively few children are referred for depressive affect alone. Rather, depression is associated with a variety of other problems. (2) Depressive symptoms are not uncommon, particularly among adolescents, with anywhere from one in five to one in three reporting depressive feelings. (3) Clinical depression increases with age. It is rare during the preschool years and is in clear evidence during middle childhood but not as prevalent as during the adolescent years. (4) Sex ratios for depressive disorders change after puberty, with the disorder becoming twice as common among females. (5) Mania becomes more common in the teenage period but is relatively uncommon prior to puberty. (6) The most rigorous studies indicate that few children in the general childhood population meet strict criteria for major depression, but approximately one fourth of clinical populations satisfy *DSM-III-R* criteria for depressive disorder (Carlson & Cantwell, 1979; Rosenstock, 1985). (7) Just as we earlier erred historically by underestimating the incidence of depression in children, we must guard against the pendulum swinging in the opposite direction and overestimating the number of children diagnosed as depressive among children referred for professional help. Once we begin to see a condition, there is a tendency to see it everywhere. For example, one study of 900 consecutive adolescents treated as inpatients showed a four-fold increase in depression as a diagnosis between 1977–1979 and 1980–1982 (Rosenstock, 1985). Depression as a diagnosis accounted for 7.6% of cases in 1977–1979 but accounted for 27.5% of adolescent diagnoses just 3 years later. In a similar vein, infantile autism used to be a very rare condition. Now we have many youngsters with this label in special education in the public schools.

ETIOLOGY

What causes childhood depression? Stress appears to trigger depression, but many factors may be at work. For purposes of discussion, we will arbitrarily divide the causes into psychosocial factors and biological factors. Although these two sets of factors are discussed separately, they most likely interact in everyday life. For example, the child who lives with a depressed mother may become depressed himself or herself by observing how the mother reacts to unpleasant events in her life. Also, the child may have a biological vulnerability that predisposes her or him to depression when stressful circumstances occur. Thus, both environmental and inherited predisposition may be operating to produce the youngster's depression. No attempt is made here to exhaust all that is known about the etiology of depression in young people. For instance, no discussion will be made of the sociological school of thought. More detailed attention is devoted in Chapter 5 to the causative role played by cognitive and behavioral factors.

Psychosocial Factors

One of the most common factors in depression is depression in the parent. In addition to clinical experience, numerous research studies indicate that having a depressed parent places the child at risk (e.g., Dodge, 1990; Downey & Coyne, 1990). First, many depressed adults retrospectively report childhoods with disturbed parents and unhealthy environments (Burbach & Borduin, 1986; Crook, Raskin, & Eliot, 1981). More direct support is available in studies of currently depressed children. Several studies find high rates of depression and psychosocial dysfunction among the parents of depressed children (Puig-Antich et al., 1985a,b). Parents of depressed children are more often found to be detached, angry, punitive, and belittling (Poznanski & Zrull, 1970). Other researchers found that depressed children and their mothers had poorer communication and less affectionate relations than did both normal and nonpsychiatric depressed controls and their mothers (Magnussen, 1991; Puig-Antich et al., 1985a,b). The clearest evidence comes from investigations in which the offspring of depressed parents consistently show high rates of dysfunction. Two major studies suggest that over 50% of offspring of depressed parents will have experienced a major depression before the age of 20 (Hammen, Barge, Burney, & Adrian 1990; Weissman et al., 1992).

Another group of studies has focused on the social and cognitive difficulties manifested by the offspring of depressed parents. A review of these studies demonstrates that the offspring of depressed parents appear to show significantly more social and cognitive difficulties than do offspring of normal parents. Among their problems are excessive rivalry with peers and siblings, a sense of social isolation, numerous classroom disturbances, inattentiveness and withdrawal, and poor comprehension. It is not known whether the frequency of these problems exceeds that of other at-risk groups such as children of a schizophrenic parent.

Another group of studies has examined the relations between depressed parents and their children. Based on an overall disturbance index, Billings and Moos (1985) found that 26% of children in depressed families had rather serious childhood dysfunction in contrast to only 7% of controls. Further, 1 year later, children whose parents showed a remission of their depressive symptoms showed little improvement. However, children of remitted parents were functioning better than those of nonremitted parents. Positive changes in family milieux may occur slowly and at different rates for different dimensions of family life, thereby leading to a delay in the children's functioning (Billings & Moos, 1985).

Despite the increasingly stronger empirical base showing the negative impact of having a depressed parent, the validity of findings is weakened by a number of methodological problems. A major difficulty centers around the *heterogeneity of the samples* used. Depression is not nearly as homogeneous an entity as one might infer from reading the research literature. For example, very few investigators have compared the adjustment of children of unipolar- and bipolar-disordered parents. Yet, based on the limited data available, it appears that children of unipolar-disordered parents are somewhat less socially competent and more clinically disturbed than offspring of bipolar-disordered parents (Downey & Coyne, 1990). Consider *severity*. Most of the better designed studies have relied on persons in hospitals and clinics who are more seriously disturbed than the typical depressed individual (Downey & Coyne, 1990). This sampling procedure limits our ability to generalize findings to the typical depressed patient. *Comorbidity* is rarely documented or even considered (Caron & Rutter, 1991). Yet, it is known that depressed parents, particularly hospitalized ones, have co-existing psychiatric disorders, such as alcoholism, drug dependence, and various forms of personality disorder. Thus, we are not sure whether the problems in these children stem from parental depression, per se, or from their other diagnoses. Similarly, numerous studies show that marital discord is commonly associated with depressive disorders in adults. Recent cross-sectional (Fendrich, Warner, & Weissman, 1990) and longitudinal research (Weissman, Fendrich, Warner, & Wickramaratne, 1992) suggests that parental depression is most strongly associated with child depression, whereas family discord (poor marital adjustment, parent-child discord, low cohesion, and affectionless control) is associated with externalizing disorders such as conduct disorder or substance abuse. Further study is needed, however, as Goodman and Brumley's (1990) claims contradict this conclusion that risk from parental mental disorders stems more from poor parenting (tenseness, rigidity, and lack of responsiveness) than from parental psychopathology, per se. The discrepant findings and conclusions may reflect the participants' demographic differences in the studies with regard to socioeconomic status, racial membership, and father absence.

The *child's age at assessment* is another issue warranting consideration. For instance, researchers have discovered different patterns of guilt in young versus older children of depressed mothers, with the pattern of older children seeming to be more maladaptive (Zahn-Waxler, Kochanska, Krupnick, & McKnew, 1990). A recent longitudinal study which charted the course of socioemotional development of young children of affectively ill parents (unipolar and bipolar) over a 3-year period showed that the children of affectively ill mothers exhibited more problems at later ages. Also, the children of unipolar and bipolar parents had different developmental trajectories. Whereas the developmental path of the children of unipolar mothers is an early and steady high level of problem behavior, children of bipolar mothers, in contrast, appeared without problems in the preschool period but exhibited an increase in depressive and disruptive problems near the end of childhood (Radke-Yarrow, Nottelmann, Martinez, Fox, & Belmont, 1992).

Establishing *cause–effect relations* is also a major concern. Bidirectional and interactional effects most likely exist. For instance, parental psychopathology may be associated with pregnancy and birth complications that could lead to congenital defects in the child, which in turn, could lead to parental unhappiness and rejection, which produce child maladjustment (Dodge, 1990). Although parents of depressed children may well be overprotective, and have more communication problems with their children (e.g., Magnussen, 1991), such behaviors may have arisen in response to certain child characteristics and behaviors. Before etiological significance can be attached to any family variable, it must be demonstrated that (a) the given variable (e.g., poor communication) is specifically linked to depressive disorder as opposed to other disorders such as delinquency or psychosis, (b) this variable has an impact on the child *prior* to the onset of the disorder, and (c) it is not confounded by an accompanying variable (e.g., a severe loss) that is the true etiological factor (Reiss, 1976).

Biological Bases

Genetic Factors

It is not difficult to trace many cases of childhood depression to stressful events such as depressive parents, rejection, and sudden losses such as death, divorce, or change of school. But the question arises as to why one person becomes depressed in response to a sudden loss or separation from a loved person or place, whereas others who have the same experience do not become depressed. Is there a biologically based predisposition to depression that is triggered by stressful events? If so, is the inherited vulnerability not only a necessary condition but also a sufficient condition? That is, does depression always have to be activated by stress? Depression does run in families (e.g., Weissman et al., 1992). Does it have a biological basis? This question has been pondered for some time, particularly with respect to adult depression.

Research evidence suggests an important role for heredity in adult affective disorders (Goodwin, 1982). Given the recency of interest in child depression as a clinical entity, it is not surprising to find that we know far less about the genetic (and social) factors operating in the affective disorders of childhood. To date there have been no twin studies with clinically depressed samples, no adoption studies, and no studies associating affective disorder with a gene whose locus is linked to that of a known gene, as is the case in color blindness. One twin study does provide modest support for a genetic influence on the symptoms associated with childhood depression (Wierzbicki, 1987). The subjects were 20 monozygotic pairs and 21 same-sex dizygotic twin-pairs ages 6 to 16 years. Mood was assessed by self, parent, and teachers. It was found that estimates of genetic variance were statistically significant for about half of the measures of both level and lability of depression. The limitations of this study (use of self and parental reports to determine twin zygosity, the absence of blind ratings with respect to twin zygosity, the small sample size, and the assumption of equal between-pair and within-pair environmental variances across groups) indicate the need for further research to establish the robustness of the present findings and to clarify the relationship between major childhood depression and subclinical depression.

Family studies constitute the primary method used to investigate the role of genetic factors in childhood depression. In one such study, it was shown that about one fourth of all parents ($FN = 29$) who were hospitalized with a primary depressive disorder had at least one child with at least five of the eight symptoms set by the researchers (moody, fearful, depressed and sad mood, significant death wishes, difficulties falling or staying asleep, being a loner, apprehensiveness around people, nervous or anxious most of the time). Seven of these eight youngsters had at least one episode lasting from 1 to 12 months. Five of the eight had received professional help. None of the children of normal parents had as many as five depressive symptoms (Welner, Welner, McCrary, & Leonard, 1977). Unfortunately, like all family studies, it is not possible to separate out the roles of environment and genetics. For example, children who are reared by depressive parents have many lessons in low self-esteem, are separated from parents due to hospitalization, and must deal more frequently with parental suicide (Goodwin, 1982). Twin and adoption studies are better suited to sort out the differential roles of psychological and genetic factors, although there are problems of interpretation even here as exemplified in the long-raging controversy on inheritability of intelligence.

In a study using empirical criteria to diagnose child depression, Puig-Antich, Perel, and Lupatkin (1979) found severe family discord or maltreatment in 11 of the 13 prepubertal cases of childhood depression. Moreover, a family history of depression, mania, alcoholism, or schizophrenia occurred in 61% of the relatives of depressed children. This study is distinctive in that it used unmodified adult criteria for the diagnosis of prepubertal major depressive disorder, divided subjects in endogenous and nonendogenous subtypes, blindly interviewed first-degree relatives over the age of 16 using a standardized interview, and arrived at diagnoses via standardized criteria (Research

Diagnostic Criteria). Again, like other family studies, the role of environmental factors was not controlled.

Family studies also suggest that children of bipolar parents are likely to be at risk for psychiatric disorder. For example, in a study using 27 patients with bipolar affective disorder, Kuyler, Rosenthal, and Igel (1980) found that 22 of 49 offspring interviewed were considered to have some type of psychiatric disorder. Almost 40% of the children with one ill parent were ill, in comparison with 50% of the children with both parents ill. Only 8%, however, had three or more symptoms associated with depressive disorder. The remaining 18 were diagnosed as having various personality disorders, adjustment reactions, attention-deficit hyperactivity disorder, as well as affective disorders. Reliance on the interview as the sole means of information may have resulted in the researchers' underestimation of depressive symptoms, in that parents may be less aware of their child's subjective feelings. The use of nonstandardized diagnostic criteria also limits the generalizability of findings.

McKnew, Cytryn, Efron, Gershon, and Bunney (1979) rated and twice interviewed 30 youngsters ages 5 to 14 whose parents had been admitted consecutively to the National Institute of Mental Health with a diagnosis of either bipolar affective disorder or unipolar depressive disorder. Weinberg's criteria were used to diagnose depression. Information from parents was also collected. Sixteen of the 30 children were judged depressed on at least one of the two structured interviews done 4 months apart and 1 was judged depressed on both interviews. No sex differences were noted. More recently, 18 of the children seen in the first study were followed up 4 years later when their mean age was 14. Interviewers did not know the previous diagnosis of either the children or the parents. Moreover, the more stringent *DSM-III-R* criteria were used. Of the 12 originally diagnosed as depressed based on Weinberg criteria, only 2 were symptomatic 4 years later (Apter et al., 1982). Of the remaining subjects, 3 had some type of psychiatric disorder: conduct disorder, overanxious disorder, and obsessive-compulsive disorder. This study provides clear evidence that children of depressed adults may have not only higher rates of psychological disorders in general but higher rates of affective disorders based on adult-like criteria.

Strober and colleagues (1989) compared 50 probands with bipolar affective disorder admitted to an adolescent psychiatric inpatient unit. Major affective disorder was found in 30% of the first-degree relatives of bipolar probands and 15% for bipolar disorder. The family loading for major affective disorder was significantly greater when the bipolar disorder in the proband was preceded by symptoms before the age of 12 years rather than in adolescence. That is, early age of onset appears to predict higher familial loading in bipolar affective disorder (Strober, 1992).

In sum, the family-genetic studies on depressed children, like the family studies of depressed adults, suggest a biological basis for affective disorders, particularly early onset bipolar and serious unipolar disorders (Rutter et al., 1990). As noted above, more rigorous studies need to be carried out with special attention devoted to the use of strict diagnostic criteria (e.g., *DSM-III-R*, psychometrically sound rating scales and interview schedules, analysis of data by subtypes, blind ratings, and a broader variety of control groups containing nonaffective psychiatric disorders). The more curious features of childhood depression (e.g., the equal sex ratio or male preponderance before puberty, overlap with conduct disorders) also deserve special attention (Rutter et al., 1990). Such studies, which are within our capabilities, will give us a clearer picture of the interactive roles played by environmental and biological forces.

Biochemical and Neuroendocrinal Factors

Biological models have also examined the role played by neuroendocrine factors in the etiology of depression (Burke & Puig-Antich, 1990). If there is a genetic predisposition underlying childhood depression, the question of what is inherited becomes critical. So far attention has been focused on four broadly defined areas (Goodwin, 1982). These are (a) the neurotransmitter systems that constitute the very specific networks of chemical messengers in the brain; (b) the membrane and functions involving salts such as sodium and potassium; (c) the neuroendocrine system comprising the pituitary gland and hypothalamus, which controls virtually all of the body's endocrine system; and (d) disturbances in the regulation of biological rhythms, namely, a disturbance in the "biological clock" that synchronizes our bodies' rhythms to the external 24-hour solar day. The major focus has been on the brain chemicals called neurotransmitters, the better known of which include norepinephrine, dopamine, and serotonin. These compounds are closely related, with the first two belonging to the chemical family known as the catecholamines and serotonin to the family of indolamines.

The catecholamine hypothesis states that something goes wrong with the amount of the transmitting substance present at the synapse. Three of several possible processes might go awry: (a) neuron-releasing transmitters may not supply enough of the chemical compound to transmit the message to the next neuron, (b) the neuron may produce too much of the substance, or (c) chemicals that break down the transmitting substances after they have carried out their mission work too rapidly thereby creating a shortage of the substance in the synaptic gap. Whatever the cause, too little neurotransmitter is believed to be associated with depression, too much to cause mania, and the right amount to be associated with a normal mood of well-being. More than two decades of research have yielded promising findings (e.g., Rogeness, Javors, Mass, & Macedo, 1990) but have failed to confirm the catecholamine hypothesis. For example, we know chemical substances effective against depression or mania also alter the amount of brain catecholamines. Nevertheless, research on new drugs shows that these are effective in treating depression even though they do not affect the neurotransmitters, evidence indicating that neurotransmitters are not critical (McNeal & Cimbolic, 1986).

Abnormalities in cortisol secretion constitute another area in which research has attempted to elucidate the neurochemical basis of affective disorders. Compared to normal persons, depressed adults excrete more daily cortisol, a hormone secreted by the adrenal glands and associated with stress. Exactly why this happens is not known. The dexamethasone suppression test (DST) is considered a neuroendocrine, biological marker for *endogenous* depression. This diagnostic procedure entails the oral administration of 0.5, 1.0, or 2.0 mg of dexamethasome at 11 p.m. followed by plasma or serum cortisol levels taken the following day. Those patients who hypersecrete on any one of the three readings taken at 8:00 a.m., 4:00 p.m., and 11:00 p.m. on day 2 are considered nonsuppressors. Results of studies are commonly reported in terms of sensitivity (the percentage of subjects who received the diagnosis of depression and who were positively identified by DST as well) and specificity (the percentage of subjects who did not receive a diagnosis of depression and who were not identified as depressed by DST). In a review of available evidence on the validity of the DST in children, Casat, Arana, and Powell (1989) found that the DST had about a 70% sensitivity and 70% specificity. Other investigators have found that the DST failed to discriminate among outpatient children with major depressive disorder, nonaffective psychiatric controls, and normal controls (Birmaher et al., 1992). Bear in mind that specificity rate is affected by the nature of the control groups. For instance, because cortisol nonsuppression is associated with other disorders influencing neuroendocrine regulation such as anorexia nervosa (Edelstein, Ray-Byrne, Fawzy, & Domfeld, 1983) and bulimia (Hudson, Laffer, & Pope, 1982), the specificity rate might be lower when the other psychiatric control groups contain youngsters with eating disorders. More than half of those diagnosed as depressed on a structured clinical interview (Kiddie-SADS) had a normal DST result (Klee & Garfinkel, 1984). Thus, cortisol suppression does not rule out a diagnosis of affective disorder. In brief, the findings indicate that very few young patients with psychiatric diagnosis other than depression will hypersecrete cortisol in response to the DST, although depressed patients are as effectively identified by psychometric measures such as inventories like the Child Behavior Checklist (Rey & Morris-Yates, 1991) and the Children's Depression Inventory (see Chapter 3), which had a 65% sensitivity. The DST might well not be the specific, sensitive, and objective measure for depression, even among adults, that has been long sought (Silver, 1986).

Other biological markers that have been investigated are sleep characteristics and growth hormones. Age and puberty have major effects on most psychobiological markers of depressive disorders, however, and the maturational differences are such that we would not expect to see adult abnormalities in prepubertal children. Given the complexities of research in this area, much remains to be learned about how beneficial the study of biological factors will be in pinpointing causal mechanisms, in diagnosing and subtyping, and in predicting outcomes and relapses of affective disorders.

SUMMARY

Of the five schools of thought regarding depression in children and adolescents, the view that depression in young people is essentially the same as depression in adults is currently popular. Major depressive disorder is characterized by either depressed mood (or possibly an irritable mood) or loss of interest or pleasure in most activities and associated symptoms, for a period of at least 2 weeks. Developmentally oriented approaches that take into account cognitive, linguistic, and socioemotional differences between young people and adults may eventually modify this prevalent view somewhat. Weinberg's criteria are the best known and most influential of the various operational criteria modified for childhood depression. In distinguishing depression from normality, the practitioner must differentiate depression from demoralization, normal grief, and stress from physical illness. Differential diagnosis also requires that depression in children and adolescents be distinguished from such related conditions as learning disabilities, attention deficit disorder, conduct disorder, school refusal, anorexia nervosa, adolescent schizophrenia, and alcohol and substance abuse. On many occasions, youth may suffer from depressive disorders as well as one of those related conditions. The best studies to date indicate that few children in the general population satisfy rigorous criteria for major depression, but about 25% of the clinical population meet *DSM-III-R* criteria for depressive disorder. Depression in young people has multiple causes. In many instances, both environmental and genetic factors may be at work to produce the youngster's depressive disorder. The single most powerful source of risk for depression among adolescents is the presence of parental depressive disorder—a circumstance that warrants intervention for the youth involved. Female predominance is age-specific, increasing from adolescence to middle age (Jorm, 1987).

REFERENCES

Achenbach, T. M., & Edelbrock, C. S. (1981). Behavioral problems and competencies reported by parents of normal and disturbed children aged 4 through 16. *Monographs of the Society for Research in Child Development, 46* (Serial No. 188).

Albert, N., & Beck, A. (1975). Incidence of depression in early adolescence: A preliminary study. *Journal of Youth and Adolescence, 4,* 301–307.

Allen-Meares, P. (1991). A study of depressive characteristics in behaviorally disordered children and adolescents. *Children and Youth Services Review, 13,* 271-286.

American Psychiatric Association. (1987). *Diagnostic and statistical manual of mental disorders* (3rd ed., rev.). Washington, DC: Author.

Apter, A., Borengasser, M., Mamovit, J., Bartko, J., Cytryn, L., & McKnew, D. (1982). A four-year follow-up of depressed children. *Journal of Preventive Psychiatry, 1,* 331–335.

Bernstein, G. (1991). Comorbidity and severity of anxiety and depressive disorders in a clinic sample. *Journal of the American Academy of Child and Adolescent Psychiatry, 30,* 43–50.

Bernstein, G., & Garfinkel, B. (1986). School phobia: The overlap of affective and anxiety disorders. *Journal of the American Academy of Child Psychiatry, 25,* 235–241.

Billings, A., & Moos, R. (1985). Children of parents with unipolar depression: A controlled 1-year follow-up. *Journal of Abnormal Child Psychology, 14,* 149–166.

Birmaher, B., Ryan, N., Dahl, R., Rabinovich, H., Ambrosini, P., Williamson, D., Novacenko, H., Nelson, B., Lo, E., & Puig-Antich, J. (1992). Dexamethasone suppression test in children with major depressive disorder. *Journal of the American Academy of Child and Adolescent Psychiatry, 31,* 291-297.

Bleuler, E. (1934). *Textbook of psychiatry.* New York: Macmillan.

Bowlby, J. (1973). *Attachment and loss: Separation and anger.* London: Hogarth Press.

Bowring, M., & Kovacs, M. (1992). Difficulties in diagnosing manic disorders among children and adolescents, *Journal of the American Academy of Child and Adolescent Psychiatry, 31,* 611-614.

Brown, G., & Harris, T. (1978). *Social origins of depression.* London: Tavistock Press.

Brumbach, R., Jackoway, M., & Weinberg, W. (1980). Relation of intelligence to childhood depression in children referred to an educational diagnostic center. *Perceptual and Motor Skills, 50,* 11–17.

Buchanan, M., & Wolf, J. (1986). A comprehensive study of learning disabled adults. *Journal of Learning Disabilities, 19,* 34–38.

Burbach, D., & Borduin, D. (1986). Parent-child relations and the etiology of depression. *Clinical Psychology Review, 6,* 133–153.

Burke, P., & Puig-Antich, J. (1990). Psychobiology of childhood depression. In M. Lewis & S. Miller (Eds.), *Handbook of developmental psychopathology* (pp. 327–339). New York: Plenum.

Cantwell, D. (1983). Depression in childhood: Clinical picture and diagnostic criteria. In D. Cantwell & G. Carlson (Eds.), *Affective disorders in childhood and adolescence: An update* (pp. 3–18). New York: Spectrum.

Cantwell, D., & Baker, L. (1991). Manifestations of depressive affect in adolescence. *Journal of Youth and Adolescence, 20,* 121-133.

Cantwell, D., & Carlson, G. (1983). Issues in classification. In D. Cantwell & G. Carlson (Eds.), *Affective disorders in childhood and adolescence: An update* (pp. 19–38). New York: Spectrum.

Cantwell, D., Sturzenberger, S., Burroughs, J., Salkin, B., & Green, J. (1977). Anorexia nervosa: An affective disorder. *Archives of General Psychiatry, 34,* 1087–1091.

Carlson, G. (1990). Bipolar disorders in children and adolescents. In B. Garfinkel, G. Carlson, & E. Weller (Eds.) *Psychiatric disorders in children and adolescents* (pp. 21-36). Philadelphia: W. B. Saunders.

Carlson, G., & Cantwell, D. (1979). A survey of depressive symptoms in a child and adolescent psychiatric population. *Journal of the American Academy of Child Psychiatry, 18,* 587–599.

Carlson, G., & Cantwell, D. (1980). A survey of depressive symptoms, syndrome and disorder in a child psychiatric population. *Journal of Child Psychology and Psychiatry, 21,* 19–25.

Carlson, G., & Garber, J. (1986). Developmental issues in the classification of depression in children. In M. Rutter, C. Izard, & P. Read (Eds.), *Depression in young people: Developmental and clinical perspectives* (pp. 399–434). New York: Guilford.

Caron, C., & Rutter, M. (1991). Comorbidity in child psychopathology: Concepts, issues and research strategies. *Journal of Child Psychology and Psychiatry, 31,* 1063–1078.

Casat, C., Arana, G., & Powell, K. (1989). The DST in children and adolescents with major depressive disorder. *American Journal of Psychiatry, 146,* 503–507.

Chambers, W., Puig-Antich, J., Tabrizi, M., & Davies, M. (1982). Psychotic symptoms in prepubertal major depressive disorder. *Archives of General Psychiatry, 39,* 921–927.

Chess, S., Thomas, A., & Hassibi, M. (1983). Depression in childhood and adolescence. *The Journal of Nervous and Mental Disease, 171,* 411–420.

Cicchetti, D., & Schneider-Rosen, K. (1986). An organizational approach to childhood depression. In M. Rutter, C. Izard, & P. Read (Eds.), *Depression in young people* (pp. 71-134). New York: Guilford.

Clark, L., & Watson, D. (1991). Tripartite model of anxiety and depression: Psychometric evidence and taxonomic implications. *Journal of Abnormal Psychology, 100,* 316–336.

Clarizio, H., & McCoy, G. (1983). *Behavior disorders in children.* New York: Harper & Row.

Clarizio, H., & Phillips, S. (1986). Sex bias in the placement of learning disabled students. *Psychology in the Schools, 23,* 44–52.

Clarizio, H., & Phillips, S. (1989). Defining severe discrepancy in the diagnosis of learning disabilities: A comparison of methods. *Journal of School Psychology, 27,* 381-389.

Clayton, P. (1982). Bereavement. In E. Paykel (Ed.), *Handbook of affective disorders* (pp. 403–415). Edinburgh & London: Churchill-Livingstone.

Cone, T., Wilson, L., Bradley, C., & Reese, J. (1985). Characteristics of LD students in Iowa: An empirical investigation. *Learning Disabilities Quarterly, 8,* 211-220.

Costello, C. (1980). Childhood depression: Three basic but questionable assumptions in the Lefkowitz and Burton Critique. *Psychological Bulletin, 87,* 185–190.

Crook, T., Raskin, A., & Eliot, J. (1981). Parent-child relationships and adult depression. *Child Development, 52,* 950–957.

Cytryn, L., McKnew, D., & Bunney, W. (1980). Diagnosis of depression in children: A reassessment. *American Journal of Psychiatry, 137,* 22–25.

de Saussure, R. (1947). A case study. *Psychoanalytic Study of the Child, 2,* 417–426.

Dobson, K. (1985). Relationship between anxiety and depression. *Clinical Psychology Review, 5,* 305–324.

Dodge, K. (1990). Developmental psychopathology in children of depressed mothers. *Developmental Psychology, 26,* 3–6.

Downey, G., & Coyne, J. (1990). Children of depressed parents: An integrative review. *Psychological Bulletin, 108,* 50–76.

Edelbrock, D., & Achenbach, T. (1980). A typology of child behavior profile patterns: Distribution and correlates in disturbed children aged 6 to 16. *Journal of Abnormal Child Psychology, 8,* 441-470.

Edelsohn, G., Ialongo, N., Werthamer-Larsson, L., Crockett, L., & Kellam, S. (1992). Self-reported depressive symptoms in first-grade children: Developmentally transient phenomena? *Journal of the American Academy of Child and Adolescent Psychiatry, 31,* 282–290.

Edelstein, C., Ray-Byrne, R., Fawzy, A., & Domfeld, L. (1983, May). *Effects of weight loss on the dexamethasone test.* Paper presented at the American Psychiatric Association Meeting, New York.

Fendrich, M., Warner, V., & Weissman, M. (1990). Family risk factors, parental depression, and childhood psychopathology. *Developmental Psychology, 26,* 40–50.

Finch, A., Lipovsky, J., & Casat, C. (1989). Anxiety and depression in children: Negative affectivity or separate constructs? In P. Kendall & D. Watson (Eds.) *Anxiety and depression: Distinctive and overlapping features* (pp. 171-196). New York: Academic Press.

Fleming, J., & Offord, D. (1990). Epidemiology of childhood depressive disorders: A critical review. *Journal of the American Academy of Child and Adolescent Psychiatry, 29,* 571-580.

Freud, A., & Burlingham, D. (1944). *Infants without families.* New York: International Universities Press.

Frommer, C. (1968). Depressive illness in childhood. In A. Coppens & A. Walk (Eds.), *Recent developments in affective disorders* (pp. 117-136). Ashford, Kent: Headley Brothers.

Garfinkel, B. (1986, June). *Major affective disorders in children and adolescents.* Paper presented at the conference on Suicide and Depression in Children and Adolescents: Assessment and Intervention Techniques, Minneapolis, MN.

Goodman, S., & Brumley, H. (1990). Schizophrenic and depressed mothers: Relational deficits in parenting. *Developmental Psychology, 26,* 31-39.

Goodwin, F. (1982). *Depression and manic-depressive illness.* Washington, DC: U.S. Department of Health and Human Services.

Graham, P.J. (1979). Epidemiological studies. In H. C. Quay & J. S. Werry (Eds.), *Psychopathological disorders of childhood* (2nd ed., pp. 185-209). New York: Wiley.

Hammen, C., Barge, D., Burney, E., & Adrian, C. (1990). Longitudinal study of diagnosis in children and women with unipolar and bipolar affective disorder. *Archives of General Psychiatry, 47,* 1112-1117.

Harrington, R., Fudge, H., Rutter, M., Pickles, A., & Hill, A. (1991). Adult outcome of childhood and adolescent depression: II. Links with antisocial disorders. *Journal of the American Academy of Child and Adolescent Psychiatry, 30,* 434-439.

Hendren, R. (1983). Depression in anorexia nervosa. *Journal of the American Academy of Child Psychiatry, 22,* 59-62.

Hudson, J., Laffer, P., & Pope, H. (1982). Bulimia related to affective disorder by family history and response to the dexamethasone suppression test. *American Journal of Psychiatry, 139,* 685-687.

Jorm, A. (1987). Sex and age differences in depression: A quantitative synthesis of published research. *Australian and New Zealand Journal of Psychiatry, 21,* 46-53.

Kandel, D. B., & Davies, M. (1982). Epidemiology of depressive mood in adolescents. *Archives of General Psychiatry, 39,* 1205-1212.

Kashani, J., Lababidi, A., & Jones, R. (1982). Depression in children and adolescents with cardiovascular symptomatology: The significance of chest pain. *Journal of the American Academy of Child Psychiatry, 21,* 187-189.

Kashani, J., & Simonds, J. (1979). The incidence of depression in children. *American Journal of Psychiatry, 136,* 1203-1204.

Kendall, P., & Watson, D. (1989). *Anxiety and depression: Distinctive and overlapping features.* New York: Academic Press.
Kendler, K., Neale, M., Kessler, R., Heath, A., & Eaves, L. (1992). Childhood parental loss and adult psychopathology in women: A twin perspective study. *Archives of General Psychiatry, 4,* 109–120.
Klee, S., & Garfinkel, B. (1984). Identification of depression in children and adolescents: The role of the dexamethasone depression test. *Journal of the American Academy of Child Psychiatry, 23,* 410–415.
Klein, D., Depue, R., & Slater, J. (1985). Cyclothymia in the adolescent offspring of parents with bipolar affective disorder. *Journal of Abnormal Psychology, 94,* 115–127.
Klein, D., Gittelman, R., Quitkin, F., & Rifkin, D. (1980). *Diagnosis and drug treatment of psychiatric disorder, adult and children.* Baltimore: Williams & Wilkins.
Klein, R., & Last, C. (1989). *Anxiety disorders in children.* Newbury Park, CA: Sage Publications.
Kovacs, M., & Beck, A. (1977). An empirical-clinical approach toward a definition of childhood depression. In J. Schulterbrant & A. Raskin (Eds.), *Depression in childhood: Diagnosis, treatment, and conceptual models* (pp. 1-25). New York: Raven Press.
Kovacs, M., Paulauskas, S., Gatsonis, C., & Richards, C. (1988). Depressive disorders in childhood: A longitudinal study of comorbidity with and risk for conduct disorders. *Journal of Affective Disorders, 15,* 205–217.
Kovacs, M., Feinberg, T., Crouse-Novak, M., Paulauskas, S., & Finkelstein, R. (1984). Depressive disorders in childhood. I. A longitudinal prospective study of characteristics and recovery. *Archives of General Psychiatry, 41,* 229–237.
Kuyler, P., Rosenthal, L., & Igel, G. (1980). Psychopathology among children of manic-depressive patients. *Biological Psychiatry, 15,* 589–597.
Laurent, J., Landau, S., & Stark, K. (1993). Conditional probabilities in the diagnosis of depressive and anxiety disorders in children. *School Psychology Review, 22,* 98–114.
Lefkowitz, M., & Burton, N. (1978). Childhood depression: A critique of the concept. *Psychological Bulletin, 85,* 716–726.
Lefkowitz, M., & Tesiny, E. (1985). Depression in children: Prevalence and correlates. *Journal of Consulting and Clinical Psychology, 53,* 647–656.
Lefkowitz, M., Tesiny, E., & Gordon, N. (1980). Childhood depression, family income, and locus of control. *Journal of Nervous and Mental Disease, 168,* 732-735.
Ling, W., Oftedal, G., & Weinberg, W. (1970). Depressive illness in childhood presenting as severe headache. *American Journal of Diseases in Children, 120,* 122-124.

Maag, J., & Behrens, J. (1989). Depression and cognitive self-statements of learning disabled and seriously emotionally disturbed adolescents. *Journal of Special Education, 23,* 17–27.

Maag, J., & Forness, S. (1991). Depression in children and adolescents: Identification, assessment and treatment. *Focus on Exceptional Children, 24*(1), 1-19.

Magnussen, M. (1991). Characteristics of depressed and nondepressed children and their parents. *Child Psychiatry and Human Development, 23,* 185–191.

Malmquist, C. (1971). Depressions in childhood and adolescence. *New England Journal of Medicine, 284,* 887–893.

McConville, B., & Boag, L. (1973, September). *Therapeutic approaches in childhood depression.* Paper presented at the annual meeting of the Canadian Psychiatric Association, Vancouver.

McConville, B., Boag, L., & Purohit, A. (1973). Three types of childhood depression. *Canadian Journal of Psychiatry, 18,* 133–138.

McKnew, D., Cytryn, L., Efron, A., Gershon, E., & Bunney, W. (1979). Off-spring of patients with affective disorders. *British Journal of Psychiatry, 134,* 148–152.

McNeal, E., & Cimbolic, P. (1986). Antidepressants and biochemical theories of depression. *Psychological Bulletin, 99,* 361–374.

Mendelson, W., Johnson, N., & Stewart, M. (1971). Hyperactive children as teenagers. A follow-up study. *Journal of Nervous and Mental Disease, 153,* 273–279.

National Institute of Mental Health. (1978). *Causes, detection and treatment of childhood depression* (DHEW Publication No. 78–612). Washington, DC: Government Printing Office.

Parker, G. (1983). *Parental overprotection: A risk factor in psychosocial development.* New York: Grune & Stratton.

Petti, T. (1978). Depression in hospitalized child psychiatry patients: Approaches to measuring depression. *Journal of the American Academy of Child Psychiatry, 17,* 49–59.

Poznanski, E., & Zrull, J. (1970). Childhood depression: Clinical characteristics of overtly depressed children. *Archives of General Psychiatry, 23,* 8–15.

Puig-Antich, J., Blau, S., Marx, J., Greenhill, L., & Chambers, W. (1978). Prepubertal major depressive disorder: A pilot study. *Journal of the American Academy of Child Psychiatry, 17,* 695–707.

Puig-Antich, J., Goetz, D., Davies, M., Kaplan, T., Davies, S., Ostrow, L., & Asnis, L. (1989). A controlled family history study of prepubertal major depressive disorder. *Archives of General Psychiatry, 46,* 406–418.

Puig-Antich, J., Lukens, E., Davies, M., Goetz, D., Brennan-Quattrock, J., & Todak, G. (1985a). Psychosocial functioning in prepubertal major depressive disorders I. Interpersonal relationships during the depressive episode. *Archives of General Psychiatry, 42,* 500–507.

Puig-Antich, J., Lukens, E., Davies, M., Goetz, D., Brennan-Quattrock, J., & Todak, G. (1985b). Psychosocial functioning in prepubertal major depressive disorders II. Interpersonal relationships after sustained recovery from affective episode. *Archives of General Psychiatry, 42,* 511–517.

Puig-Antich, J., Perel, J., & Lupatkin, W. (1979). Plasma levels of imipramine (IMI) and desmethylimipramine (DMI) and clinical response in prepubertal major depressive disorders: A preliminary report. *Journal of the American Academy of Child Psychiatry, 18,* 616–627.

Radke-Yarrow, M., Nottelmann, E., Martinez, P., Fox, M., & Belmont, B. (1992). Young children of affectively ill parents: A longitudinal study of psychosocial development. *Journal of the American Academy of Child and Adolescent Psychiatry, 31,* 68–77.

Reiss, D. (1976). The family and schizophrenia. *American Journal of Psychiatry, 133,* 181–185.

Rey, J., & Morris-Yates, A. (1991). Adolescent depression and the Child Behavior Checklist. *Journal of the American Academy of Child and Adolescent Psychiatry, 30,* 423–427.

Reynolds, W. (1985). Depression in children and adolescents: Diagnosis, assessment, intervention strategies and research. In T. Kratochwill (Ed.), *Advances in school psychology* (pp. 133–189). Hillsdale, NJ: Erlbaum.

Robins, L., & Price, R. (1991). Adult disorders predicted by childhood conduct problems: Results from the NIMH Epidemiological Catchment Area Project. *Psychiatry, 54,* 113–132.

Rogeness, G., Javors, M., Maas, J., & Macedo, C. (1990). Catecholamines and diagnoses in children. *Journal of the American Academy of Child and Adolescent Psychiatry, 29,* 234–241.

Rosenstock, M. (1985). The first 900: A nine-year longitudinal analysis of consecutive adolescent inpatients. *Adolescence, 20,* 959–973.

Rourke, B., Young, G., & Leenaars, A. (1989). A childhood learning disability that predisposes those afflicted to adolescent and adult depression and suicide risk. *Journal of Learning Disabilities, 22,* 169–174.

Rutter, M. (1986). The developmental psychopathology of depression: Issues and perspectives. In M. Rutter, C. Izard, & P. Read (Eds.), *Depression in young people* (pp. 3–32). New York: Guilford.

Rutter, M., Graham, P., Chadwick, O., & Yule, W. (1976). Adolescent turmoil: Fact or fiction? *Journal of Child Psychology and Psychiatry, 17,* 35–56.

Rutter, M., MacDonald, H., LeCouteur, A., Harrington, R., Bolton, P., & Bailey, A. (1990). Genetic factors in child psychiatric disorders II: Empirical findings. *Journal of Child Psychology and Psychiatry, 31,* 39–84.

Rutter, M., Tizard, J., & Whitmore, K. (1970/1981). *Education, health and behavior.* Huntington, NY: Krieger.

Seagull, E., & Weinshank, A. (1984). Childhood depression in a selected group of low-achieving seventh graders. *Journal of Clinical Child Psychology, 13,* 138–140.

Silver, H. (1986). Physical complaints correlate better with depression than dexamethasone suppression test results. *Journal of Clinical Psychiatry, 47,* 179–181.
Spitz, R. A. (1946). Anaclitic depression. *Psychoanalytic Study of the Child, 2,* 313–342.
Spitzer, R., Endicott, J., & Robins, E. (1978). *Research diagnostic criteria for a selected group of functional disorders* (3rd ed.). New York: New York State Psychiatric Institute.
Sroufe, A., & Rutter, M. (1984). The domain of developmental psychopathology. *Child Development, 55,* 17–29.
Strober, M., Hanna, G., & McCracken, J. (1989). Bipolar disorder. In C. Last & M. Hersen (Eds.), *Handbook of child psychiatric disorders* (pp. 299–316). New York: Wiley.
Strober, M. (1992). Relevance of early age-of-onset in genetic studies of bipolar affective disorder. *Journal of the American Academy of Child and Adolescent Psychiatry, 31,* 505–610.
Strober, M., & Carlson, G. (1982). Bipolar illness in adolescents with major depression. *Archives of General Psychiatry, 39,* 549–555.
Swartz, J. (1987). Depression often missed in teens. *APA Monitor, 42,* 29.
Teri, L. (1982). Depression in adolescence: Its relationship to assertion and various aspects of self-image. *Journal of Clinical Child Psychology, 11,* 101-106.
U.S. Department of Health and Human Services. (1986). *Mental health statistical note no. 177. Characteristics of admissions to the inpatient services of state and county mental hospitals, United States, 1980.* Washington, DC: Government Printing Office.
Vincenzi, H. (1987). Depression and reading ability in sixth grade children. *Journal of School Psychology, 25,* 155–160.
Weinberg, W., Rutman, J., Sullivan, L., Penick, E., & Dietz, S. (1973). Depression in children referred to an educational diagnostic center: Diagnosis and treatment. *Journal of Pediatrics, 83,* 1065–1072.
Weiss, G., Minde, K., Werry, J., Douglas, R., & Nemeth, E. (1971). Studies on the hyperactive child. VIII. Five-year follow-up. *Archives of General Psychiatry, 24,* 209–214.
Weissman, M., Bruce, M., Leaf, P., Florio, L., & Holzer, C. (1991). Affective disorders. In L. Robins & D. Regier (Eds.) *Psychiatric disorders in America* (pp 53–80). New York: The Free Press.
Weissman, M., Fendrich, M., Warner, V., & Wickramaratne, P. (1992). Incidence of psychiatric disorder in off-spring at high and low risk for depression. *Journal of the American Academy of Child and Adolescent Psychiatry, 31,* 640–648.
Welner, Z., Welner, A., McCrary, M.D., & Leonard, M.A. (1977). Psychopathology in children of inpatients with depression: A controlled study. *Journal of Nervous and Mental Disease, 164,* 408–413.

Wierzbicki, M. (1987). Similarity of monozygotic and dizygotic child twins in level and lability of subclinically depressed mood. *American Journal of Orthopsychiatry, 57,* 33–39.

Wright-Strowderman, C., & Watson, B. (1992). The prevalence of depressive symptoms in children with learning disabilities. *Journal of Learning Disabilities, 25,* 258–264.

Zahn-Waxler, C., Kochanska, G., Krupnick, J., & McKnew, D. (1990). Patterns of guilt in children of depressed and well mothers. *Developmental Psychology, 26,* 51-59.

Zoccolillo, M. (1992). Co-occurrence of conduct disorder and its adult outcomes with depressive and anxiety disorders: A review. *Journal of the American Academy for Child and Adolescent Psychiatry, 31,* 547–556.

2 A DEVELOPMENTAL APPROACH

Child psychopathology differs from adult psychopathology in that it has the developing child as its focus of study. Close cooperation between the fields of child psychology and child psychopathology would make eminent sense. Yet, the fields have traditionally worked apart from each other. Until very recently developmental psychologists have emphasized the development of universals, those phenomena that occur in all children, such as stages of moral development, whereas psychopathologists have emphasized the variations and idiosyncrasies of behavior. Why is it, for example, that loss of a parent results in a normal grieving experience for one child and a severe depression for another child? Why is it that one youngster experiences normal guilt over an intentional transgression while another becomes psychologically disabled and severely depressed over the same intentional transgression? As a consequence of developmental psychology's nomothetic approach and psychopathology's idiographic focus, we do not have a vast fund of knowledge regarding how cognitive, social, and emotional processes or mechanisms become distorted resulting in clinical disorders, how early experiences produce sensitizing or immunizing effects, whether these sensitizing or immunizing effects are age dependent, and how the ability to experience and to express depressive feelings varies with age.

In this chapter, we will address a variety of topics relevant to a developmental perspective on affective disorders in childhood. First, three constructs with relevance for affective disorders—the development of competence, self-understanding, and emotional awareness/expression—will be examined from the field of developmental psychology. Next, discussion will center around how depressive symptomatology varies with developmental stage. Then, the factors of age and gender will be presented as variables associated with incidence figures. Finally, the important subject of continuities and discontinuities in affective disorders will be addressed. Although our database is admittedly sketchy, and obvious gaps exist in our understanding of processes and mechanisms, a fuller realization of the potential value that can accrue from a close interplay between developmental psychology and developmental psychopathology is possible.

NORMAL DEVELOPMENT AND CHILDHOOD DEPRESSION

Three topics from developmental research are believed to play a particularly significant role in the understanding of the pathological processes seen in childhood depression. These include developmental changes in competence, self-understanding, the ontogenesis of emotions, and the awareness of emotions (Cicchetti & Schneider-Rosen, 1986).

Competence

The concept of competence has considerable relevance to depression because of the important interrelationships that exist between affect, cognition, and social relations (Cicchetti & Schneider-Rosen, 1986). The competent child is one who is able to use internal resources (specific skills and broad characteristics) and external resources to achieve a satisfactory developmental adaptation, namely, successful resolution of the developmental tasks most salient for specific periods. However, because every form of psychopathology most likely manifests itself as incompetence in the developmental period in which it occurs, there is a need to develop finer measures of competence and incompetence. For instance, a depressed preschooler and an autistic preschooler could well be assessed as incompetent but they are probably incompetent for different reasons. The depressed preschooler might lack the interest, excitement, and high activity level to persevere when frustrated, whereas the autistic youngster, incapable of secure attachment to a caregiver (among other things), would not seek parental assistance when necessary. Knowing the manner in which depression affects competence could lead to more individually tailored treatment centering around development of the specific competencies of a given developmental period. Consider further the relationship between insecure attachment, the most thoroughly studied of those stage-salient developmental tasks relevant to competence, and depression among normal infants. Ainsworth, Blehar, Waters, and Wall (1978) noted that 30% of infants are insecurely attached. Ainsworth refined the notion of insecure attachments by distinguishing two types—anxious-avoidant and anxious-resistant—in a laudable effort to describe different forms of incompetence. The anxious-avoidant type are more at risk for excessive dependency behavior in the preschool period (Sroufe, 1983). And excessive dependency has been implicated as a potential risk factor in depression (Bemporad & Wilson, 1978). Thus, a causal sequence of anxious-avoidant infant/dependent child depression may exist. Anxious-resistant infants, who explore very little and have trouble being comforted by their caregiver upon reunion, may also be at risk for subsequent depressive disorders because a means of coping with distress is missing and because later support networks are likely to be weak (Waters, Wippman, & Sroufe, 1979).

The above remarks are sketchy and speculative as no studies have been done on how depressed youngsters resolve stage-salient developmental tasks. Nonetheless, information from empirical studies and theoretical treatises (Sroufe & Rutter, 1984) on competence with normal children enables us to formulate hypotheses concerning its relationship to childhood depression. The fact that 30% of infants fail to achieve secure attachments to a caregiver (Ainsworth et al., 1978) indicates that early incompetence does not always lead to later depression, for the prevalence rate of affective disorders is not nearly this high. Early incompetence may follow any one of the seven paths discussed later in this chapter (Rutter, 1986), but it remains for future studies to clarify why incompetence leads to one form of psychological disturbance rather than another, or perhaps to none at all. Although the focus here has been on the relationship between attachment and competence, additional study of stage-salient issues such as autonomy and peer relationships is critical to further our understanding of the competence/depression issue.

Self-Understanding and Self-Esteem

The loss of self-esteem plays a central role in the psychoanalytic, cognitive, and behavioral schools of thought about depression. As described in Chapter 4, for example, cognitions involved in the loss of self-esteem could plausibly explain a large portion of a depressed person's defeating conceptions of self, world, and future that comprise Beck's (1967) "negative cognitive triad."

Many of the major changes in self-understanding, a cognitive skill or ability, are related to changes in the child's thinking. For instance, before the age of 8, children view themselves in "physicalistic" terms (Selman, 1980), that is, in terms of what they own and what they do. Beyond age 8, the self is seen as basically psychological with less emphasis on the material and activity dimensions of self. In a similar vein, children under the age of 7 tend to evaluate themselves in absolute terms. After the age of 7, children tend to evaluate their characteristics or performances by comparison to others. That is, as children move from preoperational to concrete operational thought, they tend to switch from standards (what should be) to norms (what is) when evaluating the self. Another transition at this time involves a shift from thinking of themselves in terms of what they are usually apt to do at various times and in various places (habitual actions) to thinking of themselves more often in terms of what theiractualabilitiesare(actioncompetencies).

The three transitions from physicalistic to psychological self-understanding, from absolute to relative self-appraisals, and from action-based self-cognitions to competency-based ones all have potential relevance to childhood depression. Consider, for instance, Abramson's reformulation (Abramson, Seligman, & Teasdale, 1978) of Seligman's (1975) notion of learned helplessness. Abramson et al. (1978) have suggested that individuals have characteristic attributional styles (i.e., habitual ways of explaining the causes of uncontrollable good and bad events). Three independent dimensions of attributions are deemed important: global vs. specific, stable vs. unstable, and personal vs. universal. To the extent that an individual points to personal, stable, and global causes of bad events, then that young person is increasingly likely to be helpless and depressed once a bad event is experienced. The transition from an unstable physicalistic conception of self to a psychological conception of self is a necessary precondition for attributing noncontingency between behavior and reward or punishment to *stable* characteristics of the self, and hence for an enduring depressive condition. In a similar vein, when children become capable of knowing whether others have succeeded in situations where they have failed (e.g., schoolwork), they are more apt to make *personal* attributions or explanations that reflect relatively stable conceptions of their global character, thereby leading to depressed affect across situations. Finally, the transition from cognitions of self centering on acting (which are amenable to change through conscious effort and more likely to be shared by others rather than uniquely personal) to those centering on relatively enduring, unique competencies is also a precondition for attributions leading to depressed affect. In sum, the mood of the young child's attributions tends to be unstable and specific to the situation. After about the age of 8, the transition in the nature of self-cognitions makes it possible for a child to experience a loss of self-esteem accompanying depressed affect that is associated with personal comparisons based on global and psychological qualities resulting in negative appraisals of the self. Developmental changes in competence and in self-understanding may help in understanding the causes of depression in young people. Likewise, it may be possible to shed light on the overt manifestations of depression through study of emotional development and of the awareness of emotions, the next topic of discussion.

Emotional Awareness and Expression

Emotions such as sadness, tearfulness, irritability, anger, fear, shame, and guilt are often cardinal features of childhood depression. Thus, an understanding of the development of emotion and the *awareness* of emotion are significant considerations.

Not all emotions related to depressive disorders reflect a developmental trend. For instance, Weiner and Graham's (1984) study of attributional analysis showed that when 6- to 11-year-olds were queried about incidents in their lives, only guilt followed a developmental course. The emotions of pity and anger were not age dependent in this age range. Although all children reported feelings of guilt when they engaged in wrongdoing, the 6- and 7-year-olds were much more inclined than older youngsters to feel guilty over uncontrollable or accidental outcomes. For older youth, intentionality and controllability of outcomes were clearly related to feelings of guilt. Thus, for a 7-year-old to feel guilty over his parent's death would seem normal; such an emotional reaction on the part of an 11-year-old would seem a developmentally inappropriate attribution. Other areas worthy of investigation within a developmental framework include the experiencing of conflicting emotions, the ability to have fun (hedonic capacity), and the experiencing of disappointment (Cicchetti & Schneider-Rosen, 1986).

In general, even preschoolers can distinguish basic emotions in others, can differentiate words used to describe emotion, and can identify causal events appropriately (Masters & Carlson, 1984). Emotional awareness continues to develop beyond the preschool years. Eight- and 11-year-olds can, for instance, distinguish the emotions that pertain to the self (*I* am sad) and those directed at others (I hate *him*). Yet, it is not until the adolescent years that individuals are able to locate the antecedents of emotional states within themselves (Schwartz & Trabasso, 1984).

A caveat must be mentioned. One must exercise care in extending findings about the emotional development and emotional awareness of normal youngsters to depressed children. For instance, Kovacs (1986), in her clinical experience, has found that psychiatrically referred, nonretarded outpatients have difficulty differentiating their own emotions in the absence of external cues, even though normal children accomplish this during the preschool years. Developmental studies carried out with normal children and adolescents should be replicated with depressed youngsters to guard against unwarranted extrapolations.

Much remains to be learned regarding the role that normal emotional development can play in better understanding the expression, etiology, course, and treatment of childhood and adolescent depressive disorders. First, the exact role of emotions in the etiology and expression of depression is imprecise. For instance, there is no clear account of how anger, a common symptom in childhood depression, is related to dysphoria. Second, because the topic of emotional development in normal children has been neglected in psychology, normative data are lacking against which to plot disordered emotional development. Third, the exact nature of the relationships between emotional and cognitive development in normal or abnormal populations is equivocal. Thus, the precise influence of each domain upon the other remains incomplete and unclear (Cicchetti & Schneider-Rosen, 1986). As these knowledge voids are filled, a clearer understanding will emerge of how emotions are linked to depressive disorders in young people.

DEVELOPMENTAL TRENDS IN DEPRESSIVE SYMPTOMATOLOGY

Before embarking upon a discussion of the nature of depressive symptomatology at various developmental periods, the reader should be cautioned that there has been no comprehensive study of depressive disorders across the preschool, childhood, adolescent, and adult age range (Cantwell & Baker, 1991). Indeed, studies making direct comparisons across different age groups of depressed people are rare. Because of the absence of any comprehensive study of age differences across various groups, much of what is said about the correspondence between adult symptomatology and that of younger depressed individuals has been inferred on the weak methodology of comparing the literature on depressed adults with that of younger people.

The Preschool Period

The age of onset of depression has been generally considered to be in early adulthood. Although increasing attention is being focused on prepubertal depression, there have been scattered reports on depression among children under the age of 6. Clinical descriptions have long suggested that severe sensory and social deprivation in the first year of life creates a behavioral syndrome that in many ways resembles an adult retarded depression. Spitz (1946) described "anaclitic depression," a depressive condition that occurs in the second half of the first year of life. Based on observations of infants separated from caretakers during this time period, Bowlby (1969) postulated a three-phase response—protest, despair, and detachment. Anger dominates the protest phase; sadness, withdrawal, and lack of interest characterize the despair phase; and interest increments and sadness decrements are salient features in the detachment phase. A similar pattern of apathy, lack of interest, and lack of engagement in play has been described by Gaensbauer (1980) in a 3½-month-old. Spitz (1946) regarded "anaclitic depression" as a fairly common occurrence among institutionalized children. The protest-despair-detachment sequence is seen most frequently between about 6 months and 4 years of age among those admitted to a hospital or residential nursery (Bowlby, 1969, 1980; Rutter, 1981).

Controversy continues as to whether depression in early childhood is the same condition as depression in middle childhood or adolescence. First, the emotions of fear, shame, and guilt are missing from descriptions of depression in infancy. Second, although infants can display facial anger, it is doubtful if the anger is either clearly object oriented or inner directed (Izard & Schwartz, 1986). In brief, sadness is the emotion that dominates the depressive picture during early infancy. Third, as Rutter (1986) ponders, if loss (of a loved one and personal parenting) is central to depression, and if those syndromes in institutionalized youngsters are indeed depressive disorders, why does depression decline in frequency during middle childhood only to rise again in adolescence? Separation per se is neither a necessary nor a sufficient condition for the occurrence of childhood depression for many youngsters undergo separation experiences without becoming depressed, and many depressed individuals have not experienced separation. Experiencing separation is best regarded as a facilitative condition of childhood depression. Perhaps different explanations are needed to account for changes in depression during early childhood and adolescence. For instance, Kashani and Carlson (1987) present data suggesting a strong relationship between physical abuse and neglect and symptomatology of major depressive disorder in preschool-age children. The dilemmas inherent in diagnosing major depressive disorder during the preschool years are exemplified in the case of Jenny.

Jenny

Jenny was almost 3 years old when she was referred for excessive screaming and having slapped her mother in the face. Circumstances in the home were chaotic. Jenny's mother had first married at age 16, to escape an abusive home situation. She was divorced at age 21 and became pregnant with Jenny by another man whom she subsequently married. The mother had a long history of problems—serious drug abuse, depression, four suicide attempts, and one psychiatric hospitalization. Jenny was hospitalized five times during the first 6 months of life. In sharp contrast to the problems Jenny manifested at home (e.g., persistent vomiting and diarrhea), only minimal symptoms were noted during the hospital stays. Febrile seizures occurred around age 2 and recurred when conditions at home were stressful (e.g., physical abuse of the family by the alcoholic father).

Spontaneous complaints by the mother centered around Jenny's demanding, aggressive behavior; noncompliance; and high activity level. Systematic questioning of the mother revealed Jenny's dysphoric mood (daily spontaneous crying), feelings of worthlessness ("I'm bad"), eating problems (vomiting and gagging to avoid meals, coke-and-water diet), sleep disturbances (frequent wakings), fatigue (inability to keep up with other day-care children), recurrent thoughts of death and suicide attempts (jumping in front of cars, cutting self with knives or razors, biting self, requesting others to bite her or punish her physically), hyperactivity, and limited attention span. A semistructured play interview revealed play themes centering around somebody doing something wrong, around getting spanked, and around death. Jenny appeared neither happy nor sad. Her attention with puzzles and blocks was good. Only after considerable effort on the examiner's part did she state that she was "sad." Observation of mother–child interaction showed Jenny attending well to a story read to her by her mother. A general lack of concern for her daughter's well-being was noted (e.g., ignoring Jenny's dangerous jumping from a table).

Does Jenny suffer from a major depressive disorder? Jenny did not have anhedonia nor did she show pervasive problems in concentration, but she does satisfy six of the eight criteria that *DSM-III-R* lists for this disorder. (Only five are required to meet adult criteria for this diagnosis.) But does she satisfy the letter of the law without satisfying the intent or spirit of the law? Is "meeting criteria" the same as having the disorder? Should Jenny's episodic coke-and-water diet be considered a symptom of depression? Should her sleep problem be numbered among her symptoms of depression? Frequent nighttime waking and faddish eating occur among 14% and 11%, respectively, of 3-year-olds. Moreover, they are nonspecific to and more frequent in children with various behavior problems (Richman, Stevenson, & Graham, 1982). Does Jenny's self-destructive behavior reflect genuine self-hatred, or is it an age-appropriate response of a child who has both witnessed violent behavior and been the recipient of physical punishment to master what she fears through imitation and play? Is her running in front of cars and jumping dangerously off high places an attention-getting attempt aimed to see how far she must go to elicit maternal concern? Would a *DSM-III-R* diagnosis of separation anxiety or oppositional behavior be equally or more appropriate? The answers to these questions are problematic.

Comment: Aside from illustrating how fraught with problems the diagnostic process is with young uncommunicative children showing depressive symptomatology, this case also illustrates how such youngsters are referred for problems other than depression and how more than one diagnosis might be warranted. In addition, Jenny's case depicts the potential for interplay between genetic factors and psychosocial stress and exemplifies how the child of a depressed mother is at risk.

Note. From "Major Depressive Disorder in a Preschooler" by J. Kashani and G. Carlson, 1985, *Journal of the American Academy of Child Psychiatry, 24,* pp. 490–495.

Middle Childhood

Significant developmental changes occur around the age period 6 to 9. Prominent among these are changes in moral development and the development of concrete operational thought. As youngsters enter the world of formal schooling, heightened demands are made on their self-mastery, and children's behavior is evaluated more publicly by both peers and teachers. The changes in depressive symptomatology are consistent with the changes in the cognitive and social domains. For instance, the shame component is more noticeable in reports of low self-esteem, inordinate self-criticism, and masochistic behavior (Brumbach & Weinberg, 1977; Glasberg & Aboud, 1981). There is a decrease in the frequency of affect-dominated or "feeling-thought" depression and a rise in "thought-feeling" depressive disorders in which self-deprecating thought and negative self-esteem and guilt prevail. Another common pattern in the 6-to-9 age group is the alternating pattern of acting-out behaviors with sadness and withdrawal (Carlson & Cantwell, 1980). School problems, notably underachievement, absenteeism, and school phobia, are common complaints among depressed children (Seagull & Weinshank, 1984; Tisher, 1983).

Adolescence

Substantial evidence is accumulating to suggest that depression in adolescents is similar to depression in adults (Cantwell & Baker, 1991). Available evidence indicates that loss of pleasurable experiences is a common emotional feature of depression in adolescents. Common cognitive features entail low self-esteem (Strober, Green, & Carlson, 1981); dissatisfaction with recent body changes; and feeling ugly, unattractive, weak, and unhealthy (Teri, 1982), as well as a negative view of the future. Adolescent girls report a more negative body image than boys (Turkington, 1989). Motivational features show that escapism and withdrawal are common as are thoughts about self-destruction (Strober et al., 1981). Diminished school performance has ranged widely from 13% (Strober et al., 1981) to 73% (Inamdar, Siomopoulus, Osborn, & Bianchi, 1979). Vegetative symptoms are seen in appetite and weight changes (many decreases, some increases), sleep problems (Carlson & Cantwell, 1979; Strober et al., 1981), and common complaints of fatigue (Carlson & Cantwell, 1979), which may be reflected less frequently in psychomotor behavior. Table 2.1 summarizes the changes associated with different developmental periods.

AGE TRENDS IN PREVALENCE FIGURES

Despite wide variation in general prevalence figures, it is becoming apparent that incidence figures vary with age. For instance, whereas 13% of 10- to 11-year-old children in a general population study showed a depressed mood at interview, over 40% of these same children at age 14 to 15 years reported feelings of misery and depression during a psychiatric interview (Rutter, 1980). More recent data from the Dunedin longitudinal study also reflected a doubling of major depressive episodes from age 11 to 15 (McGee, Feehan, Williams, & Anderson, 1992). The rise in depressive feelings may well be more a function of puberty than chronological age. For instance, Rutter (1980) found that scarcely any of the prepubescent boys showed depressive feelings, whereas approximately one third of the 19 postpubertal boys did. The 45 pubescent boys were intermediate on measures of depression.

Table 2.1
Developmental Changes in Depressive Symptomatology

Period	Major Symptoms
Infancy	Sadness
Toddler	Mood disturbance (irritability, excessive crying or fretfulness, anger or discontentment, grief or sadness); vegetative disturbance (insomnia, loss of appetite); behavior disturbance (absence of normal play, hyperactivity, temper tantrums).
Middle childhood	Shame, guilt, and hopelessness (after age 8), low self-esteem excessive self-criticism, masochistic behavior, increase in thought-feeling-type depression, alternating between acting-out and sadness/withdrawal, school problems (underachievement, school phobia).
Adolescence	Concern with body image, clear adult-like depressive features.

Regrettably, nearly all of the girls in this study were postpubertal so that no comparable data exist for them. Do similar findings obtain for girls? An epidemiological study of over 8,000 American high school students reported that girls at ages 14 through 18 experience consistently higher levels of depression than boys. The finding that the smallest male/female differences were recorded at age 13, with an increase occurring by age 14, suggests that puberty may be a critical turning point (Kandel & Davies, 1982.) It is not known whether this strong association with puberty is a function of endocrine changes, psychological reactions to sexual maturation, or some other source. Hormonal changes at puberty together with psychological reactions to sexual maturation and adolescent developmental tasks might well be involved (Peterson, Sarigiani, & Kennedy, 1991; Susman, Dorn, & Chrousos, 1991).

Among preschoolers referred for developmental, behavioral, or emotional problems, only 9 of 1,000 youngsters met *DSM-III* criteria for depressive disorder (Kashani & Carlson, 1987). Data provided by the U.S. Public Health Service (cited by Weiner, 1975) on over 400,000 outpatients reported that 2% to 5% of 10- to 17-year-olds were diagnosed as neurotically depressed with the rate increasing with age, particularly among females, to a high of about 10% for 10- to 19-year-old females. Public Health Service data on 380,000 inpatients indicate that 6% of 10- to 14-year-olds and nearly 12% of

15- to 17-year-olds were diagnosed as neurotically depressed. Data based on clinical samples provide a similar picture. For instance, of children first attending the Maudsley Hospital during 1968 and 1969, only 1 in 9 prepubertal children (11%) showed depressive symptomatology, whereas one fourth of postpubertal youth did so (Pearce, 1978). This represents more than a twofold increase.

GENDER DIFFERENCES

The data revealing a change in sex ratio across puberty are even more striking. Depressive symptoms were twice as common among preschoolers (Kashani & Carlson, 1987) and more common among prepubertal boys (Nolen-Hoeksema, Girgus, & Seligman, 1991), whereas such symptoms were twice as common among girls by late adolescence (Turkington, 1989). Other investigators (Albert & Beck, 1975) have also noted an increase in depressive disorders and a change in sex ratio during adolescence. Girls show more depressed affect by 12th grade. The gender difference emerged by age 14–15 years and seems to persist into adulthood (Peterson et al., 1993). Prior to puberty, being a female is not a risk factor for depression (Kashani et al., 1983; Lefkowitz & Tesiny, 1985). Hopefully, future studies will use physiological maturity indices rather than chronological age so that the influence of puberty on depressive disorders can be more fully understood. We presently lack knowledge about what specific processes underlie this change in sex ratio in depression. Body image appears to be a significant factor in depression for girls but not for boys. Girls consistently want to be thinner, and the rounded curves of a maturing adolescent body are interpreted negatively as a sign of becoming fatter. Conversely, boys see themselves as developing muscles rather than becoming fatter. Some authorities also believe that the sexes differ in their reactions to life stresses. Girls, for instance, may react in a more passive, ruminating and perhaps less autonomous way, thereby decreasing their likelihood of mastery. Girls might also experience more challenges in early adolescence. Whatever the cause(s), the gender difference appears to be a genuine difference in the experience of depression and cannot be attributed to differences in openness in reporting (Peterson et al., 1993).

Little is known regarding the age changes regarding mania or manic-depressive disorders. There are no data on the prevalence of manic-depressive disorder in the general child/adolescent population, but the general consensus is that mania has a later onset than depressive episodes (Downey & Coyne, 1990), that it rarely occurs before puberty (Anthony & Scott, 1960; Lowe &

Cohen, 1980), and that it increases during the midteens (Hassanyeh & Davison, 1980). Various interpretations of this finding are possible.

1. Bipolar disorders could begin after puberty with unipolar disorders more often having an earlier onset. Bipolar disorders could begin in childhood but for the fact that the manic component appears in adolescence or later.

2. Another possibility is that mania occurs in childhood, but it assumes a more variable form from that seen in adults (Bowring & Kovacs, 1992). For example, are certain forms of disruptive, silly, expansive, or seemingly grandiose behavior in childhood a sign of mania or hypomania? If so, why is it that depression in children looks like depression in adults but mania in children does not look like mania in adults? Can the exuberance of children sometimes render mania less noticeable? Clear answers are not available to these questions. Although we do not want to overlook manifestations of mania in childhood, we must also guard against misinterpreting topographically similar behaviors as indices of mania. For instance, hyperactivity (attention-deficit disorder, ADD) may appear similar to mania, which is often characterized by volatility, irritability or low frustration tolerance, and thoughtless impulsive interpersonal behavior. Yet, these conditions differ in essential ways. Hyperactivity has a much earlier onset, with 95% of youngsters being identifiable by entrance into school, whereas mania generally does not appear before adolescence. Also, hyperactivity is a chronic condition, and mania is episodic in nature. Finally, hyperactive youngsters do not show the gregarious, infectiously humorous charm of at least some people with mania (Carlson, 1983). The failure of follow-up studies of ADD and conduct-disordered children (Dahl, 1971; Robins, 1966) to find bipolar outcomes in percentages higher than general population predictions suggests that hyperactive children, by and large, are not suffering from bipolar disorders.

3. Another possible basis for underestimating the frequency of manic-depressive disorder might stem from diagnostic failure to distinguish this condition from schizophrenia. Retrospective analyses of case file information available at the time of admission suggested that out of 77 adolescents, 7 (9%), could be classified as manic-depressive 8 to 10 years later, according to Feighner's criteria (Welner, Welner, & Fishman, 1979). Although manic-depressive disorder may sometimes be misdiagnosed as schizophrenia, there is a dearth of empirical support (based largely on retrospective studies) to substantiate this possibility.

4. Finally, manic-depressive disorder may be missed because of our failure to recognize "masked" depression in adolescents (Preodor & Wolpert, 1979). As noted earlier, however, the concept of "masked" depression has fallen into disrepute in recent years.

It is not clear what accounts for the sharp rise in depressive disorder and the dramatic change in sex ratio. Several possibilities have been discussed, however (Rutter, 1986). One possibility is that hormonal changes are responsible for the increase in depression and change in sex ratio. It is not clear, however, why the hormonal changes experienced by girls at puberty have emotional consequences. Genetic factors also deserve consideration. Disorders arising after puberty may differ genetically from those with a childhood onset—a hypothesis consistent with the apparent increase in mania in adolescence. Yet, uncertainty continues as to whether unipolar and bipolar affective disorders are genetically distinct. Moreover, they do not seem to differ appreciably in sex distribution. Another possibility is that affective disorders arising in adolescence have a stronger genetic component, whereas those of childhood are more often reactive to environmental adversity. That is, affective disorders in adolescence are less clearly related to environmental difficulties. Moreover, psychiatric disturbances in girls are less clearly associated with family disturbance. A third possibility concerns environmental stressors. It may be that the "loss" type stressors associated with depression become more prevalent in adolescence than they were in childhood. We will be better able to test this possibility once satisfactory data on age changes in the frequency and severity of stress events are available. The limited evidence to date, however, contradicts the hypothesis of object loss as an explanation of the change in sex ratio. Longitudinal research shows that, contrary to popular opinion, boys are more affected by object losses such as death of a close friend or relative (Cordes, 1984). A fourth kind of explanation invokes developmental changes in vulnerability and protective factors. The diminution in family support associated with leaving home and becoming increasingly independent can be stress producing. This explanation fails to account for the finding that the sex ratio changes while teenagers are still attending school. A fifth explanation centers around the type of adult feedback given to boys and to girls. In one study of teacher feedback, criticism of girls referred specifically to their intellectual failings, whereas the praise given them was diffuse. For boys, praise tended to be work specific and criticism, diffuse (Dweck, Davidson, Nelson, & Enna, 1978).

Developmental changes in attributional capabilities may render adolescents more susceptible to feelings of helplessness in that they are cognitively able to view failure as a stable and lasting limitation of their performance. In brief, the type of negative adult feedback and developmental alterations in cognition might serve in part to explain the abrupt increase in affective disorders in adolescence. The notion of learned helplessness is more thoroughly discussed in the chapter on treatment (Chapter 4). Finally, developmental modifications in children's concepts of emotion, in their ability to express affect, in their awareness of others, and in their expanding awareness of the emotional significance of social situations probably all contribute to the expression of affective disorders. Yet, because most of these cognitive changes take place in early and middle childhood, they fail to explain the surge in depressive disorders in adolescence. Nor is it apparent why they should cause a shift in the sex ratio of affective disturbances. We have much to learn about the mechanisms and processes underlying the marked increase in prevalence and change in sex ratio after puberty. All of the explanations have their limitations. Future research on several fronts, such as developmental trends in social cognition among depressed children, and adequate data on age-related changes in environmental stressors for boys and girls of varying socioeconomic groups should aid in sorting out the complexities of cause–effect relations.

CONTINUITY

Is childhood depression a chronic, transitory, or recurring condition? The answer, which is of interest to practitioners, theoreticians, and parents, may vary depending on whether one studies the general population or psychiatric groups, how long one follows them, the type of design used, the criteria used to define depression, the level of diagnosis employed (symptom, syndrome, disorder, or disease), and the nature of outcome measures. Before presenting evidence on the continuity of depression from childhood to adulthood, it is instructive to examine briefly the connections between early experiences and adult psychopathology, and three types of designs that longitudinal, natural history studies commonly follow.

Connections Between Early Experiences and Adult Affective Disorder

What are ways in which early experiences might be linked with adult affective disorders (as well as other psychiatric conditions)? Numerous possibilities emerge, several of which have been delineated by Rutter (1986). Early experiences may (1) lead to immediate depression, with the disorder persisting into later life for reasons that are largely independent of the initial causation or provocation; (2) lead directly to bodily changes, which in turn affect later coping (e.g., changes in the neuroendocrine system following acute physical stresses in infancy); (3) lead directly to modified patterns of behavior, which although changed at the time of the event, assume the form of overt disorder only some years later (e.g., long-term social sequelae of institutional rearing); (4) lead to altered family interaction, which in turn predisposes to later depression; (5) lead to altered sensitivities to stress or in modifying styles of coping which either predispose toward or protect from later depression only in the presence of stressful events in adulthood; (6) lead to changes in the person's self-concept, attitudes, or cognitive set, which then in turn adversely influence responses to later circumstances; (7) lead to later behavior via the effects on the selection of environments or on the opening or shutting down of opportunities. So far, we are not knowledgeable enough to judge which of these, singly or in interaction, are most apt to link early experiences to later affective disorders.

Research Approaches

In the *prospective* study the researcher collects data at the initial point in time and then waits to collect additional follow-up data at multiple time points. In this method, data can also be collected at pretest and posttests to determine the effects of various treatments on different kinds of depressed children.

The *retrospective* study is the second type of design for assessing continuity. In the follow-back study, the investigator selects a sample (depressed adolescents or adults) and then probes the records available at the time of childhood to collect data at time one. Childhood histories are reconstructed through the use of case studies, inventories, and interviews with parents, teachers, and others. Adult control groups such as normals and/or those with anxiety disorders should also be used (but usually are not) in an effort to establish links between childhood depression and adult depression.

A third design is the *catch-up prospective* study, which combines elements of the follow-up and follow-back designs. As in the follow-up study, the sample is identified at time one, but the data have already been collected and reside in existing records. The researcher is able to select a random sample of the population chosen for study such as depressed children at time one. Lee Robins's (1966) classic study—*Deviant Children Grown Up*—is the best known example of this approach.

All of these designs have been used to assess continuity in childhood depression, and the advantages and disadvantages of these designs should be kept in mind when reading the following studies on continuity. Table 2.2 summarizes the strengths and weaknesses of the three research designs used to study continuity.

Table 2.2
Advantages and Disadvantages of Research Designs Used in Continuity Studies

Advantages	Disadvantages
Prospective design	
1. Allows collection of data at exact points of developmental importance.	1. Data are frozen for some time.
2. Permits best assessment of therapeutic outcomes by assignment of subjects to different interventions and control groups.	2. Measures and ideas change over time.
	3. Subject attrition occurs.
	4. Measures are not always isomorphically parallel.
Retrospective design	
1. Eliminates time interval between collection of initial data (childhood) and secondary data (adulthood).	1. Cause and effect relationships may be confused.
	2. Reporter error can be a problem.
Catch-up prospective design	
1. Samples are identified at point one.	1. The quality and quantity of data are limited.
2. Data have already been collected and reside in existing records.	
3. Wasted time is eliminated between investigations one and two.	

Note. From "Childhood Depression: Issues Regarding Natural History" by D. Cantwell (1983). In D. Cantwell & G. Carlson (Eds.), *Affective disorders in childhood and adolescence* (pp. 266–278), New York: Spectrum

Follow-up Studies

Some investigators have defined childhood depression as a symptom. Others have defined it as a syndrome or constellation of depressive behaviors. Still others, using stringent criteria such as *DSM-III-R*, have defined it as a disorder. The analyses of follow-up studies will be organized according to the level of diagnosis because conclusions about continuity differ in accordance with the definition of depression used. There have been no epidemiological studies of depressive syndromes in children per se, but epidemiological studies of deviant behavior have dealt with *symptoms* frequently associated with depression in children.

In a follow-up study, Kandel and Davies (1986) reassessed 1,096 young adults, who had participated in a survey of depressive *symptoms* years earlier, when they were in 10th or 11th grades. Both in high school and as young adults, respondents were administered a six-item scale of depressive symptoms, four of which measured symptoms required for the diagnoses of major depressive disorders or dysthymic disorder in *DSM-III*. However, no official *DSM-III* diagnoses were available at the time of initial assessment or at follow-up. Approximately 83% of the original subjects participated in the follow-up. The investigators concluded that depressive symptoms were relatively stable over the 9-year interval (.35 for male and .44 for female subjects). Thus, individuals reporting the experience of depressive symptoms in adolescence were more likely to do so at ages 24 to 25 years. Depressive symptoms predicted subsequent histories of psychiatric disorders by the middle twenties among women. In addition, adolescent depression was associated with heavy cigarette smoking, increased use of minor prescription tranquilizers among women, more deviant activities and accidents as young adults, and selective effects on interpersonal relationships. For example, the ability to form a close, intimate relationship with the opposite sex diminished, but the ability to maintain a circle of male and female friends was not reduced. Although these results indicate the stability and predictive value of depressive symptomatology from adolescence to young adulthood, the data also indicate considerable nonpersistence and unpredictability. Regression analyses that more precisely measure the predictive power of adolescent dysphoric mood in young adulthood accounted for less than 20% of the variance in adult dysphoric affect. Moreover, elevated scores on self-assessment depressive scales often do not indicate depression as judged by a clinician.

Tesiny and Lefkowitz (1982), who studied the short-term continuity, found that depressive symptoms in 436 fourth- and fifth-graders as measured by peer, self, and teacher ratings were stable over a 6-month period. Likewise, the performance of children, mothers, and fathers on various scales designed to assess severity of the children's depressive behaviors was also found to be relatively stable over a 6-week period among 37 depressed hospitalized children (Kazdin, French, & Unis, 1983). The correlations were in the moderate to high range. It should be noted, however, that severity of the child's depression was rated lower, particularly by mothers, at the end of the 6-week period.

The question of whether self-reported depressive symptoms in young children are a transient developmental phenomenon was studied in an epidemiological sample of 1,313 first graders (Edelsohn, Ialongo, Werthamer-Larson, Crockett, & Kellam, 1992). The investigators found that children's reports of depressive symptoms were relatively stable over a 4-month interval. The level of stability was very impressive for youngsters initially in the highest quartile of depression, all of whom remained in the top one fourth upon retesting 4 months later. Data from the Dunedin longitudinal study indicate that internalizing disorders, of which depressive disorders may be viewed as prototypic (Reynolds, 1992), show more continuity for girls than boys over the 11- to 15-year age range (McGee et al., 1992).

Not all studies indicate stability of this condition over longer time periods, however. For instance, epidemiological studies (Lefkowitz & Burton, 1978) suggest that the incidence of depressive behaviors in children is a function of age and may be a transient manifestation of developmental reactions to stress in basically normal children. For example, crying, reputedly a symptom of childhood depression, diminishes dramatically with age. Whereas 18% cried "two or three times a week" at age 6, only 2% were reported to do so at puberty. Insufficient appetite was manifested by 33% of children at age 6 but by only 7.5% at age 9 (Macfarlane, Allen, & Honzik, 1954). Likewise, whining behavior shows a dramatic decrease with age (Achenbach & Edelbrock, 1981). Discrepancies between studies suggesting persistence or nonpersistence (e.g., between the Lefkowitz and Burton, 1978, study and the Kandel and Davies, 1986, study) may be more apparent than real. The discrepancies may well be due to differences in design (longitudinal vs. cross-sectional), to the ways in which data were reported (correlation coefficients vs. percentages), and to sampling differences (homerooms wherein marijuana use was high vs. general population).

Rather than diagnosing children according to the concept of adult psychopathology, some researchers have used factor analysis to identify clusters of behavior problems that characterize troubled youngsters who then can be grouped on the basis of the clusters of problems they present. Research on *constellations* or clusters of behavior among deviant youngsters also suggests that depression may not be manifested over various developmental periods. For instance, although Achenbach and Edelbrock (1979), using a cross-sectional design, found a distinctive syndrome of depression in clinically referred children ages 6 to 11, a second phase of this study failed to find a syndrome of depression in either boys or girls ages 12 to 16. The absence of a distinctive syndrome among troubled adolescents does not mean that depressive behaviors are uncommon or unimportant. Rather, depressive behaviors among troubled adolescents appear to occur in conjunction with a wider variety of other difficulties than they do among younger disturbed children.

Long-term follow-up studies of groups of child psychiatric patients have not always suggested that depressive disorders in adulthood are a common outcome. For instance, Dahl (1971), using a catch-up prospective design, followed 146 male and 172 female patients 20 years after their initial admission to two child psychiatric departments in Denmark. By the time these subjects were 20 to 35 years old, a third of the female population and about a fourth of the males had been hospitalized in adult psychiatric facilities. In no instance was the diagnosis of manic-depressive disturbance made, but eight cases received a diagnosis of depressive neurosis at follow-up. In a catch-up prospective study Robins (1966) studied 525 children who had been referred to the same St. Louis municipal clinic between 1924 and 1929. Thirty years later the adult psychiatric and social status of these subjects was compared with that of 100 control subjects. She found that less than 1% of all disturbed children who were seen in child guidance clinics early in life later developed affective disorders. Thus, there is evidence that argues against the long-term permanence of depressive illness.

The Dahl (1971) and Robins (1966) studies are limited, however, by the fact that depressive conditions in childhood were not identified as a separate group. Zeitlin's (1972, 1985) studies are more informative. He studied a group of individuals who had been under psychiatric care at the Maudsley Hospital in London, England, both as youngsters and as adults. For purposes of comparison, however, he included a group of children who had not returned as adults and a group of adults whose disorders had their onset in adulthood. He discovered that many cases of adult depression were not preceded by any form of disorder in childhood. Furthermore, when adult depression had been preceded by psychiatric difficulties in childhood, in only a few cases were the disorders predominantly depressive. Conversely, most of the children diagnosed as depressed using Pearce's (1974) operational criteria were not diagnosed as depressed in adulthood. However, when depression was diagnosed in both childhood and adulthood solely in terms of specified symptoms of affective disorder, extremely high continuity was found. Thus, of the 37 cases of childhood depression based on Pearce's criteria, 31 fulfilled the criteria for a depressive syndrome in adult life. That is, the link between child and adult depression was highly related. It is interesting to note that the continuity was not apparent when clinical diagnoses were made because the subjects also had symptoms other than depression (fire-setting, aggression, enuresis) that dominated the clinical picture.

Studies of clinically depressed populations are extremely rare and still do not fully indicate the natural course of this disorder. The prospective study by Poznanski, Krahenbuhl, and Zrull (1976), which reassessed then-depressed children after a period of 6½ years, found that as adolescents one half were still judged to be clinically depressed. As they reached adulthood, the children resembled adult depressives. At follow-up, dependency was salient whereas overt aggression was substantially reduced. Job performance and productivity were uniformly poor. This study provided support for the belief that childhood depression and adult depression are basically the same disorder that can begin early in life and persist into adulthood. The small sample size ($N = 10$), the lack of a control group, the failure to use blind ratings, the absence of interrater reliability data, the paucity of developmental data, and the question of whether the symptoms as specified would meet recognized criteria all detract from the amount of confidence that can be placed in the findings of this study.

The well-known longitudinal study of 133 youngsters by Chess et al. (1983) found 6 children with depressive disorders: 2 with recurrent major depression, 3 with dysthymic disorder, and 1 with adjustment disorder with depressed mood. One boy who was diagnosed as having major depressive disorder at age 8 had later episodes at 15, 17, 18, and 19 years of age. Each episode lasted months. The second child with major depressive disorder was diagnosed at age 12 but failed to come to clinical attention until 21 years of age. This person's third episode occurred at age 25. A boy who had behavior problems at age 5 was diagnosed as dysthymic at age 10. Another boy only experienced a dysthymic disorder at age 17. Another child who had a behavior disorder at age 13 suffered a dysthymic disorder at 16 years of age. The last subject, a boy, experienced a secondary depression at age 13 following a divorce in the family. The findings of this study are consistent with those of Poznanski and her colleagues (1976) in supporting the notion that childhood depression and adult depression are similar conditions. It is interesting to note that the two cases of primary depression occurred in families with a strong history of major affective disorder, and their episodes were not precipitated by psychosocial stress. The four cases of secondary depression occurred in families free from a history of major depression but were precipitated by psychosocial stress. The Chess study is unique in that the subjects were selected at infancy as part of a longitudinal study examining the influence of temperamental characteristics on individuality rather than for psychopathology. The use of *DSM-III* criteria for the diagnosis of affective disorders represents another strength of this study, although the mere use of *DSM-III* criteria, particularly with children, does not guarantee interrater reliability or validity. Moreover, rater reliability was contaminated by not using blind ratings. Finally, one is not inclined to generalize these findings too widely on the basis of only 6 subjects.

In another follow-up study, by Herjanic (1976), 20 children who received a discharge diagnosis of depression from the St. Louis Children's Hospital were systematically interviewed. At the time of follow-up, only one had a true affective disorder, one had a schizoaffective disorder, and one had an undiagnosed illness that might well develop into an affective disorder later in life. These 3 children had originally met the Weinberg criteria for depression. The 17 children who did not meet the Weinberg criteria (which identify a more heterogeneous group than does *DSM-III-R,* including many who may be demoralized rather than depressed), showed more variable conditions at follow-up. Ten had no psychiatric illness, 2 had antisocial personality, and 5 were undiagnosed.

In a 4-year follow-up of 60 adolescents hospitalized for major depression, Strober and Carlson (1982) found that 12 developed mania, 11 had one or more additional episodes of major depression, 4 had intermittent episodes of depressive symptoms, and 33 were free of depressive symptomatology.

Using a catch-up prospective design, another group of investigators found that 7 of 11 hospitalized individuals diagnosed using *DSM-III* criteria (at a mean age of 14) experienced at least one episode of major depressive disorder during the 8-year follow-up period. The generalizability of these findings is limited by the small sample size, the severity of their initial episodes requiring hospitalization, the preponderance of lower socioeconomic subjects, the relative absence of subjects with a mixed pattern of depressive and other psychiatric symptomatology, and subject attrition.

In another prospective study, Eastgate and Gilmore (1984) reassessed 19 of 36 subjects some 7 to 8 years after the initial diagnosis of childhood depression was made at a children's hospital in England. The mean age at initial diagnosis was about 12 years and the mean age at follow-up was 20 years. The diagnosis of childhood depression was made on the basis of the Weinberg criteria. Ten of the children had received psychotherapy, 9 received antidepressants, and 6 received both. Seven were admitted to an inpatient psychiatric unit, and the remainder were treated as outpatients or as inpatients in a pediatric ward. Follow-up assessment involved interviews with both parents and with the young adults. Assessments at follow-up were apparently not done blind to the original diagnosis. The outcome at follow-up was highly variable, but 42% (8 of 19) still had moderate or severe disabilities. One of the 8 was schizophrenic, 4 had depression and/or anxiety, and 3 had marked personality disorders. Only 2 had been admitted to a psychiatric facility, and 1 other had attended a psychiatric outpatient department. The variable outcomes are reflected in the two case studies below, Catherine and Lisa.

From Depressed Beginnings:
Catherine

Catherine was 13 years old when she was taken to her pediatrician due to her mother's concern about Catherine's continual writing of poetry about graveyards and death. Catherine had experienced a number of major losses since age 10, including three grandparents. Both parents were exceptionally hard working, and Catherine had the responsibility for care of her two younger siblings. There was a family history of depression and anxiety, with both parents having seen mental health specialists in the past.

Catherine was unhappy, with mood swings, hypersensitivity, and intense feelings of worthlessness. She suffered marked sleep disturbances and nightmares, had lost energy as well as interest in her schoolwork and social contacts, and had lost weight in recent weeks. She was diagnosed as depressed, and family therapy was begun. She made a marked recovery.

When seen 7 to 8 years later, Catherine was in the third year of a teacher training program, living at home, and engaged to be married. She remained anxious and depressed, however. She was bothered by frequent bad dreams, excessive fatigue, and had lost 16 pounds before her last exams. She also had periods during which she lost interest in her usual pursuits and had difficulty concentrating and making decisions. She thought about death daily, fearing that she or someone close to her would die. She was afraid to stay in the house by herself. She had numerous somatic complaints such as stomachaches and sore throats, visiting her general practitioner at least 10 times during the past year and her college physician at exam times. She had no close friends except for her fiance, on whom she was very dependent.

Catherine's parents described her as "a very lonely girl," easily upset, who had to be handled gently by other family members. As a young adult, Catherine appeared to be extremely vulnerable and troubled, and it seems unlikely that she will avoid further psychiatric difficulties in the years to come.

Lisa

Lisa first began showing symptoms of depression at age 10, following a viral infection. Initially, the symptoms were primarily somatic in nature—head, abdominal, and limb pains; sore throat; and weight loss. Three months later she was admitted to a children's hospital, bed-bound, unable to stand, and suffering blackouts. She was unhappy and had premonitions of death. She felt useless because she could not walk. Prior to admission, she had been unable to focus any effort on her schoolwork and had become socially withdrawn. She was the older of two girls from a professional family which was free of other significant social or emotional problems.

During her 2-month stay in the psychiatric unit she responded well to psychotherapy and ward milieu. Two months after treatment, her parents reported that she was back at school and socializing with friends.

When seen 8 years later, Lisa was at college and leading a full social life. She described herself as a "happy person" but a bit of a "perfectionist." Her mother stated that Lisa was now a normal girl, friendly, warm-hearted, and a thoroughly nice person.

Note. From "Long-Term Outcome of Depressed Children" by J. Eastgate and L. Gilmore, 1983, *Developmental Medicine and Child Neurology, 26,* pp. 68–72.

In one of the best-known longitudinal, naturalistic studies to date, Kovacs, Feinberg, Crouse-Novak, Paulauskas, and Finkelstein (1984) and Kovacs, Feinberg, Crouse-Novak, Paulauskas, Pollack, and Finkelstein (1984) studied the eventual adjustments of 65 school-aged students spread across four psychiatric groups—those 8- to 13-year-olds with a major depressive disorder (MDD), those with dysthymic disorder (DD) or minor depression, those with adjustment disorder with depressed mood (ADDM), and a heterogeneous comparison group whose nonaffective illnesses (e.g., attention-deficit disorder) were common among the depressed cohorts. The mean age at entry into the study was 11.2 years. Four important findings were noted: (a) the three depressive disorder groups were distinguishable from the psychiatric controls on the basis of age of onset and pattern of recovery; (b) depressive disorders during childhood tend to have a longer duration than was previously believed; (c) earlier age of onset predicts a lengthier course of illness of MDD and DD but does not predict the likelihood of becoming depressed in the future; and (d) whereas childhood depressive disorders are often associated with other psychiatric disorders, only the presence of DD as an associated diagnosis increased the risk of relapse.

Adjustment disorder with depressed mood (ADDM) emerged as the most "benign" of the three depressive disorders, with a high likelihood of recovery in the first 3 months. More than 90% of these children were symptom-free at 9 months and, as a group, they were no more likely than the psychiatric controls to become depressed within 5 years (none of the controls became depressed). Furthermore, they had the least chance of receiving another concurrent psychiatric diagnosis of all the depressed children. When they had two or more diagnoses, the second tended to be some form of an anxiety disorder.

Children diagnosed as having major depressive disorder (MDD) were more like those with DD than those in the ADDM or psychiatric control groups because of the protracted nature of their illness. In fact, these children were not likely to recover during the first 3 months of their illness and exhibited a strong, but very gradual, recovery rate over time (92% recovered within 1½ years) with a mean episode length of 7½ months. Concurrent psychiatric diagnoses were common among almost 80% of the subjects, with anxiety and dysthymic disorders being overrepresented. During follow-up, those with MDD were likely to relapse (72% probability over 5 years), and remissions tended to be brief with a maximum symptom-free interval of no more than 2 years. The risk of relapse was greatest in those with an underlying dysthymic disorder.

Dysthymic disorder (DD) proved to be the most chronic of the three depressive disorders, with a mean episode length of 3 years and a median recovery time of 3½ years. Unlike MDD, there seems to be a low probability of recovery with each successive year, and the maximum recovery rate of 89% was not reached before 6 years. This group was also found to have the highest percentage of other associated diagnoses (93%), most commonly anxiety disorders and MDD. The overall clinical course of DD not only emerged as lengthy, but was likely to be punctuated by recurrent episodes of MDD. Approximately 70% of these children will suffer from a first episode of major depression within 5 years of becoming dysthymic.

In short, the Kovacs data indicate that the diagnosis of either MDD or DD does not signal a favorable course. Indeed, these data indicate that the outcome is worse for children than for adults.

Despite the thoroughness of the Kovacs study, generalizability of these findings is limited for several reasons:

1. The overwhelming majority of MDD and DD cases had another psychiatric disorder such as anxiety (79% and 93%, respectively). The outcome may be worse for youngsters with dual conditions than for those with "pure" MDD or DD.

2. No data are yet available concerning the outcome regarding nondepressive psychiatric disorders (fire-setting, enuresis, delinquency, aggression) that may persist after recovery from the initial depressive episode. That

is, depressed youngsters often have other forms of psychiatric disturbance that may persist after recovery from the initial depressive episode (Eastgate & Gilmore, 1984).

3. The nondepressive comparison group was not closely matched on symptomatology. For example, although 33% of MDD and 36% of DD subjects had anxiety disorder as a nonaffective psychiatric condition, only 10% of comparison subjects were so diagnosed.

4. African Americans and low socioeconomic cases were overrepresented, thereby raising questions about the extent to which the findings can be generalized to other groups.

5. It appears that the follow-up assessments were made with knowledge of the original diagnosis, thus spuriously inflating the degree of continuity.

6. No data were provided as to whether the depression was primary or secondary in terms of onset.

7. It might have been instructive if subjects had been classified as prepubescent or pubescent at the time of initial diagnosis of depression to see if these two groups have different outcomes.

The longitudinal study by McGee and Williams (1988) found that 9-year-old children identified as having a current depressive disorder ($N = 17$) or a postdepressive disorder ($N = 23$) reported significantly more depressive symptoms than the comparison group when studied at ages 11 and 13. These findings are consistent with Kovacs's data, indicating that most prepubertal children experience continuous or recurrent episodes of depression.

The protracted course and the chronicity of depressive disorder is also evident in a recent prospective, naturalistic study of 58 adolescent inpatients (Strober, Lampert, Schmidt, & Morrell, 1993). The cumulative probability of recovery was high (92%) by 24 months. However, the recovery process was often painstakingly slow. The average time to recovery is more than 27 weeks. Less than one third of the sample recovered by week 20 although the majority are symptomatically improved. Surprisingly, the psychotic–nonpsychotic distinction had no prognostic significance as far as recovery is concerned. Psychotically depressed adolescents were more likely than those nonpsychotically depressed to switch over time from unipolar to bipolar, however. The Ontario Health Study longitudinal data based on adolescents identified in the community as depressed show that adolescent depression is a persistent condition and that referral biases cannot account for the substantial pathology found in studies using patients as subjects (Fleming, Boyle, & Offord, 1993).

The above follow-up studies were all carried out on depressed youth. What do we know about the fate of bipolar manic-depressive youth? The early onset of childhood depression as well as childhood/adolescent schizophrenia suggests a poorer prognosis than adult onset. Coping with a severe disorder during the formative years of development may be more disruptive than when the individual's schooling has been completed, stable interpersonal relationships have been established, and a sense of firm identity has been achieved. Thus the question naturally arises as to whether early onset of bipolar manic-depressive illness is prodromal of a more severe natural history than adult onset. To answer this question, Carlson, Davenport, and Jamison (1977) compared 28 bipolar manic-depressive adolescents with a mean age of 15.8 years with 20 individuals whose onset occurred at a mean age of 50.6 years. No significant differences were found in mean episode frequency per year, educational achievement, or adaptive behavior with respect to job, family, or community settings. Sixty percent were found to be functioning well, and 20% were chronically ill. Those figures do suggest continuity for a sizeable minority of manic-depressive youth but they do not indicate that earlier onset patients experience a more devastating bipolar manic-depressive disorder than later onset patients.

Retrospective Studies

Various retrospective studies (Crook, Raskin, & Eliot, 1981; Jacobson, Fasman, & DeMascio, 1975; Munro, 1966; Perris, 1966) suggest continuity in depressive disorders. For example, researchers using symptom summaries from children who had attended the Maudsley Hospital in London examined the adult psychiatric status of 52 individuals who initially manifested a significant number of depressive symptoms and 52 matched nonpsychiatric controls. Some 40% of the childhood depressed group met Research Diagnostic Criteria for depression within 5 years of reaching adulthood with 58% showing a history of affective disorder at the time of follow up (mean age 31) in comparison to a 25% figure for the control subjects (Harrington, Fudge, Rutter, Pickles, & Hill, 1990). These studies varied markedly with respect to sample characteristics, control groups, and depression measures. The findings are consistent in showing that, as children, adult depressive patients remembered perceiving their parents as making more negative/punitive evaluations, receiving less parental affection, parents' inducing guilt frequently and having minimal involvement, being the object of parental abuse, family discord, and high rates of parental mental illness. However, numerous methodological limitations seriously question the validity of the findings. For example, none reported interrater reliability coefficients for diagnostic procedures.

Conclusions

What can we conclude in the light of available evidence? It should be noted that the conclusions must be tentative as there has been no study specifically designed to measure the continuity of depression over time, because of the dearth of research studies relating to this topic and because of the methodological shortcomings of past studies. Bearing the above limitations in mind, the following tentative conclusions are advanced:

1. Level of Diagnosis. Normal "depressive" symptoms (e.g., crying) that occur as developmental phenomena seem to have a high probability of being resolved with increasing age. That is, certain depressive symptoms commonly seen in children may be transitory and decrease or disappear with age (Lefkowitz & Burton, 1978). In a similar vein, many depressive behaviors are regarded as transient because they are highly responsive to environmental events. Factor-analytic studies designed to discover depressive constellations or syndromes fail to provide evidence of continuity. Thus, when depression is defined in terms of isolated symptoms or a syndrome, the notion of continuity in depression is challenged.

Although the database is small, it appears that severe depressive disorders, particularly those meeting stringent, operationally defined clinical criteria, have a low probability of improvement. Those youngsters receiving a diagnosis of major depression or dysthymic disorder are at far greater risk for later affective disorder than are those receiving a diagnosis of adjustment disorder with mood disturbance or other psychiatric diagnoses (Kovacs, Feinberg, Crouse-Novak, Paulauskas, & Finkelstein, 1984; Kovacs, Feinberg, Crouse-Novak, Paulauskas, Pollack, & Finkelstein, 1984). The low rates of improvement are comparable to those of the most debilitating psychopathological conditions of childhood (Clarizio & McCoy, 1983).

2. Age of Onset. If the onset of a depressive disorder is early (e.g., prepubertal), the depressive disorder might well be more severe. That is, if depressed adolescents experienced a prior depressive episode in childhood, they are more likely than other adolescents to experience subsequent episodes (Carlson, 1984).

3. Research Design. *Retrospective studies* indicate that it is very difficult to postulate any direct, causal connection between early childhood experiences and later depressive disorders. Adult depressives showed no distinctive clinical picture when they were children. Specific patterns of parent-child interactions may be involved in the etiology, maintenance, and expression of depressive disorder in children, adolescents, and adults, but several methodological shortcomings seriously limit the confidence that can be placed in these findings (Burbach & Borduin, 1986). The search for a "de-

pressogenic" environment has proved unsuccessful thus far. Likewise, no particular premorbid personality appears to predispose individuals to bipolar manic-depressive disorder (Carlson, 1983; Zeitlin, 1972, 1985). Premorbid personality varies as does intellectual and school performance. Affective disorders can arise in adults for reasons that may have little to do with childhood events (Zeitlin, 1972, 1985).

The best-known *longitudinal research* to follow up psychiatrically referred children into their adult years indicates that both MDD and DD youngsters are at high risk for a later major depressive episode (Kovacs, Feinberg, Crouse-Novak, Paulauskas, & Finkelstein, 1984; Kovacs, Feinberg, Crouse-Novak, Paulauskas, Pollack, & Finkelstein, 1984). Our best clues as to whether the child's depressive disorder is likely to be transitory or chronic seems to be the severity of incapacitation, knowing whether the child has had a previous depressive episode and its pervasiveness and duration (Carlson, 1984; Kovacs, Feinberg, Crouse-Novak; Paulauskas, & Finkelstein, 1984; Kovacs, Feinberg, Crouse-Novak, Paulauskas, Pollack, & Finkelstein, 1984).

4. Individual Prediction. Although the outlook appears bleak for youngsters experiencing a major depressive disorder or dysthymic disorder as judged by *DSM-III-R* criteria, we must guard against being excessively pessimistic in our forecasts. Much remains to be learned about the natural course and responsiveness to treatment before the information on continuity will have practical value in working with depressed youth. Although we have preliminary data on the outlook for certain groups of depressed youngsters (e.g., those with major depressive disorders, dysthymic disorders, and primary depression), we cannot predict with any degree of assurance which youngsters will spontaneously improve or under what circumstances. Later research will most likely provide clues to ameliorating and exacerbating factors.

5. Future Research. Among the significant issues to be addressed by future studies on continuity of childhood depression are (a) the analysis of data according to depressive subtypes; (b) the fate of those diagnosed according to various criteria (e.g., *DSM-III-R* vs. Weinberg, in community surveys vs. those referred); (c) continuity as assessed from an organizational, developmental perspective which takes adaptive patterning of behavior into account as well as static symptoms as outlined in *DSM-III-R;* (d) closer attention to outcome variability as it relates to socioeconomic status, age of onset, and gender; (e) more analytic study of different outcome criteria with particular reference to neglected areas such as extrafamilial domains, notably school adjustment and the finer aspects of peer relations; (f) whether depression in young people has the same natural course if it occurs in conjunction with

other psychopathological disturbances; (g) a broadening of informants to include teachers, peers, and employers rather than relying solely or primarily on parents; and (h) an examination of the natural history of depression in prepubertal children as it relates to eventual suicidal behavior.

SUMMARY

Despite the fact that child psychopathology differs most obviously from adult psychopathology in its focus on the developing child, the fields of development and psychopathology had not merged their research efforts until relatively recently. A developmental perspective of abnormality implies a concern with (a) processes and mechanisms of development throughout the age span; (b) the relationship, or lack thereof, between normal emotions and/or behaviors and clinical disturbances; and (c) the effects of the course of development on psychopathology and vice versa.

Three topics from current developmental research are thought to bear upon the understanding of childhood depression. These include the development of competence, of self-understanding and self-esteem, and of emotions. It should be remembered that findings based on research or theories of normal development are not always generalizable to disordered youth. In some instances, the developmental phenomena under consideration may make their appearance at a later age in depressed youth (e.g., differentiating their own emotions in the absence of external cues) or at an earlier age than believed developmentally possible (e.g., excessive self-criticism).

Given the cognitive, linguistic, and social changes that occur in the course of development, it is not surprising to find that depressive symptomatology varies with age. Sadness predominates as a symptom of depression during infancy. Mood disturbance, vegetative symptoms, and disruptive behavior are salient features during the toddler period. With the advent of middle childhood, cognitive factors assume a more prominent role in mood disturbances with guilt, hopelessness, excessive self-criticism, and school problems clearly evident. In adolescence, the major depressive symptoms closely resemble those of adults.

Depression increases with age throughout the childhood and adolescent years. Boys appear to be more at risk than do girls up until the teenage years when depressed girls outnumber depressed boys. There is no clear-cut explanation that accounts for the age and sex changes in prevalence figures. Native American adolescents may have increased depression but further research is needed before the relationship between race and depression is clarified (Peterson et al., 1993).

The continuity between childhood and adult depressions continues to be a source of controversy. Conflicting evidence can be attributed to differences in the populations studied, diagnostic criteria, length of follow-up, type of research design, level of diagnosis, and nature of outcome measures. The best evidence to date suggests that depressive disorders in childhood have a more protracted duration than was previously believed.

REFERENCES

Abramson, L., Seligman, M., & Teasdale, J. (1978). Learned helplessness in humans: Critique and reformulation. *Journal of Abnormal Psychology, 87,* 49–74.

Achenbach, T., & Edelbrock, C. (1979). The Child Behavior Checklist II: Boys aged 12–16 and girls aged 6–11 and 12–16. *Journal of Consulting and Clinical Psychology, 47,* 223–233.

Achenbach, T., & Edelbrock, C. (1981). Behavioral problems and competencies reported by parents of normal and disturbed children aged 4 through 16. *Monographs of the Society for Research in Child Development, 46*(Serial No. 188).

Ainsworth, M., Blehar, M., Waters, E., & Wall, S. (1978). *Patterns of attachment: A psychological study of the strange situation.* Hillsdale, NJ: Erlbaum.

Albert, N., & Beck, A. (1975). Incidence of depression in early adolescence: A preliminary study. *Journal of Youth and Adolescence, 4,* 301–307.

Anthony, J., & Scott, P. (1960). Manic-depressive psychosis in childhood. *Journal of Child Psychology and Psychiatry, 1,* 53–72.

Beck, A. (1967). *Depression: Clinical, experimental and theoretical aspects.* New York: Harper & Row.

Bemporad, J., & Wilson, A. (1978). A developmental approach to depression in childhood and adolescence. *Journal of the American Academy of Psychoanalysis, 6,* 325–352.

Bowlby, J. (1969). *Attachment and loss: Attachment.* New York: Basic Books.

Bowlby, J. (1980). *Attachment and loss: Loss.* New York: Basic Books.

Bowring, M., & Kovacs, M. (1992). Difficulties in diagnosing manic disorders among children and adolescents. *Journal of the American Academy of Child and Adolescent Psychiatry, 31,* 611–614.

Brumbach, R., & Weinberg, W. (1977). Relationship of hyperactivity and depression in children. *Perceptual and Motor Skills, 45,* 227–251.

Burbach, D., & Borduin, D. (1986). Parent-child relations and the etiology of depression. *Clinical Psychology Review, 6,* 133–153.

Cantwell, D. (1983). Issues regarding natural history. In D. Cantwell & G. Carlson (Eds.), *Affective disorders in childhood and adolescence* (pp. 266–278). New York: Spectrum.

Cantwell, D., & Baker, L. (1991). Manifestations of depressive affect in adolescence. *Journal of Youth and Adolescence, 20,* 121–133.

Carlson, G. (1983). Bipolar affective disorders in childhood and adolescence. In D. Cantwell & G. Carlson (Eds.), *Affective disorders in childhood and adolescence* (pp. 61–84). New York: Spectrum.

Carlson, G. (1984). A comparison of early and late onset adolescent affective disorder. *Journal of Operational Psychiatry, 15,* 46–50.

Carlson, G., & Cantwell, D. (1979). A survey of depressive symptoms in a child and adolescent psychiatric population. *Journal of the American Academy of Child Psychiatry, 18,* 587–599.

Carlson, G., & Cantwell, D. (1980). A survey of depressive symptoms, syndrome and disorder in a child psychiatric population. *Journal of Child Psychology and Psychiatry, 21,* 19–25.

Carlson, G., Davenport, Y., & Jamison, K. (1977). A comparison of outcome in adolescent and late bipolar manic depressive illness. *American Journal of Psychiatry, 134,* 919–922.

Chess, S., Thomas, A., & Hassibi, M. (1983). Depression in childhood and adolescence. *The Journal of Nervous and Mental Disease, 171,* 411–420.

Cicchetti, D., & Schneider-Rosen, K. (1986). An organizational approach to childhood depression. In M. Rutter, C. Izard, & P. Read (Eds.), *Depression in young people* (pp. 71–134). New York: Guilford.

Clarizio, H., & McCoy, G. (1983). *Behavior disorders in children.* New York: Harper & Row.

Cordes, C. (1984). The triumph and tragedy of longitudinal research. *APA Monitor, 15,* 318.

Crook, T., Raskin, A., & Eliot, J. (1981). Parent-child relationships and adult depression. *Child Development, 52,* 950–957.

Dahl, V. (1971). A follow-up study of child psychiatric clientele, with special regard to manic-depressive psychosis. In A. Arnell (Ed.), *Depressive states in childhood and adolescence* (pp. 534–541). Stockholm: Almquist & Wiksell.

Downey, G., & Coyne, J. (1990). Children of depressed parents: An integrative review. *Psychological Bulletin, 108,* 50–76.

Dweck, C., Davidson, W., Nelson, S., & Enna, B. (1978). Sex differences in learned helplessness, II. The contingencies of evaluative feedback in the classroom, III. An experimental analysis. *Developmental Psychology, 14,* 268–276.

Eastgate, J., & Gilmore, L. (1984). Long-term outcome of depressed children: A follow-up study. *Developmental Medicine and Child Neurology, 26,* 68–72.

Edelsohn, G., Ialongo, N., Werthamer-Larson, L., Crockett, L., & Kellam, S. (1992). Self-reported symptoms in first-grade children: Developmentally transient phenomena? *Journal of the American Academy of Child and Adolescent Psychiatry, 31,* 282–290.

Fleming, J., Boyle, M., & Offord, D. (1993). The outcome of adolescent depression in the Ontario Health Study. *Journal of the American Academy of Child and Adolescent Psychiatry, 32,* 28–33.

Gaensbauer, R. (1980). Anaclitic depression in a three-and-one-half-month child. *American Journal of Psychiatry, 137,* 841–842.

Glasberg, R., & Aboud, F. (1981). A developmental perspective on the study of depression: Children's evaluative reaction to sadness. *Developmental Psychology, 17,* 195–202.

Harrington, R., Fudge, H., Rutter, M., Pickles, A., & Hill, J. (1990). Adult outcomes of childhood and adolescent depression. *Archives of General Psychiatry, 47,* 465–473.

Hassanyeh, F., & Davison, K. (1980). Bipolar affective psychosis with outset before age 16 years: Report of 10 cases. *British Journal of Psychiatry, 137,* 530–539.

Herjanic, B. (1976, June). *Follow-up study of 20 children given a discharge diagnosis of depression at St. Louis Children's Hospital.* Paper presented at the meeting of the American Psychiatric Association, Miami.

Inamdar, S., Siomopoulus, G., Osborn, M., & Bianchi, E. (1979). Phenomenology with depressed moods in adolescents. *American Journal of Psychiatry, 136,* 156–159.

Izard, C., & Schwartz, G. (1986). Patterns of emotion in depression. In M. Rutter, C. Izard, & P. Read (Eds.), *Depression in young people: Developmental and clinical perspectives* (pp. 33–70). New York: Guilford.

Jacobson, S., Fasman, J., & DiMascio, A. (1975). Deprivation in the childhood of depressed women. *Journal of Nervous and Mental Disorders, 166,* 5–14.

Kandel, D., & Davies, M. (1982). Epidemiology of depressive mood in adolescents. *Archives of General Psychiatry, 39,* 1205–1212.

Kandel, D., & Davies, M. (1986). Adult sequence of adolescent depressive symptoms. *Archives of General Psychiatry, 43,* 255–262.

Kashani, J., & Carlson, G. (1985). Major depressive disorder in a preschooler. *Journal of the American Academy of Child Psychiatry, 24,* 490–495.

Kashani, J., & Carlson, G. (1987). Seriously depressed preschoolers. *American Journal of Psychiatry, 144,* 348–350.

Kashani, J. H., McGee, R. O., Clarkson, S. E., Anderson, J. C., Walton, L. A., Williams, S., Silva, P., Robins, A., Cytryn, L., & McKnew, D. (1983). Depression in a sample of 9-year-old children. *Archives of General Psychiatry, 40,* 1217–1223.

Kazdin, A. E., French, N., & Unis, A. (1983). Child, mother, and father evaluations of depression in psychiatric inpatient children. *Journal of Abnormal Child Psychology, 11,* 167–180.

Kovacs, M. (1986). The clinical interview. In M. Rutter, C. Izard, & P. Read (Eds.), *Depression in young people* (pp. 435–465). New York: Guilford.

Kovacs, M., Feinberg, T., Crouse-Novak, M., Paulauskas, S., & Finkelstein, R. (1984). Depressive disorders in children. I. A longitudinal prospective study of characteristics and recovery. *Archives of General Psychiatry, 41,* 229–237.

Kovacs, M., Feinberg, T., Crouse-Novak, M., Paulauskas, S., Pollack, M., & Finkelstein, R. (1984). Depressive disorders in childhood. II. A longitudinal study of the risk for a subsequent major depression. *Archives of General Psychiatry, 41,* 643–649.

Lefkowitz, M., & Burton, N. (1978). Childhood depression: A critique of the concept. *Psychological Bulletin, 85,* 716–726.

Lefkowitz, M., & Tesiny, E. (1985). Depression in children: Prevalence and correlates. *Journal of Consulting and Clinical Psychology, 53,* 647–656.

Lowe, T., & Cohen, D. (1980). Mania in childhood and adolescence. In B. Belmaker & H. vanPraag (Eds.), *Mania: An evolving concept* (pp. 111–117). New York: Spectrum Press.

MacFarlane, J., Allen, L., & Honzik, M. (1954). *A developmental study of the behavior problems of normal children between twenty-one months and fourteen years.* Berkeley: University of California Press.

Masters, J., & Carlson, C. (1984). Children's and adults' understanding of the causes and consequences of emotional states. In C. Izard, J. Kagan, & R. Zajonc (Eds.), *Emotions, cognition and behavior* (pp. 438–463). New York: Cambridge University Press.

McGee, R., Feehan, M., Williams, S., & Anderson, J. (1992). DSM-III disorders from age 11 to age 15 years. *Journal of the American Academy of Child and Adolescent Psychiatry, 31,* 50–59.

McGee, R., & Williams, S. (1988). A longitudinal study of depression in 9-year-old children. *Journal of the American Academy of Child and Adolescent Psychiatry, 27,* 342–348.

Munro, A. (1966). Some familial and social factors in depressive illness. *British Journal of Psychiatry, 112,* 429–441.

Nolen-Hoeksema, S., Girgus, J., & Seligman, M. (1991). Sex differences in depression and explanatory style. *Journal of Youth and Adolescence, 20,* 233–245.

Pearce, J. (1974). *Childhood depression.* M. Phil. thesis. University of London.

Pearce, J. (1978). The recognition of depressive disorder in children. *Journal of the Royal Society of Medicine, 71,* 494–500.

Perris, C. (1966). A study of bipolar (manic-depressive) and unipolar recurrent depressive psychoses, Part 2 Childhood environment and precipitating factors. *Acta Psychiatrica Scandinavica* (Suppl. 194), *42,* 45–57.

Peterson, A., Compas, B., Brooks-Gunn, J., Stemmler, M., Ey, S., & Grant, K. (1993). Depression in adolescence, *American Psychologist, 48,* 155–168.

Peterson, A., Sarigiani, P., & Kennedy, R. (1991). Adolescent depression: Why more girls. *Journal of Youth and Adolescence, 20,* 247–271.

Poznanski, E., Krahenbuhl, V., & Zrull, J. (1976). Childhood depression—A longitudinal perspective. *Journal of the American Academy of Child Psychiatry, 15,* 491–501.

Preodor, D., & Wolpert, E. (1979). Manic-depressive illness in adolescence. *Journal of Youth and Adolescence, 8,* 111–130.

Reynolds, W. (1992). *Internalizing disorders in children and adolescents.* New York: Wiley.

Richman, N., Stevenson, J., & Graham, P. (1982). *Preschool to school: A behavioral study.* London: Academic Press.

Robins, L. (1966). *Deviant children grown up.* Baltimore: Williams & Wilkins.

Rutter, M. (1980). *Changing youth in a changing society: Patterns of adolescent development and disorder.* Cambridge, MA: Howard University Press.

Rutter, M. (1981). *Maternal deprivation reassessed* (2nd ed.). Harmondsworth, Middlesex, England: Penguin Books.

Rutter, M. (1986). The developmental psychopathology of depression: Issues and perspectives. In M. Rutter, C. Izard, & P. Read (Eds.), *Depression in young people* (pp. 3–30). New York: Guilford.

Schwartz, R., & Trabasso, T. (1984). Children's understanding of emotions. In C. Izard, J. Kagan, & R. Zajonc (Eds.), *Emotions, cognition and behavior* (pp. 409–437). New York: Cambridge University Press.

Seagull, E., & Weinshank, A. (1984). Childhood depression in a selected group of low achieving seventh graders. *Journal of Clinical Child Psychology, 13,* 138–140.

Seligman, M. (1975). *Helplessness.* San Francisco: Freeman.

Selman, R. (1980). *The growth of interpersonal understanding.* New York: Academic Press.

Spitz, R. A. (1946). Anaclitic depression. *Psychoanalytic Study of the Child, 2,* 313–342.

Sroufe, L. (1983). Infant-caregiver attachment and patterns of adaptation in preschool: The roots of maladaptation and competence. In M. Perlmutter (Ed.), *Minnesota symposia in child psychology* (pp. 41–83). Hillsdale, NJ: Lawrence Erlbaum.

Sroufe, L., & Rutter, M. (1984). The domain of developmental psychopathology. *Child Development, 55,* 17–29.

Strober, M., & Carlson, G. (1982). Bipolar illness in adolescents with major depression. *Archives of General Psychiatry, 39,* 549–555.

Strober, M., Green, J., & Carlson, G. (1981). Phenomenology and the subtypes of major depressive disorder in adolescence. *Journal of Affective Disorders, 3,* 381–390.

Strober, M., Lampert, C., Schmidt, S., & Morrell, W. (1993). The course of major depressive disorder in adolescents: I. Recovery and risk of manic switching in a follow up of psychotic and nonpsychotic subtypes. *Journal of the American Academy of Child and Adolescent Psychiatry, 32,* 34–42.

Susman, E., Dorn, L., & Chrousos, R. (1991). Negative affect and hormone levels in young adolescents: Concurred and predictive perspectives. *Journal of Youth and Adolescence, 20,* 167–182.

Teri, L. (1982). The use of the Beck Depression Inventory with adolescents. *Journal of Abnormal Child Psychology, 10,* 277–284.

Tesiny, E., & Lefkowitz, M. (1982). Childhood depression: A six month follow-up study. *Journal of Consulting and Clinical Psychology, 50,* 778–780.

Tisher, M. (1983). School refusal: A depressive equivalent? In D. Cantwell & G. Carlson (Eds.), *Affective disorders in childhood and adolescence* (pp. 129–144). New York: Spectrum.

Turkington, C. (1989). Body image in girls pushes rate of depression up. *APA Monitor, 20,* 33.
Waters, E., Wippman, J., & Sroufe, L. (1979). Attachment, positive affect, and competence in the peer group: Two studies in construct validation. *Child Development, 50,* 821–829.
Weiner, B., & Graham, S. (1984). An attributional approach to emotional development. In C. Izard, J. Kagan, & R. Zajonc (Eds.), *Emotions, cognition and behavior* (pp. 167–191). New York: Cambridge University Press.
Weiner, I. B. (1975). Depression in adolescence. In F. F. Flach & S. C. Draghi (Eds.), *The nature and treatment of depression* (pp. 99–118). New York: Wiley.
Welner, A., Welner, Z., & Fishman, R. (1979). Psychiatric adolescent inpatients. *Archives of General Psychiatry, 36,* 698–700.
Zeitlin, H. (1972). *A study of patients who attended the children's department and later the adults' department of the same psychiatric hospital.* M. Phil. dissertation, University of London.
Zeitlin, H. (1985). *The natural history of psychiatric disorder in children.* Institute of Psychiatry Maudsley Monograph: Oxford University Press.

3 DIAGNOSIS AND ASSESSMENT

The area of diagnosis of childhood depression is very active at this time. Important subjects to be assessed include (1) facial expression and motoric behavior; (2) social responsivity and adjustment, particularly the way the child relates to parents, peers, and teachers; (3) task performance; (4) affective, behavioral, and cognitive problem-solving strategies; (5) concepts of the self, world, and motivation; and (6) mood and affective expression.

Four basic objectives have been formulated for coverage in this chapter. First, we discuss levels of diagnosis as they relate to assessment of childhood depression. Second, the better known self-report inventories, psychiatric interviewing schedules, parent rating scales, and peer nomination techniques are described and evaluated. Third, the importance of a multistage, multimethod approach to screening and identification will be discussed. Finally, diagnostic issues associated with reliability, validity, consistency across raters, settings, and time, and requirements for symptom duration are examined.

LEVELS OF DIAGNOSIS

Considerable diagnostic confusion arises from the different uses of the term *depression* (Cantwell & Baker, 1991). The diagnostician should bear in mind that approaches to diagnosis vary in their levels of analysis in accordance with their definition of depression (Kazdin, 1983). At one level of analysis is the *symptom,* which refers to a given overt behavior (withdrawal), affect (depressed mood), cognition (irrational belief), or vegetative functioning (somatic concerns). In behavioral analysis, these would be referred to as target behaviors. In *DSM-III-R,* symptoms also refer to a description of the presenting complaint. Despite the everyday use of the term *depression* to mean sad mood, feeling miserable, and so on, individual symptoms do not necessarily signal a depressive disorder. To illustrate, Achenbach and McConaughy (1992) report that the phrase "unhappy, sad, or depressed," although one of the best discriminators between referred and nonreferred children in teachers' ratings, was reported for between 39% and 80% of referred cases in parent, teacher, and self-reports. That is, these problems were very common among referred children and appear to be general symptoms of malaise rather than indicative of a single disorder such as depressive disorder.

A second level of analysis involves the term *syndrome,* which implies that behaviors may covary. That is, affective, cognitive, motivational, and vegetative changes occur regularly in combination. Whether a constellation of behaviors exists is, of course, an empirical matter. As noted earlier, there is evidence that behavior often comes in packages, at least at certain ages (Achenbach & McConaughy, 1992). Behaviorally oriented diagnoses have no concept that is clearly analogous to that of a syndrome even though they do treat multiple symptoms. Even at this level, the term *depression* may or may not be a primary psychiatric disorder. Although a syndrome may occur as a primary problem, it may occur with and secondary to various medical, environmental, or psychiatric (e.g., anxiety disorder) antecedents, and, in adolescents, from disruptive behavior disorders (Cantwell & Baker, 1991). The notion of a syndrome has therapeutic implications as well. Interventions that focus on one area have been found to alter, in an empirically predictable way, the type and direction of changes in the behaviors with which the target behavior is related (Wahler & Fox, 1980). The possibility of modifying several depressive behaviors by treating a correlated target behavior is an exciting one that awaits empirical investigation.

A third level of conceptualization involves the notion of *disorder.* To demonstrate that disorder exists, more information is needed than the mere clustering of behavior. For a syndrome to be considered a disorder, it must be shown that the syndrome cannot be accounted for by a more pervasive condition. Major depression in adults is a disorder because this syndrome cannot be accounted for by other disorders of which it is a part (e.g., anxiety disorders). Also, information is available about the course of the depression, family history, and biological markers. Subtypes also respond differentially. In short, much more is known about depression than the mere covariation of symptoms. The fourth level of analysis centers around the concept of *disease,* which states that there is a specific known etiology and an identifiable biological abnormality.

DSM-III-R deals with the first three levels of analysis, whereas behavioral approaches focus primarily on the first level. The classification system associated with Public Law 94-142 also uses a level one analysis, equating childhood depression with the symptom of dysphoria. As you read about the major scales for measuring childhood depression, ask yourself what is the level of analysis upon which each relies.

ASSESSMENT TECHNIQUES

The methods used to assess childhood depression will be grouped into four categories: self-report inventories; psychiatric interviewing; clinician, parent, or teacher ratings or reporting; and peer ratings. The most commonly used methods are based on self-report inventories and clinical interviews. Although self-report inventories and clinical interviewing will be discussed separately, it should be recognized that the assessment approaches with children are not as distinct as is commonly viewed. Many self-report inventories are routinely read aloud to children to enhance their comprehension of the questions and the various response alternatives. Moreover, both formats depend on information given by children and on their ability to evaluate adequately their own symptoms (Kazdin & Petti, 1982). The discussion will present some of the better known inventories of each of the four types.

Self-Report Inventories

Before examining some of the better known self-report scales, it is well to recognize the distinction between a formal diagnosis of depression in the syndromal sense and assessment of depression with respect to the depth or *severity* of its symptomatology. The scales discussed herein are designed to provide clinical measures of severity of depressive symptomatology and not to yield a formal diagnosis of depression. Self-report measures of depression do not differentiate whether symptom endorsement is specific to depression, a related condition, or a normal response to everyday events (Reynolds, 1992). Nor do they take into account the inclusionary and exclusionary criteria of diagnostic classification systems.

Children's Depression Inventory

Self-rated depressive inventories have long been used in clinical research on adults. Despite the availability of self-report symptom scales for adults, there were no corresponding measures for children. In response to this need, Marie Kovacs, using the Beck Depression Inventory (Beck, 1967) for adults as a starting point, devised the Children's Depression Inventory (CDI). The CDI, initially developed in 1977 and made commercially available in 1992 (Kovacs, 1992), is the most commonly cited and thoroughly researched self-report measure of childhood depression (Finch, Saylor, & Edwards, 1985). It is a 27-item questionnaire designed to assess depression in school-aged children and adolescents aged 7 to 12 years. The items are to be answered in relation to behaviors experienced or manifested over the previous 2 weeks. Although its readability is at the 1st-grade level, the examiner reads the items aloud, at least for the first few items, and the child marks the answer on the inventory. A 10-item Short Form is also available. Its high correlation with the long form ($r = .89$), its brevity, and the omission of the controversial item on suicide ideation will contribute to its acceptability as a screening instrument in schools.

There is evidence that CDI scores obtained in group administration do not differ significantly from those obtained in individual administration (Saylor et al., 1984). Each item is scored on a 0- to 2-point scale. There are five subscales: Negative Mood, Interpersonal Problems, Ineffectiveness, Anhedonia, and Negative Self-Esteem (Kovacs, 1992). The total CDI mean score for public school children is about 9.5 (Finch et al., 1985; Green, 1980; Kovacs, 1992; Smucker, Craighead, Craighead, & Green, 1986). A total cutoff score of 20 identifies the upper 10% of normal children and adolescents (Kovacs, 1992). Although a cutoff score of 20 might correspond to an epidemiologically defined level of "deviance," further research is needed before finalizing a cut point for general screening. For clinical settings, a cutoff score of 12 is suggested given the higher base rate of depression in clinically referred children (Garvin, Leber, & Kalter, 1991). As you will read later in this chapter, cutoff scores also need to vary depending on whether the scale is self-completed or parent-completed.

Analysis of additional normative data on 1,463 second- through eighth-graders in Florida public schools revealed small but significant gender and grade differences, with boys reporting more depressive symptoms than girls at all but the third-grade level, where the number of subjects was small ($N = 38$). Young children reported fewer symptoms than other groups (Finch et al., 1985). Item analysis of CDI scores by Smucker and colleagues (1986) revealed significant gender differences. Starting around junior high school age for adolescent males, acting-out behaviors such as disobedience and general misbehavior were more highly correlated with overall depression score than was true for adolescent females. Whereas males may exhibit more externally focused characteristics of depression, adolescent girls tend to internalize their depression, as evidenced by the higher correlation of dysphoric mood (sadness, loneliness, crying, and somatic preoccupation) and negative body image with total depression scores for both preadolescent and adolescent females than for same-aged males. Taken together, findings pertaining to gender differences on the CDI have been inconsistent (Kovacs, 1992). Findings regarding age trends have been more consistent, showing that youth aged 13 and above score higher on the CDI than do children 12 and below (Kovacs, 1992). There are no systematic data on which to develop separate norms for different ethnic groups in North America (Kovacs, 1992), although there is research showing that Hispanics (Worchel et al., 1990), Japanese (Koizumi, 1991), and Egyptians (Ghareeb & Beshai, 1989) score higher on the CDI.

Scores on this scale are negatively correlated with school performance and positively with self-reported adjustment problems among 7th and 8th graders. Internal consistency reliability is adequate (.86) based on a sample of 875 normal children. Clinicians' global rating of depression correlated .55 with CDI scores.

The inventory has acceptable internal consistency ranging from an alpha of .87, based on a large sample ($N = 860$) of Toronto public school children, to .71 in a pediatric-medical outpatient group ($N = 61$). Test-retest data yielded correlation coefficients ranging from .72 to .84 in various samples (normals, diabetics, depressed) over time periods ranging from 4 to 13 weeks. There is some evidence to suggest that CDI depression scores are significantly more stable for females across a 1-year time interval than they are for males, which might indicate that depression may stabilize earlier in life for females than for males (Smucker et al., 1986).

In large samples of normal juveniles, the CDI appears to function as a unidimensional scale. In psychiatric clinic-referred children, the CDI's factor structure is more diverse and multidimensional. Concurrent validity studies show that children who score high on the CDI also tend to have high levels of anxiety ($r = .65$) and low self-esteem ($r = -.59$), two phenomena that are theoretically and clinically related to depression (Kovacs, 1985). Also, unpopular children have significantly higher levels of self-rated depression than do their popular peers (Vosk, Forehand, Parker, & Richard, 1982).

Finally, the inventory differentiates diagnostic categories (i.e., children with major depression score higher than youngsters with other nondepressive psychiatric conditions). This scale does not, however, differentiate those less severe forms of depression (major depressive disorder in partial remission and adjustment disorder with depressed mood) from psychiatric conditions that are not in the depressive domains (conduct disorder). Moreover, although the CDI does quantify severity of a major depressive syndrome, its "hit rate" or diagnostic precision vis-à-vis the more depressive conditions falls short of what is psychometrically desirable. For example, Kazdin, Colbus, and Rodgers (1986) found that more than 70% of psychiatrically hospitalized children with a diagnosis of depression would not have been identified as clinically depressed using a cutoff score of 19. Because depressive symptoms, per se, are not unique to depressive *disorders,* empirically derived cutoff scores must be used cautiously (Kovacs, 1983). Finally, no validity scales are included to check the accuracy of the child's responses. The CDI's factorial structure appears to depend on the population being studied. Most factor-analytic studies using normal and clinical samples find from three to eight factors, although most studies have found one factor to explain a large amount of the variance (Kovacs, 1992). The CDI's ability to discriminate among heterogeneous child psychiatric populations also warrants further scrutiny (Kovacs, 1992; Nelson, Politano, Finch, Wendel, & Mayhall, 1987). It does appear to discriminate within psychiatric outpatient groups, but the magnitude of between-group differences suggests that the scale not be used alone. It does, however, serve the purpose for which it was designed, namely, to provide a *severity* rate for depressed children and adolescents. We must remember that the CDI was not intended to be a diagnostic tool.

One further use deserves mention. In addition to its use as an index of the severity of depression in children and adolescents, it has also been viewed as a good index of therapeutic change (e.g., Garvin et al., 1991). It is well known that there is a significant drop in CDI scores from the first to the second testing (Meyer, Dyck, & Petrinack, 1989). This phenomenon, which is not limited to the CDI, highlights the need to establish multiple baselines before evaluating the efficacy of any given treatment so that measurement artifacts are not mistaken for treatment effects (Kovacs, 1992). Because youngsters may not like to complete a self-report again and again, some clinicians prefer a less aversive and time-consuming procedure such as completing a checklist of symptoms experienced during the previous week.

Children's Depression Scale

The Children's Depression Scale (CDS), developed by Tisher and Lang (1978), consists of 66 items based on close inspection of psychotherapy records and sentence completion protocols of depressed children as well as on descriptions of childhood depression in the literature. The CDS contains 48 items dealing with depression and 18 positive items ("I enjoy myself most of the time"). The depressive scale items are divided into five subscales: affective response, social problems, self-esteem, preoccupation with one's own sickness and death, and guilt. Sample items include:

Subscale: Affective Response
   Sometimes I don't know why I feel like crying.
Subscale: Social Problems
   Often I feel I am no use to anyone.
Subscale: Self-Esteem
   Often I feel ashamed of myself.
Subscale: Preoccupation with Own Sickness and Death
   I often imagine myself hurt or killed.
Subscale: Guilt
   Often I feel I deserve to be punished.

The CDS is unique in several respects. Each of the 66 items is printed on separate cards, which are presented individually. The child reads the item, which is rated on a 1- to 5-point scale by placing it in one of five boxes labeled, from left to right, "very wrong," "wrong," "don't know," "right," and "very right." The focus on one item at a time might serve to reduce the influence of the child's response to earlier items. The manipulative activity forces the child to take a more active role than is the case with other self-report scales. Because of the CDS's gamelike format, children often enjoy the scale more than other self-report measures. This scale is also unique in that duplicate items can also be answered by parents, teachers, and therapists to describe the child. The inclusion of a positive scale to measure pleasurable experiences is yet another unique feature.

Psychometric evaluation of the CDS is somewhat better than that for other similar scales. Internal consistency reliability is high. Scores on the CDS distinguish depressed children from both normals and other diagnostic groups (Kazdin, 1987). Factor analysis of the CDS suggests that a single dimension accounts for most of the items, a finding that raises questions about the empirical basis of the various subscales. No specific time period is stated regarding the length of time required before a symptom is considered indicative of childhood depression. In brief, the CDS is a promising scale with many positive features.

Reynolds Child Depression Scale (RCDS)

This 30-item self-report scale is designed for use with children 8 through 13 years of age (Reynolds, 1989a,b). Twenty-nine of the items refer to clinically defined symptoms of depression (e.g., I feel that no one cares about me) and are rated for frequency of occurrence over the past 2-week period on a 4-point scale ("almost never," "sometimes," "a lot of the time," and "all of the time"). The 30th item provides a global dysphoric mood-state rating by asking the child to place an X on one of the five "smiley-type" faces that best describes how the individual feels.

A test manual is available that includes information on administration, scoring, and psychometric data. The RCDS was normed on more than 1,600 children from diverse ethnic and socioeconomic backgrounds. Internal consistency reliability is high for both normal and depressed children (.86 to .91). Test-retest reliability is also adequate (.85) over a 4-week interval (Reynolds, 1992). A wide variety of validity data are presented (e.g., correlations with other depression scales) (Reynolds, 1989b). All in all, the RCDS is one of the most useful self-report scales of depression in this age group.

Reynolds Adolescent Depression Scale

The Reynolds Adolescent Depression Scale (RADS) (Reynolds, 1987) is the only scale specifically designed to assess depression among adolescents. The scale consists of 30 paper-and-pencil items to assess severity of depressive symptoms reflecting cognitive, somatic, psychomotor, and interpersonal domains. Not all symptoms associated with depression are assessed by the RADS. Normative data have been collected on over 11,000 adolescents aged 13 through 18. Sample items include "I feel sad" and "I feel like crying" and, with reverse scoring, "I feel happy" and "I feel like talking to other students." The adolescent is asked about the frequency of each item ranging from "almost never" to "most of the time." The scale also asks how the student has felt during the past week or so. If the student indicates either "somewhat depressed" or "very depressed," then he or she must explain why he or she feels depressed. The scale takes about 10 minutes to complete. Test-retest reliability with a sample of 124 adolescents over a 6-week interval was .84, and coefficient alpha varied from .90 to .96 based on various samples from around the United States (Reynolds, 1986). Validity studies (Reynolds, 1992) provide a firm foundation for clinical and research use of this scale. The psychometric properties of this scale indicate that it is a promising instrument.

Evaluation

Despite the fact that children may be the best source of information for rating their inner feelings, most authorities would urge that information from other sources be obtained. Although reading obstacles are readily overcome by presenting the items to the child orally, comprehension may not be easily achieved. The low but inverse relationship between depression and achievement indicates that depressed youngsters will possess below average reading ability and underscores the need to ensure that they comprehend the items. Fortunately, the readability of commonly used self-report scales ranges from 1st- to 3rd-grade levels and is below the age levels proposed for the various measures (Kazdin & Petti, 1982). Even if youngsters understand the items, it is doubtful whether they have sufficient cognitive and/or experiential maturity to rate accurately the frequency, severity, and duration of such depressive symptoms as self-regard, sleep disturbances, sad looks, and withdrawn posturing. There is also the danger that self-report measures reflect what happened in the child's life that day rather than reflecting a more stable behavioral pattern. The finding that 40% of children who scored above the CDI cutoff score on an initial assessment subsequently scored below the cutoff score when retested a short while later (Tharinger & Stark, 1990) indicates that scales exaggerate the frequency and severity of depression in young people. Radloff (1991) also cautions that the scores of junior high school students may be inflated by an excess of transient symptoms. It is important to note that psychiatric inpatient youngsters aged 5 to 13 years consistently rate themselves as less depressed across various measures of depression than do their parents (Kazdin, French, & Unis, 1983). This finding indicates the need for different cutoff scores for parent-completed and child-completed inventories (Kazdin et al., 1986). Unfortunately, there are no well-established cutoff scores that have been used to delineate clinical levels of depression among most scales for children (Kazdin et al., 1986). Kovacs (1981) noted that further research must be undertaken to establish the scale's relationship to independent diagnoses and its short-term stability on clinical samples before recommending it for wider use.

Diagnosis of childhood depression should not rely solely or even primarily upon short questionnaires or checklists. Although useful for research purposes, the readiness of these scales for clinical usage is questionable. Further, those clinicians who advocate the concept of masked depression will deplore the absence of such symptomatology from current questionnaires and checklists. In any event, clinical diagnosis should incorporate information from various measures (e.g., interviews) and informants rather than relying on individual scale scores. The value of a multistage, multimethod approach to identification will be discussed later in the chapter. The need for adequate normative data as well as a developmental perspective is readily apparent. Regrettably, existing self-report scales do not reflect a developmental perspective. Without it, there can be no valid method for assessing childhood depression. How might a developmental perspective be implemented? Items, for example, could be designated by experts as specific to childhood, adolescence, or adulthood, or as common to some or all of these age periods. In addition, items could be designated as specific or common to various stages of cognitive development (preoperational, concrete operational, or formal operational stages). Another possibility would be to have similar content but to weight the item differentially. For instance, items such as "wanting to leave home" or "concern about how my body looks" could be given greater weight during the adolescent years. Conversely, another possibility might be to place more emphasis on affect-oriented items at younger ages and on more ideational-oriented items at the older years. At times, item content might even be scored in a reverse direction depending on the child's age. To illustrate, experiencing guilt over an event beyond one's control (e.g., accidental breaking of a valued possession) would be scored as normal for a young child but perhaps as pathological for an older child. In addition to a developmental perspective, functional analyses of depressive behaviors in children are sorely needed. To know that a child seems tired most of the time is of limited value without a functional analysis of her tiredness. Unfortunately, behaviorally oriented investigators have not paid much attention to childhood depressive disorders.

Parent Ratings

Parent ratings, like clinician, teacher, and peer ratings, have many disadvantages and advantages. The disadvantages include (1) the unobservable nature of many of the inner aspects of depression (e.g., suicidal ideation, excessive guilt feelings), (2) the ambiguity in the meaning of the symptoms to be appraised (e.g., depressed mood), and (3) the wide individual differences among raters such as leniency, severity, or tendency to rate everybody as average.

As summarized by Barkley (1990), the advantages include (1) drawing upon a rater's often substantial previous experience with the child over long periods of time and in different settings, (2) gathering data on rare and infrequent behaviors, (3) low cost and efficiency in gathering valuable information, (4) the availability of normative data to show whether treatment has brought the child closer to the average child, (5) the existence of numerous scales on which substantial information has been collected regarding their psychometric properties and practical value, (6) ecological validity in that the opinions of various "significant others" are incorporated, and (7) the quantification of qualitative aspects of child behavior not readily available through other means.

General Psychopathology Scales

Use of a general scale of childhood psychopathology can be helpful for at least two reasons. First, most measures of childhood depression focus solely on *severity* of symptomatology rather than on a formal diagnosis. Second, childhood depression frequently occurs in conjunction with other psychopathological disorders which can affect treatment plans and future research on etiology. Two of the best general scales of childhood psychopathology are reviewed in this section together with adaptations of self-report measures for parents.

The Personality Inventory for Children

The Personality Inventory for Children (PIC) (Wirt, Lachar, Klinedinst, & Seat, 1977) has been selected to illustrate how parental reports can be used to obtain accurate information about the child and his or her relationships with others. The PIC contains clinical subscales of which one is designed to measure depression in children. The PIC can be used with children between 3 and 16 years of age and is to be completed by someone who has had ample opportunity to observe the child, usually the mother. The Depression Scale consists of 46 items dealing with such factors as moodiness, social isolation, crying spells, lack of energy, pessimism, serious attitude, indecisiveness, uncommunicativeness, concern with death and separation, and sensitivity to criticism. Sample items include:

My child tends to pity him (her) self.
My child hardly ever smiles.
My child has little self-confidence.
My child doesn't seem to care for fun.
Several times my child has threatened to kill him (her) self.
Often my child locks him (her) self in the bedroom.
My child speaks of him (her) self as stupid or dumb.
My child often will cry for no apparent reason.

All of the 46 items had to be nominated by at least four of seven judges to be included in the scale. The test-retest reliability of this scale based on 34 psychiatric outpatients was .94 over a 15-day average period and .93 for 45 normal children over a 2-week interval. No validity data are available for this scale except for data indicating that the scale's scores are high for various clinical samples. Although profile analysis is not yet well developed with the PIC, other scales of the instrument, such as the Anxiety Withdrawal Scale and Social Skills Scale, should be considered in the interpretation of childhood depression because the correlation of these three subscales with the depression subscale is .81, .62, and .62, respectively, due in part to overlap of items on these subscales.

Criticisms questioning the utility of the PIC center around the out-of-date norms; the inconsistency between mother, father, and teacher ratings; and the question of whether the scale should be completed at home or at the clinic or school (Leon, Kendall, & Garber, 1980; Reynolds & Tuma, 1985; Rothermel & Lovell, 1985). Despite its shortcomings, the PIC remains one of the most sophisticated and best developed personality scales available for children.

The Child Behavior Checklist

The Child Behavior Checklist (CBCL) (Achenbach, 1991a) also relies on parental report as a means of assessing childhood depression and other clinical conditions. The CBCL is designed to assess in standardized format the social competencies and childhood problems among youngsters aged 4 through 16 as reported by their parents or teachers. Of the 118 childhood behavior problems, some pertain to depressive phenomena. The items, which are rated on a 3-point scale, contain specific observable child behaviors (e.g., talks about killing self) that require more general inferences (e.g., unhappy, sad, or depressed) and behaviors that require considerable judgment on the part of others (e.g., feels too guilty). A 5th-grade reading capability is required to complete the CBCL (Mooney, 1984). It is easy to administer, well normed with respect to age and gender as well as to normal and clinical populations, psychometrically sound, and clearly appropriate for a wide variety of clinic-referred children. It is quite useful in distinguishing clinical from nonclinical groups and in providing a broad overview of the child's problems from the parents' and teachers' perspectives. The usefulness of this checklist in differentiating among clinical samples is reflected in the finding that follow-up scores on social involvement differentiated between suicidal children and depressed children. The depressed tended to withdraw from others whereas the suicidal tended to maintain contact with friends and family (Cohen-Sandler, Berman, & King, 1982). Although the CBCL is helpful in distinguishing clinically impaired youngsters from the general population, its usefulness with normal children may be limited (Mooney, 1984). The reliability of the depression items due to their less observable nature is also lower than the average of other individual scales. And, like most rating scales, the CBCL tends to locate the problems in the individual child's pathology and to neglect the impact of environmental forces such as the family system or classroom on the child's problems. Despite these limitations, the CBCL has deservedly gained a respected role in the psychological assessment of children's problems.

Recent research (Rey & Morris-Yates, 1991) has demonstrated that a measure of depression extracted from the CBCL by Nurcombe et al. (1989) was able to discriminate between adolescents with and without major depression with an accuracy comparable to that reported for the Dexamethasone Suppression Test. The subjects consisted of 667 adolescents aged 12 to 16 years, referred to the Rivendell Adolescent Unit in Sydney, Australia. Two senior clinicians made independent *DSM-III* diagnoses. Using analyses of the receiver operating characteristic (ROC) of signal detection theory, the only technique that yields an overall index of diagnostic accuracy uninfluenced by decision biases and prior probabilities (Swets, 1988), the investigators found that the 22 items of the CBCL-NUR scale (see Table 3.1) were most accurate when discriminating between patients with and without major depression. The scale discriminates almost as accurately between major depression and separation anxiety. The scale was least accurate when discriminating depression from dysthymia, although even here, the scale did better than chance.

Adaptations of Self-Report

Almost all of the self-report measures of childhood depression have been reworded so that parents can report on their children's depression. Thus far, no single measure has clearly demonstrated superior reliability and validity (Kazdin, 1990) despite the use of parent-report scales in several investigations. As is the case with self-report scales with children, the primary purpose of these adapted parent-related scales is to rate the *severity* of depression, not to achieve a diagnosis. For instance, both the CDI, the most cited and thoroughly researched questionnaire designed to assess depression in school-aged children and adolescents, and the Children's Depression Scale (CDS) developed by Tisher and Lang (1978) have also been used as parent-rated depression measures. By and large, there seems to be limited consistency across raters. Children's self-report of depression on the CDI and CDS shows a modest relationship with parents' ratings of children's depression (Moretti, Fine, Hales, & Marriage, 1985). In general there is a reliable but low agreement ($r = .25$) for parent and child assessments of problem behav-

Table 3.1
CBCL-NUR Items

CBCL Item	
13	Confused or seems to be in a fog
14	Cries a lot
18	Deliberately harms self or attempts suicide
30	Fears going to school
31	Fears he/she might think or do something bad
32	Fears he/she has to be perfect
35	Feels worthless or inferior
42	Likes to be alone
47	Nightmares
50	Too fearful or anxious
52	Feels too guilty
54	Overtired
56B	Headaches
75	Shy or timid
77	Sleeps more than most children during day and/or night
80	Stares blankly
91	Talks about killing self
100	Trouble sleeping
102	Underactive, slow moving, or lacks energy
103	Unhappy, sad, or depressed
111	Withdrawn, doesn't get involved with others
112	Worrying

Note. Adapted from Nurcombe et al., 1989. "Is Major Depressive Disorder in Adolescence a Distinct Diagnostic Entity?" *Journal of the American Academy of Child and Adolescent Psychiatry, 28,* 333–342.

ior (Achenbach, McConaughy, & Howell, 1987). Children see their impairment as less severe than their parents. Direct observation of overt depressive behavior among child psychiatric inpatients shows that behavioral measures are consistently related to parent-completed ratings of depression and *DSM-III* diagnoses but not to child-completed ratings (Kazdin, Esveldt-Dawson, Sherick, & Colbus, 1985). This finding does not invalidate parent-rated scales, self-report inventories, and interviews of children. Both parental reports and self-reports might well be valid measures of different external criteria even though they do not correlate highly with each other. There is no need to assume that one source of information is correct and the other inaccurate, given what we know from personality research about the situational specificity of behavior and low relationships between various measures of a construct. Indeed, research indicates that parental reports correlate with decreased social participation on the youngster's part and visible signs of emotion (Kazdin, et al., 1985), and that child self-reports of depression correlate with suicide attempt and ideation, low self-esteem, negative attributional style (Kazdin, French, Unis & Esveldt-Dawson, 1983). Research in validating rater reports is often plagued by criterion contamination. For instance, clinical ratings are sometimes used as an external criterion to validate parental reports when, in fact, they are based on parental input.

Clinician-Rated Inventories

The Children's Depression Rating Scale—Revised

The Children's Depression Rating Scale—Revised (CDRS-R) was developed by Poznanski and colleagues (1984) by modifying the Hamilton Scale, which has been used successfully with adults. The CDRS-R, which takes about 30 minutes to complete, is designed to measure both the presence and severity of depression in children aged 6 to 12 years. The child is rated following an interview with the clinician. There are 17 items, 14 of which are rated on the basis of the youngster's responses to a series of standardized questions. Items are rated from 1 to 7 for 14 items and from 1 to 5 for sleep, appetite, and tempo of speech. A rating of 5 or higher indicates definite abnormal symptomatology, and a total score of 40 is a reliable indicator of depression.

The items rated cover schoolwork, capacity to have fun, social withdrawal, sleep, appetite, physical complaints, irritability, guilt, self-esteem, depressed feelings, morbid ideation, suicidal ideation, weeping, and nonverbal items such as depressed affect, tempo of speech, and hypoactivity.

Reliability studies indicate that both test-retest reliability and interrater reliability are high. The scale's strengths include its ease and brevity of administration, its high reliability, and its correlation with global ratings. Potential drawbacks center around the subjective nature of the ratings, lack of clarity as to weighting of various data sources, potential "halo effect" in determining correlation with the global rating (Strober & Werry, 1986), and exclusive attention to major depressive disorders (Petti, 1985).

Bellevue Index of Depression and Children's Affect Rating Scale

Another noteworthy clinician-rated scale is the Bellevue Index of Depression (BID) (Petti, 1978), which is designed for children aged 6 to 12 years. Based on Weinberg's diagnostic criteria, the BID consists of 40 symptoms (e.g., looking sad, crying easily). Each problem is rated on two separate 4-point scales: one for severity and one for duration. Petti (1978) recommends an arbitrary cutoff score of 20 to designate a child as depressed. The BID is completed by interviewing the child and other informants and by examination of referral documents. It is unclear as to how the information sources are weighted. Combining scores and weighting them warrant careful consideration especially since parents and children differ in their reporting of depressive severity (Kazdin et al., 1986). There are no subscales. This scale has the advantages of covering a wide variety of symptoms and the potential to monitor for remission or deterioration of symptoms because of its graded scoring system (Kashani et al., 1981). Classificatory agreement between the BID and a clinician's designation of depression was high (83%), but the data are difficult to interpret because all assessments were made by the same clinician. Although much remains to be learned about the scale's psychometric properties, the BID does exemplify a pragmatic approach toward clinical scale construction; that is, the quantifying of all the symptoms required by a particular research diagnostic standard (Kovacs, 1981).

The Children's Affect Rating Scale (Cytryn & McKnew, 1972) is another well-known clinician-rated scale.

Teacher-Rated Scales

There are several reasons why input from teachers is important for the assessment of childhood depression. First, children and adolescents spend approximately 12,000 hours in school settings during the formative years of their lives. Second, next to parents, teachers know the children better than perhaps any other adult. Third, because young people exhibit different types of behaviors at home and at school (Leon et al., 1980), data from the teacher can aid in developing a broader view of the youngster's adjustment. Teacher-rated scales and direct observation are two methods available to teachers and specialists in the schools for assessing depression in young people.

The Behavior Evaluation Scale-2 (BES-2) was developed by McCarney and Leigh (1990) in response to the need for an operational definition of emotional impairment as defined under Public Law 101-476, Individuals with Educational Disabilities Act (IDEA), formerly known as the Education for All Handicapped Act (EHA) or more commonly as Public Law 94-142. This scale, originally developed in 1983 and revised in 1990, devotes 17 of its 76 items to the assessment of depression, which under PL 101-476 is defined as "a general pervasive mood of unhappiness or depression." Items are weighted to reflect the seriousness of the behaviors rated. Each item is rated for frequency from 1 (never or not observed) to 7 (continuously throughout the day). Consistent with the federal government's definition of emotional impairment, this scale also has a related subscale of 14 items designed to measure "a tendency to develop physical symptoms or fears associated with personal or school problems."

Sample Items from the depression subscale of the BES-2 include:

Demonstrates a facial expression of sadness or displeasure (e.g., frowning) (1, weighted score)

Appears to be bored with or disinterested in daily activities (e.g., says he/she doesn't care what happens, etc.) (3)

Cries in response to personal or school situations (3)

Makes derogatory comments about self (e.g., I'm dumb, ugly, etc.) (3)

Makes comments or writes notes about suicide (5)

Makes comments that he/she feels helpless (3)

The BES-2 is designed to serve students from kindergarten through grade 12. It has six primary purposes: (1) to screen for behavior problems, (2) to assess the behavior of referred pupils, (3) to aid in the diagnosis of serious emotional disturbance/behavior disorders (e.g., depression), (4) to link assessment with specific behavioral interventions (assessment utility), (5) to evaluate the outcomes of behavioral interventions, and (6) to record data for research (McCarney & Leigh, 1990).

The scale was restandardized on 2,772 students in grades K-12 from 31 states selected to provide representation of those demographic characteristics in the U.S. population as reported in the U.S. Census data. Internal consistency coefficients ranged from .87 to .89 for four different age groups on the depression subscale. Test-retest reliabilities were .94 with a group of normal youngsters and .90 for a group of behaviorally disordered youth. Standard errors of measurement are reported for the total scale as well as for the subscales. Content validity was established by subjecting the item pool to a sample of 675 professionals from 31 states to judge the appropriateness of each item. All items selected for inclusion on the final scale were deemed appropriate as stated by a minimum of 95% of the respondents. Evidence of criterion-related validity was based on a study that correlated the scores of 26 behaviorally disordered pupils on the RES-2 with scores on the Teacher Rating Scale of the Behavior Rating Profile (BRP) by Brown and Hammill (1990). The resulting correlation coefficient was .44 between the depression subscales on these two instruments. Although the BES-2 appears to differentiate between behaviorally disordered and normal youngsters, no evidence is available regarding its ability to distinguish among specific groups of psychiatrically disordered youth. Contrary to the authors' assertions (McCarney & Leigh, 1990), the high intercorrelations between the subscales ($r = .57$ to .90) suggest that differential diagnosis among various emotionally impaired subgroups would be difficult. Strengths of the scale include an adequate norm group, minimal time to administer (15–20 minutes), and the linkage between assessment and intervention.

The Behavior Disorders Identification Scale (BDIS) by Wright (1988) is similar to the BES-2 in that it is also modeled after the federal definition of seriously emotionally disturbed as outlined under Public Law 101-476. Like the BES-2, only one of the five subscales deals with the assessment of depression in young people. This 81-item scale is for use with individuals ages 4.5 to 21 years. The BDIS was standardized on 3,188 students based on ratings obtained from 867 teachers in 71 school districts across 23 states. Each of the 10 items on the depression subscale is rated for frequency but not for severity. Males received higher scores than females on all five subscales. Interrater reliability ranged from .88 to .94 from all age levels. Test-retest reliability of the depression subscale is .92. The intercorrelations among the BDIS subscales range from .67 to .75 which indicates that students with problems in one area are also likely to have problems in other areas. Content validity was based on input from the test author and on an unknown number of "diagnosticians and educational personnel." Criterion-related validity was established by correlating the BDIS subscale scores with the BES (original version) subscale scores. The depression subscale on the BDIS showed a .65 correlation with the BES depression subscale. This scale is also designed for use with parents. Like the BES-2, teacher intervention strategies are designed for each elevated item on the depression subscale. The effort to link assessment with intervention is commendable. It remains for future research to establish whether this tie-in between assessment and intervention leads to superior outcomes over traditional approaches to assessment/intervention.

A Teacher Report Form (TRF) of the CBCL is available for classroom use (Achenbach, 1991c). Like the CBCL completed by the parent, the TRF consists of 118 items, the vast majority of which (85) are identical on both forms. Some 9 items were changed only slightly in wording to make them more suitable to the classroom. For example, in TRF Item 25, the word "pupils" was substituted for the word "children" in CBCL Item 25 which reads "Doesn't get along with the other children." For the remaining 24 items, the content was altered so that the items would be appropriate to the classroom setting. For example, an item on allergies in the CBCL might be replaced by the school-oriented item "Hums or makes odd noises in class." Each of the 118 items is rated on a 3-point scale (0 = "not true"; 1 = "somewhat or sometimes true"; 2 = "very true or often true"). The TRF can usually be completed in 8–10 minutes. Ratings are based on the previous 2-month period rather than the previous 6-month period for the CBCL. When pupils have more than one teacher, as is often the case with secondary schools and departmentalized elementary schools, the opportunity is present to compare students' functioning in different classes and to explore why teacher perceptions vary from one setting to another. It is also possible to average scale scores to form a composite picture. No scales are designed to detect various kinds of informant bias such as denying, exaggeration, and social desirability sets. Because teacher ratings did not prove to provide as a good a basis for typology as do the parent profiles, the TRF does not use "profile types." Socioeconomic and racial differences are regarded as too small to warrant the use of separate norm groups.

The Teacher Affect Rating Scale (TARS) is devoted solely to the assessment of depression in children by teachers in contrast to the three scales discussed above that attempt to assess various aspects of student psychopathology, only one of which involves depression. Developed by Petti (no date), this scale consists of 26 items, each of which is rated on a scale of 0 to 3. The ratings are based on the child's behavior during the past week. Sample items, which are rated on a 4-point scale from "not at all" to "very much," include "poor work effort," "irritable, easily annoyed," and "lacks enjoyment". This scale seems to measure three factors: a behavior factor, a learning factor, and a depression factor.

Because the scale is still in its developmental stage, there is no manual and little information exists on its psychometric properties. Like most rating scales, it probably does not differentiate between the *demoralized* child and the child with a depressive *disorder*. For example, many learning disabled children may be demoralized but do not have depressive disorders. Having the ratings based on the past week, say versus the past 4 weeks, will also result in an increased number who are called depressed when, in reality, they are not. Finally, the value of teacher ratings of depression remains to be established. It might well be that teachers are better at identifying disruptive students than they are depressed students.

Direct Observation

Teachers are in a unique position to observe students over an extended period of time, not only with respect to educational performance but also in social interactions with classmates. Thus, a major practical limitation of observational methods—their time-consuming nature—is obviated by the teacher's having to spend so much time with students. Observational techniques are particularly well suited to the assessment of the *overt* behaviors characteristic of depression such as diminished social and motor activity, sad facial expression, on-task classroom pursuits, and playground/lunch room interactions. Despite the obvious and natural suitability of observational methods to assess depression in classrooms, development of observational codes for teachers has been neglected.

Kazdin (1990) reports on an observational system that divides behaviors into three categories: (1) *social,* which in turn consists of talking, playing a (structured) game, and participating in a group activity; (2) *solitary* behavior, which in turn is divided into playing a game alone, working on an academic task, listening and watching, straightening one's room, and grooming (self-care); and (3) *affect-related* expression, which subsumes smiling, frowning, arguing, and complaining. Although the behavioral code was developed for use with inpatient children during free-period times, it could easily be adapted for teacher use in a classroom. Such an adaptation would be welcomed, particularly if it were structured so that antecedents and consequences could be systematically studied.

The CBCL has a Direct Observation Form (DOF) which is designed for use by an experienced observer who monitors the target child in settings such as classrooms and lunchrooms. The general practice is for the experienced observer to write a narrative description of the student's behavior as it occurs over a 10-minute interval and then to rate the pupil on the 96 behavior problems. The 4-point rating scale capitalizes on the finer-grained discriminations made by experienced observers. Of the 96 items, 49 are similar to those of the TRF, 11 have no direct counterpart on the TRF, and 36 items differ only slightly from items on the TRF. The DOF also permits the scoring of on-task behavior at 1-minute intervals. Interrater agreement based on total problem score is quite acceptable for both children in residential treatment centers ($r = .96$) and in public school classes ($r = .92$). As no standardized scoring profile yet exists, the authors suggest that a child's deviance be judged by comparing the target student's scores with the scores of two control students of the same sex observed under the same conditions.

It is also possible for the teacher to use *DSM-III-R* criteria as a basis for observation. Relying on observational data the teacher might ask questions, presented in Table 3, that relate to diagnostic criteria of major depressive disorder derived from *DSM-III*.

The questions raised in Table 3.2 can prove helpful in structuring teacher observations of possible major depressive disorders. Some major limitations

Table 3.2
Symptoms Checklist for Major Depressive Disorders
(Derived from *DSM-III*)

		YES	NO
1A.	Does the student appear sad, unhappy, depressed, low, cranky, or down in the dumps most of the time?		
2A.	Does the student seem to think that there is nothing to enjoy at all?		
3A.	Has the student lost interest in homework or the job?		
4A.	Does the student seem to think that things are not going to work out and are hopeless?		
5A.	Is the student easily irritated? (Does he/she get mad very easily?)		
6B.	Has the student lost his/her appetite?		
7B.	Has his/her appetite increased tremendously?		
8B.	Has the student lost 4 or more pounds during the last year?		
9B.	Has the student gained 4 or more pounds during the last month or 10 or more pounds during the last year?		
10C.	Does the student need more sleep than previously?		
11D.	Does the student feel tired most of the time?		
12E.	Is the student more restless than before? (Observer should look for inability to sit still, pacing, pulling or rubbing his/her hair, skin, clothing, or pressure of speech.)		
13E.	Has the student slowed down? (Observer should look for slowed speech, increased pauses before answering, monotonous speech, or slowed body movement.)		
14F.	Has the student lost interest in activities that were pleasurable in the past? (Hobbies, art, music, TV, sports, social gatherings, etc).		
15G.	Does the child often blame him/herself excessively when things go wrong?		
16G.	Does the child seem to feel very bad or guilty for minor mistakes?		
17G.	Does the child feel worthless, useless, or no good at all?		
18H.	Does the child find it difficult to concentrate and focus on what he/she is doing?		

Table 3.2

(Continued)	YES	NO
19H. Is it difficult for the student to make decisions quickly?		
20I. Has the student been thinking about hurting him/herself? (*If yes, please explain.*)		

Note. Adapted from McKnew and Cytryn, cited in "Scales of Potential Use in the Psychopharmacological Treatment of Depressed Children and Adolescents, by T. Petti, *Psychopharmacological Bulletin,* 1985, *21,* 957–958.

To diagnose depression, the person must have at least one symptom from group A and four symptoms from the eight groups lettered B through I.

should be kept in mind, however. First, teachers might not be able to rate observable behaviors pertinent to depression because they occur outside of the school setting (e.g., Does the child have difficulty falling asleep and/or wake up earlier than usual?). Also, teachers might have difficulty making judgments about certain observable behaviors even though they do occur within the school setting (e.g., the amount of weight gain or loss). Finally, some aspects of major depressive disorder are not observable (e.g., suicidal ideation). An individual's internal states frequently do not lend themselves to observational assessment. Despite these limitations, teachers should be encouraged to be more sensitive observers of depressive states, conditions that teachers might well overlook. No professional group spends more time with young people than teachers, and their observational powers should be honed and tapped in the detection of depressive disorders.

Another observationally based measure is the Emotional Disorder Rating Scale developed by Kaminer, Feinstein, Seifer, Stevens, and Barrett (1990). This instrument has 54 items spread across eight subscales, which are rated on the basis of frequency and severity. It relies on direct observation and inferences of behaviors and cognitions related to depression. Preliminary data regarding its psychometric data indicate that the subscales vary widely with respect to test-retest reliability (.35 for a 1-day interval) and internal consistency.

Peer Ratings

Though not widely used, peer nominations offer a fascinating and promising tool for assessing childhood depression. Ratings by peers suffer from the same problems noted earlier in the discussion of ratings by parents, teachers and clinicians. In addition, raters may tend to overestimate the relationship between popularity and positive mood, as well as the relationship between rejection or neglect and depression. Despite its limitations, this method has numerous advantages that are often overlooked or deemphasized. Many of the symptoms of depression such as dysphoria, loss of energy, or lack of involvement in activities can be readily observed by peers in the give-and-take of social interaction. Peers also have the opportunity to observe across a number of settings in the neighborhood and school. There is also the advantage of having several raters rather than just one. Finally, the raters are already knowledgeable about many of the behaviors in question in that they too have experienced them in the process of growing up.

The Peer Nomination Inventory of Depression (PNID) (Lefkowitz & Tesiny, 1980) is the best known technique of this type. It consists of 20 items designed to sample four areas of functioning related to depression: affective, cognitive, motivational, and vegetative.

The content validity of these 20 items was determined by the judgment of nine "experts." From a list of 29 potential manifestations of depression gathered from the clinical literature, these experts chose the items they believed most indicative and relevant to the definition of depression provided. Of the 20 items finally selected, 14 were presumed to measure depression, 4 were presumed to measure happiness, and 2 were presumed to measure popularity. The happiness and popularity items were added to temper the negative tone of the depression items, as well as to assist in the examination of construct validity. Children are asked in a group setting questions like "Who often thinks they are bad?" "Who plays alone?" "Who often looks sad?" "Who often sleeps in class?" and "Who doesn't have much fun?" Each child nominates other classmates for each question, with a child's score equaling the total number of nominations received.

The scale was originally normed on 452 boys and 492 girls from 61 fourth- and fifth-grade classrooms in New York City. Internal consistency reliabilities are adequate, ranging from reliability coefficients of .71-.85 (e.g., Cole & Carpentieri, 1990). Test-retest coefficients for the total depression score are adequate ($r = .79$). Factor analyses cross-validated across samples indicate that the symptoms of childhood depression may be represented by three factors—loneliness, inadequacy, and dejection (Lefkowitz & Tesiny, 1980). The normative data base was later expanded to 3,020 youngsters in grades 3 through 5 in New York City (Lefkowitz & Tesiny, 1985). PNID performance is predictive of school performance, self-concept, teacher rating of work, skill and school behavior, peer rating of happiness and popularity and locus of control (Lefkowitz & Tesiny, 1985; Lefkowitz & Gordon, 1980; Tesiny & Lefkowitz, 1982), but it is not clear whether the variables predicted by the PNID could be predicted as well or better by other general measures of personality disturbance. Further, the degree of relationship between peer and teacher ratings of depression is moderate at best ($r = .41$) and the correlation between peer ratings and self-report on the CDI is low ($r = .23$). Another study by these authors based on 58 third-, fourth-, and fifth-grade students reported lower correlations between mothers' ratings of depression on the CBCL and PNID ratings for boys ($r = .14$) than for girls ($r = .26$) (Tesiny & Lefkowitz, 1982). Later research based on 752 fifth-, sixth-, and ninth-grade public school children from a midsize city in central Texas and 142 fifth-graders from a large metropolitan area in southwest Texas confirmed previous research showing a higher relationship between two other-reports of depression (from peers and teachers) than between self-report and other-reports of depression. For instance, the correlation between teacher reports as measured by the TRF and scores from peer reports as measured by the PNID was .35. The correlations between teacher reports and self-report as measured on the CDI was only .13, and the correlation between peer and self-report was .27 (Worchel et al., 1990). The low correlations might be explained, in part, by the fact that the nature of the items on the three scales used varies appreciably. Whereas the CDI attempts to assess internal states such as not liking oneself, the PNID measures more observable behaviors such as sleeping in class and the TRF includes items of both overt and covert nature (Worchel et al., 1990).

This same study (Worchel et al., 1990) also raises questions about the generalizability of PNID normative data gathered on pupils in New York City as scores in both of the Texas samples were significantly lower than those obtained from the New York City samples. Whereas a PNID cutoff score of 4.00 identifies the upper 5% of the New York sample, only 1.2% of the Texas sample received a PNID score of 4.00 or higher. Whether the differences in normative data can be explained solely on differences in geographical area and racial difference between the Texas and New York samples awaits further research. One conclusion is clear, however. We will need additional local normative data before a cutoff score can be confidently set for children of different racial/gender groups from a given geographical area.

The use of the PNID can pose other problems when used in a public school setting. Although informed consent is most likely not needed from all classmates and their parents for a preliminary screening of the class, it would be required by federal guidelines if a given child is suspected of being seriously emotionally handicapped due to depression. Moreover, because this scale has been used with public school populations, we do not know how well the PNID discriminates between children with depressive *symptoms* and children with depressive *disorder*. Finally, the PNID's usefulness within *clinical* settings is severely limited by the absence of a stable peer group who knows the child well enough to rate accurately. Despite its limitations, the PNID is a well-developed, reliable scale with validity studies showing consistently moderate correlations with such variables as competence (Blechman, McEnroe, Carella, & Audette, 1986), lower social interaction time (even though depressed children initiated a greater number of interactions and were approached more frequently than nondepressed children) (Altmann & Gotlib, 1988), and success on an anagram task (Ward, Friedlander, & Silverman, 1987). It remains a one-of-a-kind scale for assessing depression in children.

Psychiatric Interviewing

The psychiatric interview might well be the most commonly used method to assess childhood depression. Many research-oriented clinicians contend that school-aged youngsters can and should be interviewed directly about their symptoms and concerns. Moreover, such data are viewed as indispensable to the diagnostic process. Advocates of the direct diagnostic interview view free play as a distraction and not as an aid in this regard. Proponents of the direct interview method emphasize oral-vocal dialogue between the clinician and the child to learn about the child's symptoms and complaints. Given that many youngsters may not be able to recognize, properly label, accurately monitor, or estimate frequency, severity, and duration, observation of nonverbal behaviors is also highlighted (Kovacs, 1986). The approach underlying the interview techniques reviewed herein is the same in that they all use a semistructured format guaranteeing that certain questions are asked about certain symptomatic areas. They differ in the age range of the youngsters for whom they are to be used, the comprehensiveness of the psychopathology covered, the extent and structure of the probes in various symptomatic areas, and certain aspects of coding (Cantwell, 1983).

Kiddie-SADS

Prominent among the several interviews developed to assess depression in children is the Kiddie-SADS (K-SADS) by Puig-Antich and Chambers (1978). The authors used the adult Schedule of Affective Disorders (Endicott & Spitzer, 1978) as a point of departure. The 1983 revision of the K-SADS is designed for use with children between the ages of 6 and 16 and covers symptoms of depression, conduct disorders, neurosis, and psychosis. It is administered first to parents, then to the child alone, and finally summary ratings are achieved by including all sources of information (parent, child, teacher). Specific criteria are given for rating the severity of each symptom. All symptoms are rated separately for the previous week and for past and current episodes. Because clinical judgment plays a central role in guiding the interview (for example, questions to be asked) and in scoring the information, the services of a trained clinician are required. The first part of the K-SADS is relatively unstructured. The informant is asked to identify presenting problems and symptoms so that the interviewer can know the chronology of the ongoing episode, its mode of onset, and its duration. Treatment history is recorded as well as the time period when symptoms were most severe (during the current episode or during the following year, whichever is shorter). In the second part of the interview, approximately 200 questions are asked about specific symptoms or behaviors relevant to Axis I, *DSM-III* diagnoses. The K-SADS is organized primarily according to diagnostic category. The third part includes 16 observational items rated by the interviewer and a rating of the children's version of the Global Assessment Scale.

An interrater reliability ($r = .54$) has been reported for the diagnosis of major depressive disorder among a sample of 52 outpatients, aged 6 to 17 years. Internal consistency data are adequate. Test-retest reliabilities for depressive symptoms ranged from .32 to .88, with the majority of ratings over .50. Internal consistency correlations ranged from .65 to .94 (Chambers et al., 1985). Later research studies have reported a mean interrater kappa coefficient for affective symptoms of .70 (Apter, Orvaschel, Laseg, Moses, & Tyano, 1989) and .83 (Ambrosini, Metz, Prabucki, & Lee, 1989). The interrater reliability figure of .83 from the Ambrosini study may be inflated as the ratings were based on watching a videotape rather than on data from separate interviewers. Other investigators find a correlation of .62 between mother's and children's severity scores on the K-SADS, present episode version, and a correlation of .38 between scores by fathers and children (Stark, Reynolds, & Kaslow, 1991). Because interview measures typically sample the criteria for affective disorders, it is assumed that they possess content validity. This assumption, of course, is based on the adequacy of the criteria and the clinician's interviewing skills in using unstructured or semistructured interview schedules. Evidence of criterion validity is suggested by the finding that interview scores reflect changes in response to the use of antidepressant drugs (Puig-Antich et al., 1981). This finding highlights the importance to be accorded to biological markers of depression as they relate to interview and self-report measures in future attempts to establish criterion validity.

The current widespread concern about linking assessment with intervention warrants comment. When using unstructured or semistructured interviews, the clinician is free to ask additional questions that may be helpful in planning intervention *targets* and *strategies*. Illustratively, the interviewer can prioritize treatment targets (body image, eating problems, inability to concentrate, sleep problems,). Further, the interview may indicate which treatment procedure may be the method of choice (social skills training, monitoring positive/negative cognitions, progressive muscle relaxation). Finally, information can be elicited as to the success or lack thereof for previous treatment approaches with the youth in question. In brief, much valuable treatment information can be gathered during the course of an interview. The practitioner can tailor questions to acquire significant clues as to the *what, how,* and likely *success* of intervention. Whether clinicians can achieve these objectives in a reliable, valid way that enhances therapeutic outcomes remains for future research to establish.

Other interviews designed to assess depression in children include the Child Assessment Schedule (CAS) by Hodges (1983); the Interview Schedule for Children (ISC) (Kovacs & Beck, 1977); the Diagnostic Interview Schedule for Children and Adolescents by Reich, Herjanic, and Welner (1982); and the Diagnostic Interview Schedule for Children—Revised (Shaffer et al., 1993). (A summary of the characteristics and partial content of these interviews is provided in Table 3.3.) For a further discussion of selected interview schedules, the reader is referred to Hodges and Cools (1990).

Evaluation

Despite the fact that the direct interview of the child has long been known to be feasible, reliable, and valid (Rutter & Graham, 1968), many legitimate questions remain regarding its use. Are schoolchildren sufficiently mature to grasp the interpersonal constructs invoked in a clinical interview? Can they respond in accordance with their assigned role as informant? That is, do they truly comprehend the interviewer's questions about symptoms and complaints? Most of these issues will now be addressed. After examining the general demands of the clinical interview on the child, discussion will focus on three specific interviewee competencies required in the assessment of childhood depression.

Interview Demands and Developmental Abilities

The clinical interview makes both general and specific demands on the child's social and cognitive development. The general demands include (1) recognizing that one has a problem, (2) viewing the clinician as a helping person, and (3) trusting the clinician. All three demands could influence the

Table 3.3
Characteristics and Content of Interviews

Interview properties	CAS	DICA	DISC	ISC	K-SADS
Number of items	128	267–311	264–302	200+	200+
Time period assessed	current or past 6 months	current or ever	past year	2 weeks or past 6 months	current or life-time
Age assessed	7–17	6–17	6–17	8–17	6–17
Completion time	45–60 min	60–90 min	50–70 min	60–90 min	45–120 min
Structured		X	X		
Semistructured	X			X	X
Symptom oriented	X		X	X	
Category oriented		X			X
Severity ratings				X	X
Pre-coded	X	X	X	X	X
Computer scoring		X	X		
Administration					
Lay interviewer		X	X		
Clinician	X	X	X	X	X
Reliability data	X	X	X	X	X
Axis I disorders: Affective disorders Adjustment disorders with depressed mood				X	
Cyclothymia	X		X		X
Dysthymia	X	X	X	X	X
Hypomania				X	X
Major depression	X	X	X	X	X
Mania	X	X	X	X	X
Minor depression					X

Table 3.3
(Continued)

Note. From "Psychiatric Interview Suitable for Use in Research with Children and Adolescents" by H. Orvaschel, 1985, *Psychopharmacology Bulletin, 21,* p. 739.

outcome of the interview. For instance, not until age 10 or so do children have sufficient cognitive development to recognize that personal problems involve internal events (e.g., psychological distress) as well as external observable components. This suggests that young children's (6- to 8-year-olds') answers to questions can be interpreted more parsimoniously as reflecting developmental status rather than as denial. Further, the clinician who relies on indirect action such as discussing the problem or giving advice might not be seen as so helpful as one who engages in direct action on behalf of the child. Last, the adult conception of trusting the expert is most likely irrelevant to self-disclosure in that preadolescents do not cite trustworthiness as an attribute of the effective helper (Barnett, Darcie, Holland, & Kobasigawa, 1982). For further discussion of the clinical interview's general demands on young patients, see Hughes and Baker (1990) and Kovacs (1986).

Specific Competencies Demands

To be an effective informant about depressive symptoms, the child must have a functional understanding of certain psychological, interpersonal, and intellectual concepts. Although it has been traditionally assumed that the emotional immaturity of children—their denial, fear, or extensive anxiety—precludes direct questioning (Simmons, 1981), evidence suggests that many of the concepts implicated in the assessment of depression follow a developmental path. Foremost among these developmental constructs are knowledge of emotion and mood, understanding of the self, memory, and notions of time.

An understanding of emotion and mood. The interview process requires that the young child have the ability to recognize and distinguish between various emotions. Assessment of the cardinal features of depression via interview is facilitated if the child has an understanding of mood disturbance and emotional indicators such as sadness, tearfulness, and crying; self-pity, irritability, and whininess; and an inability to have fun.

Developmental research indicates that younger children consistently rely on public, observable components of emotions, as well as situational cues. Physiological and behavioral cues (e.g., "I get a headache," "I bang the table,'') are used by similar proportions of children ages 6 to 15. The private or inner mental aspects of emotional experience are rarely recognized or acknowledged by 1st-graders, however. In brief, there is a developmental shift from physicalistic to mentalistic understanding of inner experience between ages 6 to 11 (Harris, Olthof, & Terwogt, 1981). It is not until adolescence that youth are typically able to locate the antecedents of emotional states within themselves (Schwartz & Trabasso, 1984).

Using an attributional framework, Weiner and Graham (1984) found that guilt followed a developmental trend whereas pity and anger did not. All youngsters reported feeling guilty when they engaged in wrongdoing, but 6- and 7-year-olds were much more likely than older children to feel guilty for uncontrollable or accidental outcomes, such as death of a parent. This finding underscores the need for clinicians to use developmental guidelines in determining whether guilt is normal or pathological. To sum up, it is clear that young children can satisfy the interview's demands for differentiation of emotions as well as words for emotion (except for the distinction between "typical" sadness and an autonomous quality of dysphoria, a distinction required by *DSM-III* for the subtyping of a melancholic depression). However, inquiries about sadness, self-pity, and other affects should be posed in the context of specific environmental events or recent somatic experiences. Moreover, it is important to remember that the developmental norms cited are based on normal children and may not be generalizable to disturbed youth who may develop these competencies at later ages.

Understanding of self. Beside mood disturbance, depressed children may feel inadequate or worthless and show a decreased ability to concentrate or think. The assessment of such symptoms presupposes the capacity for introspection and social perspective-taking. The inquiries require that the child think about his or her own thinking (metacognition). Again, we find that the ability to introspect and to evaluate oneself undergoes developmental changes with genuine self-reflection emerging only in adolescence (Damon & Hart, 1982). Because metacognitive phenomena appear to be components of self-as-knower, it is doubtful that the typical 1st- or 2nd-graders could provide accurate information on the quality of their thinking (e.g., "slowed thinking").

Is the young child developmentally capable of feeling worthless? A sense of worthlessness implies self-deprecation of the self-as-knower, organizer, and interpreter of "I" attributes (as opposed to the "me" physical and psychological attributes of self), a mentalistic conception of self, and a social evaluation capability. With young children, say, 6-year-olds, the interviewer might best focus on the child's physicalistic, action-related, or possession-connected descriptions. With 8- to 10-year-olds, it is possible to elicit stable self-derogatory statements of a social-evaluative nature ("I am a lot dumber than other kids") or self-perceived inability to live up to one's own expectations ("I learn as much as other kids but not as much as I should"). (Although developmental research on normal youngsters suggests that self-deprecation arising from a social-evaluative basis does not appear until age 8 or so, practitioners report that this ability is seen in younger depressed children. Additional study involving both normal and depressed children might well clarify this issue.) Finally, we might well expect inconsistent or contradictory responses to questions about self-esteem from younger children in that conceptual integration of various aspects of the self does not occur until adolescence.

Time concepts and memory. Diagnosing depression involves the examination of the temporal covariation and duration of symptoms. As such, it demands a reasonably well-developed awareness of time. Notions of temporal order (succession of events) and temporal duration (the length of intervals between events) do not appear until concrete operational thinking is well established, around age 8 or 9. An elaborated sense of personal and historical time does not develop until adolescence (Wessman & Gorman, 1977).

Youngsters in the primary grades can most likely provide reliable temporal information about current depressive symptoms given their understanding of absolute durations and their here-and-now self-description. They should be able to estimate if it takes a long or short time to fall asleep or if a symptom has been present for a day or for a week. However, providing accurate information on the duration of one symptom relative to another or on the overall persistence of their complaints is often beyond their cognitive capacities even when marker events are used. Only adolescents are likely to provide temporally accurate information about previous episodes of depression or about the time of onset of long-lasting symptoms. Because the research on the origins of temporal awareness was conducted with small samples of bright and mentally healthy youngsters, caution must be exercised in extending these findings to disturbed youth. The most prudent course of action is to interview parents and other significant adults for historical and temporal functioning of depressed young people.

Summing Up

Do available measures of depression in children and adolescents take into account the developmental aspects of interpersonal, psychological, and cognitive factors that impinge on assessment? Many of the available instruments

(K-SADS, ISC, DICA) do combine uniformity with flexibility, especially with regard to specific semantic inquiries used to attain information from youngsters. Although these scales, which were originally designed for research purposes, do not explicitly address the general requirements of a sound interview—how or whether a child should be prepared beforehand, the need to establish a trusting relationship, the maturity level needed to recognize that a personal problem implies internal events as well as external correlates—it is to be hoped that they are used by skilled clinicians who are sensitive to these requirements. Further, the K-SADS, ISC, and DICA's references to a child's problems are embedded in questions about specific symptoms. This practice is consistent with the developmental literature showing that context or situationally related discussions of problems are more meaningful to younger children than general pre-interview preparatory statements about the clinician's intent. Attempts are also made to gear questions to the child's linguistic, semantic, and conceptual levels. This sensitivity is evidenced in the simple sentence structure of the DICA, the relatively plain vocabulary and alternative symptom inquiries of the K-SADS and ISC, and the down-to-earth, direct approach to information that characterizes all three interview schedules (Kovacs, 1986). Unfortunately, the vocabulary level is not uniformly low enough to assure ready use with 6- or 7-year-olds. Both the K-SADS and ISC are administered initially to the parent in an effort to compensate for the child's inability to give a full and reliable report. This practice is desirable given what is known about the child's sense of temporal awareness, a developmental variable important to the establishment of symptom onset and duration. Moreover, in keeping with the child's present orientation, these schedules require only fairly crude or absolute judgments on the child's part (e.g., Have you felt this way "a lot," "a little," or "all day," "part of the day?"). Finally, available measures start with the simplest formulation of the construct in question and then advance semantically and conceptually to more complex levels. For example, in the case of assessing guilt, exemplars are used instead of the word "guilt."

Relying on their clinical experience, sophisticated intuition, and knowledge of the developmental literature, the authors of interview schedules have generally been responsive to the developmental demand that interviews place on young people. Nonetheless, much remains to be accomplished in order to make interview schedules more developmentally oriented and sensitive. For instance, the K-SADS requires that the child have the ability to tell when the depression was worst (a demand that taxes or exceeds the youngster's past time perspective), the ability to make comparative judgments about severity of symptoms, and the capacity for long-term memory. One certainly wonders if children at the concrete operational stage, especially 6- to 8-year-olds, have the cognitive capabilities to cope with such demands. Moreover, even adjustments in vocabulary level may not ensure the child's comprehension of concepts such as worthlessness. Her or his developmental status precludes an understanding of "self as knower." Additionally, we need more practical methods to assess the child's developmental status in order to know how to interpret the child's self-report. It is normal, for instance, for the young child to feel guilty over an unfortunate event even though he or she was not responsible for it. The same attribution by a 13-year-old would be age-inappropriate, however. Constructing more sensitive interviews necessitates the gathering of norms on the cognitive and emotional constructs specifically assessed in the diagnosis of childhood depression. Although developmental theory is helpful in alerting clinicians to certain diagnostic pitfalls, it is no substitute for empirical evidence. For instance, although children lacking formal operational thought are believed to be incapable of experiencing hopelessness and despair for the future, clinical observation showed that pessimism for the future was evident with almost equal frequency among both depressed prepubertal children and adolescents (Carlson & Cantwell, 1982).

MULTISTAGE MODEL

The need for a multistage screening program with depressed children and adolescents is underscored by studies on adult depressives that demonstrate that an unacceptably large number of false positives are identified when only a single self-report measure is administered (Lewinsohn & Teri, 1982). For whatever reasons, adults, adolescents, and children report greater depressive symptomatology on the first administration of a self-report measure of depression than on the second administration of the same scale a short while later (Nelson & Politano, 1990; Reynolds, 1986). In light of this finding, various multistage procedures have been advanced. Some have recommended three successive interviews (Dohrenwend & Shrout, 1981). Others have suggested a two-stage self-report method wherein either two different self-report inventories are administered back-to-back or the same self-report is administered on several successive occasions (Lewinsohn & Teri, 1982). Reynolds (1986) has proposed a three-stage model. The first stage involves group screening of young people with one or more self-report scales such as the Children's Depression Inventory, the Children's Depression Scale, or the Reynolds Adolescent Depression Scale. This could be done by the classroom teacher, taking about 20 to 40 minutes. Those who scored above the cutoff score on the scale would be involved in Stage 2. The second stage entails a reassessment of those youngsters who scored at depressed levels. The original depression measures are readministered 3 to 6 weeks after the initial screening. Stage 2 administrations are given in a small group setting by either a teacher or the school psychologist. The Stage 2 screening would eliminate students who initially overendorsed depressive symptomatology or who suffered a transient depressed mood disturbance. Students identified as depressed in both stages 1 and 2 are then individually evaluated at Stage 3 of this model. This last stage uses an individual clinical interview (e.g., Children's Depression Rating Scale) that requires a trained mental health specialist. The amount of time required ranges from 30 to 90 minutes depending on the interview schedule used. Research on this model over a 3-year period in a number of school districts shows that 18% to 20% of students are identified at Stage 1, that only between 12% to 15% of the total tested at Stage 2 now score in the depressed range, and that the percentage identified as depressed (7% to 12%) is further reduced by the clinical interviews used in Stage 3.

Few, if any, professionals would dispute the value of a multistage, multimethod approach to screening. Like any approach, the multistage model has its drawbacks and potential problems, however. First, we do not know the percentages of students that would be identified as depressed by the various types of multistage models. For instance, would a model using two successive self-report measures followed by a clinical interview identify more, less, or the same percentage of students as depressed as would three successive interviews? Future research on this issue should assist in the selection of a given model. Second, we need to do additional research to determine the amount of risk, say for suicide, to which students who score at various points above the cutoff score on a given depression scale are exposed. For instance, are those falling at the 85th percentile at risk to the same extent as those scoring at the 98th percentile or do their treatment needs differ? Given the tendency of certain scales to identify large numbers of youth as depressed and the limited availability of mental health facilities, the answer to the above kind of question becomes critical. Third, mental health specialists in the schools are often not trained in the relevant interview schedules (e.g., K-SADS). Fourth, self-report measures typically lack validity scales designed to detect random responding and "faking good" or "faking bad." Fifth, schools have typically taken a reactive approach to the identification of emotionally impaired children. Asking them to take a proactive stance in this regard is inconsistent with the culture of the school. Sixth, school authorities would not be cheered to find that 7% to 12% of their student population is depressed and in need of treatment. Many of these youngsters could conceivably be entitled to special education services under Public Law 101-476, Individuals with Educational Disabilities Act, thereby increasing school costs. If schools are to spend additional dollars, they might prefer to spend them on learning disabled youth and acting-out emotionally impaired youngsters rather than on quiet, withdrawn, depressed students. Seventh, the overidentification of youngsters at Stage 1 is appropriate in that it decreases the likelihood of missing a youngster who is depressed. Nonetheless, it does not eliminate the problem of false negatives. Illustratively, one group of youngsters who scored at or above the cutoff score on the initial CDI were given a second CDI plus a psychiatric interview *regardless* of their score on the second CDI. The results indicated that 6% of the children were falsely identified as normal by the second administration of the CDI (Stark, Reynolds, Kaslow, & Kelley, 1991). Eighth, because of the episodic nature of depression, the screening procedures conducted, say in the fall of the school year, might well miss a child who becomes depressed later in the school year. For example, an adolescent boy who is functioning satisfactorily in November might become depressed and suicidal in January as a result of breaking up with his girlfriend.

Last, we need additional research showing how the results of a multistage process might be influenced by the age of the children assessed. Relatedly, we may want to use a different cutoff point for younger (aged 12 and below) and older children (13 and above) as the latter group score higher than the former on the CDI (Kovacs, 1992).

Despite the above concerns, many of which are remediable, the multistage model is an appropriate procedure for use in the schools. The model has worked well, even when identification is compared to diagnoses based on interviews (Evert & Reynolds, 1986), and is socially valid as suggested by the positive evaluation of principals and school boards, as well as funding by the legal staff of at least one State Department of Public Instruction.

ADDITIONAL DIAGNOSTIC CONCERNS

Having addressed diagnostic difficulties such as the difficulty in rating depressed children; the impact of age, cognitive development, and the degree of pathology on the accuracy of children's self-reports; the consistent tendency of children to rate themselves as less depressed than do parents; the tendency of certain scales to identify one third of children as depressed; and the continuity of depression in young people, the present discussion will center on other major assessment concerns. These include the issues of symptom duration requirements, stability across raters and settings, and further discussion of reliability and validity concerns.

Duration of the Problem

Self-report measures vary in terms of the time required for a given behavior to be deemed a sign of childhood depression. Some scales such as the Modified Zung (Lefkowitz & Tesiny, 1980), Children's Depression Scale, and the Face Valid Scale for Adolescents (Mezzich & Mezzich, 1979) do not specify any time frame for symptom duration.

In general, interview techniques pay the greatest attention to symptom duration. For instance, the Bellevue Index of Depression assesses each item separately on a 4-point scale, from absent (0) to severe (3). A score of 1 point is accorded for symptoms manifested for 1 month or less, and 2 points for behaviors lasting from 1 to 2 months. This type of scoring system guards against the danger of referring youngsters who are not depressed or in need of professional care.

Stability Across Settings and Raters

In this section we will examine the stability of depressed behavior as measured across raters and settings. The criterion of stability of behavior across raters and settings is consistent with sound diagnostic practice as well as legal mandates. If one is to speak of a generalized depressive syndrome, then the behaviors characteristic of depression should be manifest across a variety of raters and situations. The child's self-report should be consistent with the parents' ratings of the child's depression, and teachers' and parents' ratings should indicate agreement.

Child vs. Parent Ratings

By and large, there seems to be limited consistency across settings and raters. Children's self-reports of depression on the CDI and CDS show a modest relationship with parents' ratings of children's depression (Moretti et al., 1985). Children see their impairment as less severe than do their parents. Direct observation of overt depressive behavior among child psychiatric inpatients shows that behavioral measures are consistently related to parent-completed ratings of depression and *DSM-III* diagnoses but not to child-completed ratings (Kazdin, et al., 1985). This finding does not challenge the validity of self-report inventories and interviews for children, as child-ratings of depression do correlate with other characteristics of depression including independent reports of suicide attempt and ideation and self-rated helplessness and self-esteem (Kazdin, French, & Unis, 1983; Kazdin, French, Unis, & Esveldt-Dawson, 1983). When there are disagreements in severity of impairment between parent and child, the child's rating is more apt to provide a lower bound estimate of dysfunction.

Parent vs. Teacher Ratings

Parents and teachers show little agreement. Whereas parents rated depressed children as manifesting a significantly greater frequency of behavior problems than nondepressed children, teachers noted only more inattentive-passive behavior among depressed children (Leon et al., 1980). Similar findings were obtained by Lefkowitz and Tesiny (1980), who reported low correlations (.23 and .14) between depression scores on the PNID and two self-report measures. Teacher-rated depression yielded a somewhat higher (.41) relationship with the PNID. Later research by these same investigators also yielded low correlations (.12 to .26) between three measures of childhood depression: peer, self, and parent ratings (Tesiny & Lefkowitz, 1982). Graham (1974) notes that teachers' and parents' ratings of sadness and misery were not related.

This lack of consistency between home and school may (a) indicate that depression in children does not possess the pervasiveness or generalizability of adult depression, that is, depressed children may actually behave differently in different settings; (b) be due to different assessment devices used by informants (e.g., children, CDI; parents, PIC; and teachers, Conner's Teacher Questionnaire) (Goyette, Conners, & Ulrich, 1978); (c) reflect a lack of a common frame of reference for judging depressive behavior; or (d) suggest that parents have a response set that endorses negative characteristics of their children (Leon et al., 1980). Discrepancies between informants' reports about a youngster can be as informative as agreements in that they provide clues about the child's functioning across settings and people. Such disparities can lead to more focused interventions (e.g., changing of informant's behavior or perceptions; Achenbach et al., 1987).

Same Rater, Different Scales

Research studies discussed above agree in their finding of only limited agreement across raters but they leave unanswered the issue of whether a given individual is consistent across various measures of depression. In contrast to the research on consistency across raters and settings, different measures of depression completed by the *same* rater (be it child, mother, or father) tend to be moderately to highly intercorrelated (Kazdin, French, Unis, & Esveldt-Dawson, 1983; Reynolds, 1992). Even so, children consistently rate themselves as less depressed than do their parents. It is not known whether children tend to underestimate their symptoms or whether adults overestimate them. As noted above, there is some evidence to show that direct observations of overt depressive behavior among psychiatric inpatients relate more closely to parental ratings of the child's depression than do child ratings (Moretti et al., 1985).

Reliability

It is a rare inventory that has been thoroughly evaluated with respect to various types of reliability such as internal consistency, test-retest, and interjudge agreement. The reliabilities of some measures are based on samples of normal children; fewer are based on clinical populations. Thus, we are not sure how reliable the majority of scales are with children who manifest severe problems. Although internal consistency measures have been commonly established, very little consideration has been given to test-retest reliability. In those instances where test-retest reliability has been investigated, the correlations based on nonclinic samples have been in the low .70s, indicating moderate reliability over periods from 1 to 4 weeks (Kovacs, 1981; Tisher & Lang, 1983). In one of the few studies using a clinical sample, the test-retest reliabilities were slightly lower (CDI = .50; BID = .63; Depression Symptom Checklist = .47) over a 6-week interval (Kazdin, French, Unis, & Esveldt-Dawson, 1983). If childhood depression is like some adult depressions in being episodic, then it would be better to use brief intervals (e.g., 2 weeks) on which to base test-retest reliabilities rather than longer intervals.

With regard to clinical interviews, the most commonly reported reliability measure is interjudge agreement. Interjudge agreement is often reported in one of two ways: through the percent of agreement on the presence of symptoms or through more sophisticated measures of relationship such as kappa. High interjudge agreements have been generally reported for the presence of specific symptoms and overall diagnosis using various interview schedules, but Kazdin and Petti (1982) note that some of these estimates have been obtained by comparing the ratings of clinicians who conducted the interview with ratings of those who observed the same interview. Independent interviews might well lower interjudge agreements. Moreover, the agreement figures are based on the presence or absence of symptoms or diagnosis and not on judgments of the severity of symptoms or the overall disorder.

Validity

Given the recency of efforts to assess childhood depression, it is not surprising to find a dearth of validation research. Few self-report and interview measures have been subjected to rigorous validation studies. Yet, considerable strides are being made. Following the lead of Kazdin and Petti (1982), four types of validity will be presented: content validity, criterion validity, convergent validity, and discriminant validity. The topic of masked depression is omitted from the discussion.

Content Validity

Content validity has to do with insuring that the items used in a given measure represent the universe of the relevant domain. The content validity of childhood depression measures has been studied in four different ways.

Diagnostic criteria. Several scales designated to assess the severity of depression in young people (ISC, K-SADS, BID) used specific diagnostic criteria for affective disorders as a basis for item selection. A one-to-one correspondence between diagnostic criteria and items for measures of severity minimizes questions that can be raised about item content. The problem with this approach is that all questions about item content revert to the adequacy of the original diagnostic criteria. As noted earlier, universal agreement about diagnostic criteria is yet to be achieved.

The evaluation of clinically depressed children. Careful clinical evaluation of depressed children, particularly the characteristics commonly associated with or peculiar to this disorder, has formed the basis for the development of the CDI and CDS scales. When this approach is used, input from the depressed children themselves may be of particular value. For instance, Kovacs and Beck (1977) in the development of the CDI and Tisher and Lang (1978) in the development of the CDS asked children to comment upon items and revised the items to make them more appropriate to their experiences and developmental level. The reluctance or inability of many depressed children to communicate freely limits the extent to which client feedback can be relied upon to revise items.

The use of expert judges. Using expert clinicians is another means to achieve content validity. For example, in development of the PIC, Wirt and colleagues (1977) insisted that four of seven clinicians agree that an item measured depression before including it in the Depression Scale. Tisher and Lang (1978) had child psychiatrists rate several items in terms of whether they reflected depression, anxiety, or neither. Of course, an item does not necessarily measure what a small group of experts believe it does. Many of us have been in error, but not often in doubt. By and large, rationally derived personality scales based on expert judgment are not as valid as empirically derived scales.

Factor analysis. Factor analysis, a systematic method for identifying a small number of underlying factors that can account for the complete set of relationships among the test variables, has also been used to assess whether a given scale measures certain types of content. For instance, factor analysis of DSA (Depression Scale for Adolescents; Mezzich & Mezzich, 1979) items yielded six factors (lack of self-confidence, social abandonment, loss of interest, sadness, somatic symptoms, and acting out) which are consistent with some of the symptom areas outlined by RDC. Despite the objective status accorded to factor-analytic techniques, their subjective nature is reflected in the nature of the items included, the type of statistical rotation used, and the name given the factor.

Criterion Validity

Criterion validity is established by demonstrating that performance on a given measure is correlated with a more established or accepted criterion. A common practice is to analyze statistically the difference in total scores for two separate clinical groups on a given measure of depression. It is reasonable to expect that children suffering from depression would score higher on a depression inventory than children suffering from other disorders. Using this approach, several investigators (e.g., Kashani & Simonds, 1979; Mezzich & Mezzich, 1979; Tisher & Lang, 1978) have shown that depressed children do indeed score higher on measures of depression than do children with other diagnoses.

The use of known criterion groups can yield valuable validity data but this approach, too, has its limitations. Again we encounter definitional problems. We must have agreement on basic characteristics before we can say that a child belongs in this criterion group or not. Also, measures of severity should not only distinguish depressed from nondepressed groups but they should also accurately quantify the degree of severity. The use of criterion groups that can be expected to vary in the degree of depression (e.g., those who just lost a parent or contracted a severe disease) could prove helpful in providing validity data about the severity of depression. Furthermore, studies using known criterion groups have relied primarily on mean differences and failed to provide information about the number of false positives and false negatives.

Convergent and Discriminant Validity

All in all, content and criterion validity have been established to a moderate degree for the measures discussed in this review. Little has been done along the lines of convergent and discriminant validity, however. Convergent validity refers to evidence that a given measure correlates with other measures with which it is expected to correlate, whereas discriminant validity refers to evidence that the measure does not correlate significantly with other measures with which it would not be expected to correlate. Although global clinical ratings of depression correlate positively with performance on a given self-report or interview measure (Kovacs & Beck, 1977), the reasons for the interrelationship are not clear. It is conceivable that both measures reflect the severity of psychological impairment across a wide range of disorders rather than depression per se. Further, common response biases (e.g., social desirability and similarities, for example), in method of self-report inventories preclude univocal interpretation of the data (Kazdin, 1981). In general, very little has been done to demonstrate convergent or discriminant validity of the measures covered in this review. Available evidence is consistent, however, in indicating that there is little relationship between parent and child scores for the same measures (CDI, BID) although mothers' and fathers' ratings of their children are moderately related (Kazdin, French, & Unis, 1983; Leon et al., 1980; Weissman, Orvaschel, & Padian, 1980).

GUIDELINES FOR ASSESSMENT

The following guidelines should prove helpful to practitioners in their assessment of depression in young people.

1. Bear in mind the distinction between depressive symptoms and depressive disorder. Just as a fever accompanies many medical conditions, depressive symptoms accompany many kinds of distress. Distinguishing demoralization and bereavement from depressive disorder is essential to the diagnostic process.

2. Depression in children and adolescents involves both internalizing and overt symptoms. This means that assessment of childhood and adolescent

depression requires a comprehensive diagnostic evaluation involving multiple sources (e.g., child, parent, teacher, possibly peers) and methods (self-report, report by others, direct observation, interviews).

3. Select a method and scale appropriate to the young person's developmental level and gender. For example, diagnostic evaluations of adolescents should tap symptomatology that is unique or appropriate to their developmental level and gender (e.g., body image and/or eating problems among adolescent girls, more suicidal behaviors among adolescents than adults or children).

4. Remember that depressed young people commonly have at least one other disorder (e.g., conduct disorder, anxiety, eating problems, attention-deficit disorder, possibly a learning disability). This means that the assessment must focus on all aspects of functioning. Thus, a general measure of psychopathology and competence should be a part of the diagnostic workup (e.g., Achenbach 1991a; Child Behavior Checklist). Treatment plans must also take into account *comorbidity* as it can complicate interventions.

5. Psychoeducational evaluation is as necessary as psychological evaluation for at least two reasons. First, federal laws pertaining to handicapped students require demonstration that the emotional impairment has an adverse impact on school performance. Second, many of the depressive symptoms can impair school functioning (e.g., inability to concentrate, fatigue).

6. Bear in mind the correlates of depressive disorder in young people. For instance, depressive youngsters are more likely to have one or more depressed parents. This fact may have relevance for diagnosis as well as treatment.

7. The possible presence of subtypes of depression must also be considered. For example, in the case of bipolar disorder, the choice of assessment methods and type of treatment (e.g., use of lithium) will be altered.

8. Remember that parent ratings tend to yield higher estimates of depression than do their children's self-reports.

9. Determining whether a child is depressed or not does not necessarily determine whether the youngster is also suicidal. Many depressed youngsters never attempt suicide and many suicidal youngsters are not depressed.

10. There is a genuine danger the child with dysthymia might be overlooked by school personnel. Given the chronic, yet mild nature of the symptomatology, teachers may view such behavior as a natural, temperamental characteristic.

11. Do not overlook the benefits that can accrue to the "what," the "how," and the "success" of treatment by asking additional questions during the interview.

SUMMARY

Various definitions of depression differ in their level of diagnostic analysis in that they focus on symptom, syndrome, disorder, or disease. The psychological assessment methods receiving the most attention fall into four categories: self-report techniques, ratings by adults, peer ratings, and clinical interviews. Self-report measures can provide valuable insights regarding inner feelings, but there are no well-established cutoff points to delineate clinical levels of depression among most scales for children. Parents', teachers', and clinicians' ratings, which offer an adult's view of the problem, can be particularly helpful regarding the more observable aspects of depression. Parents usually rate depressive conditions as more severe than do the children themselves. Peer ratings are a unique adjunct to adults' reports because they are based on experiences that are seldom fully visible to adult observers. The psychiatric interview is perhaps the most commonly used method to assess depression in young people. No interview measures have been specifically designed for adolescents, although those for children can also be used with teenagers. Interviewers must be sensitive to the general and specific demands that this approach places on the child's social and cognitive abilities.

There is only limited consistency across raters (children, parents, teachers) and across settings (home and school), but there is moderate to high consistency across different measures of depression completed by the same rater. The wisest course of action for practitioners is to take account of variations in functioning across domains and informants. Remember that disagreement between informants can be as instructive as agreement. The multistage method appears to offer a worthwhile method of identification in school settings. Cutoff scores must be used cautiously as they would vary with the age of the child/adolescent, the severity of the affective problem, and the type of the informant (child self-report versus parent).

REFERENCES

Achenbach, T. (1991a). *Manual for the Child Behavior Checklist/4-18 and 1991 Profile.* Burlington, VT: Child Psychiatry, University of Vermont, Department of Psychiatry.

Achenbach, T. (1991b). *Manual for the Youth Self-Report and 1991 Profile.* Burlington, VT: University of Vermont Department of Psychiatry.

Achenbach, T. (1991c). *Manual for the Teacher's Report Form and 1991 Profile.* Burlington, VT: University of Vermont Department of Psychiatry.

Achenbach, T., & McConaughy, S. (1992). Taxonomy of internalizing disorders of childhood and adolescence. In W. Reynolds (Ed.) *Internalizing disorders in children* (pp. 19–60). New York: Wiley.

Achenbach, T., McConaughy, S., & Howell, C. (1987). Child/adolescent behavioral and emotional problems: Implications of cross-informant correlation for situational specificity. *Psychological Bulletin, 101,* 213–232.

Altmann, E., & Gotl, B. (1988). The social behavior of depressed children: An observational study. *Journal of Abnormal Psychology, 16,* 29–44.

Ambrosini, P., Metz, C., Prabucki, K., & Lee, J. (1989). Videotape reliability of the third revised edition of the K-SADS. *Journal of the American Academy of Child and Adolescent Psychiatry, 28,* 723–728.

Apter, A., Orvaschel, H., Laseg, H., Moses, T., & Tyano, S. (1989). Psychometric properties of the K-SADS in an Israeli adolescent inpatient population. *Journal of the American Academy of Child and Adolescent Psychiatry, 28,* 61–65.

Barkley, R. A. (1990). *Attention deficit hyperactivity disorder: A handbook for diagnosis and treatment.* New York: Guilford.

Barnett, K., Darcie, G., Holland, C., & Kobasigawa, A. (1982). Children's cognitions about effective helping. *Developmental Psychology, 18*(2), 267–277.

Beck, A. (1967). *Depression: Clinical, experimental and theoretical aspects.* New York: Harper & Row.

Blechman, E., McEnroe, M., Carella, E., & Audette, D. (1986). Childhood competence and depression. *Journal of Abnormal Psychology, 95,* 223–227.

Brown, L., & Hammill, D. (1993). *Behavior Rating Profile* (2nd ed.). Austin, TX: Pro-ed.

Cantwell, D. (1983). Assessment of childhood depression: An overview. In D. Cantwell & G. Carlson (Eds.), *Affective disorders in childhood and adolescence* (pp. 146–156). New York: SP Medical and Scientific Books, Spectrum.

Cantwell, D., & Baker, L., (1991). Manifestations of depressive affect in adolescence. *Journal of Youth and Adolescence, 20,* 121–133.

Carlson, G., & Cantwell, D. (1982). Suicidal behavior and depression in children and adolescents. *Journal of the American Academy of Child Psychiatry, 21,* 361–368.

Chambers, W., Puig-Antich, J., Hirsch, M., Paez, P., Ambrosini, P., Jabrizi, M., & Davies, M. (1985). The assessment of affective disorders in children and adolescents by semistructured interview: Test-retest reliability of the K-SADS-P. *Archives of General Psychiatry, 42,* 696–702.

Cohen-Sandler, R., Berman, A., & King, R. (1982). Life stress and symptomatology: Determinants of suicidal behavior in children. *Journal of the American Academy of Child Psychiatry, 21,* 178–186.

Cole, D., & Carpentieri, S. (1990). Social status and comorbidity of child depression and conduct disorders. *Journal of Consulting and Clinical Psychology, 58,* 748–757.

Costello, A., Edelbrock, C., Duncan, M., Kalas, R., & Klaric, S. (1984). *Development and testing of the NIMH Diagnostic Interview Schedule for Children in a clinic population.* Final Report. Rockville, MD: Center for Epidemiologic Studies, NIMH.

Cytryn, L., & McKnew, D. (1972). Proposed classification of childhood depression. *American Journal of Psychiatry, 129,* 149–155.

Damon, W., & Hart, D. (1982). The development of self-understanding from infancy through adolescence. *Child Development, 53,* 841–864.

Dohrenwend, B., & Shrout, P. (1981). Toward the development of a two-stage procedure for case identification and classification in psychiatric epidemiology. In R. Simmons (Ed.), *Research in community mental health* (Vol. 2, pp. 295–323). Greenwich, CT: JAI.

Edelbrock, C. (1979). Empirical classification of children's behavior disorders: Progress based on parent and teacher ratings. *School Psychology Digest, 8,* 355–369.

Endicott, J., & Spitzer, R. (1978). A diagnostic interview: A schedule for affective disorders and schizophrenia. *Archives of General Psychiatry, 35,* 837–844.

Evert, T., & Reynolds, W. (1986). *Efficacy of a multistage screening model for depression in adolescents.* Unpublished manuscript.

Finch, A., Saylor, C., & Edwards, G. (1985). Children's Depression Inventory: Sex and grade norms for normal children. *Journal of Consulting and Clinical Psychology, 53,* 424–425.

Garvin, V., Leber, D., & Kalter, N. (1991). Children of divorce: Predictors of change following preventive intervention. *American Journal of Orthopsychiatry, 61,* 438–447.

Ghareeb, G., & Beshai, J. (1989). Arabic version of the Children's Depression Inventory: Reliability and validity. *Journal of Clinical Child Psychology, 18,* 323–326.

Goyette, C., Conners, C., & Ulrich, R. (1978). Normative data on revised Conners Parent and Teacher Rating Scales. *Journal of Abnormal and Child Psychology, 6,* 221–236.

Graham, P. (1974). Depression in pre-pubertal children. *Developmental Medicine and Child Neurology, 16,* 340–349.

Green, B. (1980). Depression in early adolescence: An exploratory investigation of its frequency, intensity and correlates (Doctoral dissertation, Pennsylvania State University). *Dissertation Abstracts International, 41,* 3890B.

Harris, P., Olthof, T., & Terwogt, M. (1981). Children's knowledge of emotion. *Journal of Child Psychology and Psychiatry, 22,* 247–262.

Hodges, K. (1983). *The Child Assessment Schedule* (CAS). Unpublished manuscript.

Hodges, K., & Cools, J. (1990). Structured diagnostic interviews. In A. La Greca (Ed.) *Through the eyes of the child: Obtaining self-reports from children* (pp. 109–149). Boston: Allyn & Bacon.

Hughes, J., & Baker, D. (1990). *The clinical child interview.* New York: Guilford.

Kaminer, Y., Feinstein, C., Seifer, R., Stevens, L., & Barrett, R. (1990). An observationally based rating scale for affective symptomatology in child psychiatry. *Journal of Nervous and Mental Disease, 178,* 750–754.

Kashani, J., Husain, A., Shekim, W., Hodges, K., Cytryn, L., & McKnew, D. (1981). Current perspectives on childhood depression: An overview. *American Journal of Psychiatry, 138,* 143–153.

Kashani, J., & Simonds, J. (1979). The incidence of depression in children. *American Journal of Psychiatry, 136,* 1203–1204.

Kazdin, A. (1981). Assessment techniques for childhood depression. *Journal of the American Academy of Child Psychiatry, 20,* 358, 375.

Kazdin, A. (1983). Psychiatric diagnosis, dimensions of dysfunction and child behavior theory. *Behavior Therapy, 14,* 73–99.

Kazdin, A. (1987). Children's Depression Scale: Validation with child psychiatric inpatients. *Journal of Child Psychology and Psychiatry, 28,* 29–41.

Kazdin, A. (1990). Assessment of childhood depression. In A. LaGreca (Ed.), *Through the eyes of the child: Obtaining self-reports from children and adolescents* (pp. 189–233). Boston: Allyn & Bacon.

Kazdin, A., Colbus, D., & Rodgers, A. (1986). Assessment of depression and diagnosis of depressive disorder among psychiatrically disturbed children. *Journal of Abnormal Child Psychology, 14,* 499–515.

Kazdin, A., Esveldt-Dawson, K., Sherick, R., & Colbus, D. (1985). Assessment of overt behavior and childhood depression among psychiatrically disturbed children. *Journal of Consulting and Clinical Psychology, 53,* 201–210.

Kazdin, A., French, N., & Unis, A. (1983). Child, mother, and father evaluations of depression in psychiatric inpatient children. *Journal of Abnormal Child Psychology, 11,* 167–180.

Kazdin, A., French, N., Unis, A., & Esveldt-Dawson, K. (1983). Assessment of childhood depression: Correspondence of child and parent ratings. *Journal of the American Academy of Child Psychiatry, 22,* 157–164.

Kazdin, A., & Petti, T. (1982). Self-report and interview measures of childhood and adolescent depression. *Journal of Child Psychology and Psychiatry, 23,* 437–457.

Koizumi, S. (1991). The standardization of Children's Depression Inventory. *Syoni Hoken Ken Kyu* (The Journal of Child Health) *50,* 717–721.

Kovacs, M. (1981). Rating scales to assess depression in school-aged children. *Acta Paedopsychiatrica, 46,* 305–315.

Kovacs. M. (1983). *The Children's Depression Inventory: A self-rated depression scale for school-aged youngsters.* Unpublished manuscript.

Kovacs, M. (1985). The Children's Depression Inventory. *Psychopharmacology Bulletin, 21,* 995–998.

Kovacs, M. (1986). A developmental perspective on methods and measures in the assessment of depressive disorders: The clinical interview. In M. Rutter, C. Izard, & P. Read (Eds.), *Depression in young people* (pp. 435–465). New York: Guilford.

Kovacs, M. (1992). *The Children's Depression Inventory.* North Tonawanda, NY: Mental Health Systems.

Kovacs, M., & Beck, A. (1977). An empirical-clinical approach toward a definition of childhood depression. In J. Schulterbrant & A. Raskin (Eds.), *Depression*

in childhood: Diagnosis, treatment, and conceptual models (pp. 1–25). New York: Raven Press.
Lefkowitz, M., & Tesiny, E. (1980). Assessment of childhood depression. *Journal of Consulting and Clinical Psychology, 48,* 43–50.
Lefkowitz, M., & Tesiny, E. (1985). Depression in children: Prevalence and correlates. *Journal of Consulting and Clinical Psychology, 53,* 647–656.
Leon, G., Kendall, P., & Garber, J. (1980). Depression in children: Parents, teachers, and child perspectives. *Journal of Abnormal Child Psychology, 8,* 221–235.
Lewinsohn, P., & Teri, L. (1982). Selection of depressed and nondepressed subjects on the basis of self-report data. *Journal of Consulting and Clinical Psychology, 50,* 590–591.
McCarney, S., & Leigh, J. (1990). *Behavior Evaluation Scale.* Austin, TX: Pro-Ed.
Meyer, N., Dyck, D., & Petrinack, R. (1989). Cognitive appraisal and attributional correlates of depressive symptoms in children. *Journal of Abnormal Child Psychology, 17,* 325–336
Mezzich, A., & Mezzich, J. (1979). Symptomatology of depression in adolescence. *Journal of Personality Assessment, 43,* 267–275.
Mooney, K. (1984). Child Behavior Checklist. In D. Keyser & R. Sweetland (Eds.), *Test critiques* (Vol. 1, pp. 168–184). Kansas City, MO: Test Corporation of America.
Moretti, M., Fine, S., Haley, G., & Marriage, K. (1985). Childhood and adolescent depression: Child-report versus parent-report information. *Journal of the American Academy of Child Psychiatry, 24,* 298–302.
Nelson, W., & Politano, P. (1990). Children's Depression Inventory: Stability over repeated administrations in psychiatric inpatient children. *Journal of Clinical Child Psychology, 19,* 254–256.
Nelson, W., Politano, P., Finch, A., Wendel, N., & Mayhall, C. (1987). Children's Depression Inventory: Normative data and utility with emotionally disturbed children. *Journal of the American Academy of Child and Adolescent Psychiatry, 26,* 43–48.
Nurcombe, B., Seifer, R., Scioli, A., Tramontana, M., Grapentine, W., & Beauchesne, H. (1989). Is major depressive disorder in adolescence a distinct diagnostic entity? *Journal of the American Academy of Child and Adolescent Psychiatry, 28,* 333–342.
Orvaschel, H. (1985). Psychiatric interview suitable for use in research with children and adolescents. *Psychopharmacology Bulletin, 21,* 737–745.
Petti, T. (1978). Depression in hospitalized child psychiatry patients: Approaches to measuring depression. *Journal of the American Academy of Child Psychiatry, 17,* 49–59.
Petti, T. (1985). Scales of potential use in the psychopharmacologic treatment of depressed children and adolescents. *Psychopharmacology Bulletin, 21,* 957–958.
Petti, T. (no date). *Teacher Affect Rating Scale* (TARS). Unpublished manuscript.
Poznanski, E. (1982). The clinical phenomenology of childhood depression. *American Journal of Orthopsychiatry, 52,* 308–313.

Poznanski, E., Grossman, J., Buchsbaum, Y., Banegas, M., Freeman, L., & Gibbons, R. (1984). Preliminary studies of the reliability and validity of the Children's Depression Rating Scale. *Journal of the Academy of Child Psychiatry, 23,* 191–197.

Puig-Antich, J., & Chambers, W. (1978). *Schedule for affective disorders and schizophrenia for school-age children. Kiddie SADS (K-SADS).* Unpublished manuscript.

Puig-Antich, J., Tabrizi, M., Davies, M., Goetz, R., Chambers, W., Halpern, F., & Sachar, E. (1981). Prepubertal endogenous major depressives hyposecrete growth hormone in response to insulin induced hypoglycemia. *Journal of Biological Psychiatry, 16,* 801–818.

Radloff, L. (1991). The use of the Center for Epidemiologic Studies Depression Scale in adolescents and young adults. *Journal of Youth and Adolescence, 20,* 149–166.

Reich, W., Herjanic, B., & Welner, Z. (1982). Development of a structured psychiatric interview for children: Agreement on diagnosis comparing child and parent interviews. *Journal of Abnormal Child Psychology, 10,* 325–336.

Rey, J., & Morris-Yates, A. (1991). Adolescent depression and the Child Behavior Checklist. *Journal of the American Academy of Child and Adolescent Psychiatry, 30,* 423–427.

Reynolds, C., & Tuma, J. (1985). Review of Personality Inventory for Children. In J. Mitchell (Ed.), *The ninth mental measurements yearbook* (pp. 1154–1159). Lincoln, NE: The Buros Institute of Mental Measurement.

Reynolds, W. (1986). A model for screening and identification of depressed children and adolescents in school settings. *Professional School Psychology, 1,* 117–129.

Reynolds, W. (1987). *RADS Manual.* Odessa, FL: Psychological Assessment Resources.

Reynolds, W. (1989a). *Reynolds Child Depression Scale.* Odessa, FL: Psychological Assessment Resources.

Reynolds, W. (1989b). *Reynolds Child Depression Scale: Professional manual.* Odessa, FL: Psychological Assessment Resources.

Reynolds, W. (1992). Depression in children and adolescents. In W. Reynolds (Ed.), *Internalizing disorders in children and adolescents* (pp. 149–253). New York: Wiley.

Rothermel, R., & Lovell, M. (1985). Personality Inventory for Children. In D. Keyser & R. Sweetland (Eds.), *Test critiques* (Vol. 2, pp. 570–578). Kansas City, MO: Test Corporation of America.

Rutter, M., & Graham, P. (1968). The reliability and validity of the psychiatric assessment of the child: I. Interview with the child. *British Journal of Psychiatry, 114,* 563–579.

Saylor, C., Finch, A., Baskin, C., Saylor, C., Darnell, G., & Furey, W. (1984). Children's Depression Inventory: Investigation of procedures and correlates. *Journal of the American Academy of Child Psychiatry, 23,* 626–628.

Schwartz, R., & Trabasso, T. (1984). Children's understanding of emotions. In C. E. Izard, J. Kagan, & R. Zajonc (Eds.), *Emotions, cognition, and behavior* (pp. 409–437). New York: Cambridge University Press.

Shaffer, D., Schwab-Stone, M., Fisher, P., Cohen, P., Piacentini, J., Davies, M., Conners, C., & Regier, D. (1993). The Diagnostic Interview Schedule—Revised (DISC-R): I Preparation, field testing, interrater reliability, and acceptability. *Journal of the American Academy of Child and Adolescent Psychiatry, 32,* 643–650.

Simmons, J. (1981). *Psychiatric examination of children* (3rd ed.). Philadelphia: Lea & Febiger.

Smucker, M., Craighead, W., Craighead, L., & Green, B. (1986). Normative and reliability data for the Children's Depression Inventory. *Journal of Abnormal Child Psychology, 14,* 25–39.

Stark, K., Reynolds, W., & Kaslow, N. (1991). *Assessment of depressive symptomatology in school children: An exploration of variables that mediate rater variance.* Unpublished manuscript.

Stark, K., Reynolds, W., Kaslow, N., & Kelley, A. (1991). *Mothers', fathers', and children's ratings of childhood depression: A study of variables that mediate differences in ratings.* Unpublished manuscript.

Strober, M., & Werry, J. (1986). Assessment of depression in children and adolescents. In N. Sartorius & T. Ban (Eds.), *Assessment of depression* (pp. 324–342). New York: Springer Verlag.

Swets, J. (1988). Measuring the accuracy of diagnostic systems. *Science, 240,* 1285–1293.

Tesiny, E., & Lefkowitz, M. (1982, August). *Assessing childhood depression: Cumulative data.* Presented at the Annual Meeting of the American Psychological Association, Washington, DC.

Tharinger, D., & Stark, K. (1990). A qualitative versus quantitative approach to evaluating the Draw-a-Person and Kinetic family drawing: A study of mood- and anxiety-disorder children. *Psychological Assessment: A Journal of Consulting and Clinical Psychology, 2,* 365–375.

Tisher, M., & Lang, M. (1978). *Children's Depression Scale* (Research Edition). Palo Alto, CA: Consulting Psychologists Press.

Tisher, M., & Lang, M. (1983). The Children's Depression Scale: Review and further development. In D. Cantwell & G. Carlson (Eds.), *Affective disorders in childhood and adolescence* (pp. 181–203). New York: SP Medical & Scientific Books.

Vosk, B., Forehand, R., Parker, J., & Rickard, K. (1982). A multimethod comparison of popular and unpopular children. *Developmental Psychology, 18,* 571–575.

Wahler, R., & Fox, J. (1980). Solitary toy play and time out: A family treatment package for children with aggressive and oppositional behavior. *Journal of Applied Behavior Analysis, 13,* 23–39.

Ward, L., Friedlander, M., & Silverman, W. (1987). Children's depressive symptoms, negative self-statements and causal attributions for success and failure. *Cognitive Therapy and Research, 11,* 215–227.

Weiner, B., & Graham, S. (1984). An attributional approach to emotional development. In C. Izard, J. Kagan, & R. Zajonc (Eds.), *Emotions, cognition and behavior* (pp. 167–191). New York: Cambridge University Press.

Weissman, M., Orvaschel, H., & Padian, N. (1980). Children's symptom and social functioning self-report scales: Comparison of mothers' and childrens' reports. *Journal of Nervous and Mental Disorders, 168,* 736–740.

Wessman, A., & Gorman, B. (1977). The emergence of human awareness and concepts of time. In B. Gorman & A. Wessman (Eds.), *The personal experience of time* (pp. 3–55). New York: Plenum.

Wirt, R., Lachar, D., Klinedinst, J., & Seat, P. (1977). *Multidimensional description of personality.* Los Angeles: Western Psychological Services.

Worchel, F., Hughes, J., Hall, B., Stanton, S., Stanton, H., & Little, V. (1990). Evaluation of subclinical depression in children using self-, peer-, and teacher-report measures. *Journal of Abnormal Child Psychology, 18,* 271–282.

Wright, F. (1988). *Behavior Disorders Identification Scale.* Columbia, MO: Hawthorne.

4 TREATMENT OF CHILDHOOD DEPRESSION

Jack

Jack, a 9-year-old, was depressed. His father worked long hours at a very successful practice. Jack believed that his father did not love him. The initial intervention was to help Jack to make an operational definition of loving behaviors and then to see how many of these behaviors his father performed and how frequently. After a few sessions of defining the list and empirically verifying his father's responses, we unfortunately came to the conclusion that Jack's father did not fare too well on this empirical test. Although he performed most of the behaviors on the caring list, he did so at a low frequency.

Did the father love Jack? That was the next question that Jack struggled with. How many loving behaviors does one have to perform toward another to demonstrate love? How frequently does one have to perform loving behaviors toward a person to receive that person's love? I tried to convince Jack that any decision we made about a cutoff score of frequency of loving behaviors and types of loving behaviors was arbitrary. My cutoff score might be different from his. Someone else's might be different altogether. Love is what one person defines it to be. Any definition that we made of love would be just that, our definition, and might not represent a universal reality. We could not define whether or not Jack's father loved him, and we also did not know how Jack's father *felt*. Although we could infer his affective state toward Jack from his behavior, the result would be just that, an inference. I used lots of examples to show how Jack very often felt quite differently from the way he acted. Jack was still left with one real adversity. He experienced fewer loving behaviors from his father than he wanted. It was evident that Jack's father demonstrated caring behaviors much less frequently than the fathers of Jack's peers. So Jack's lack of received affection was real. The important issue I pointed out to Jack was not whether his father loved him, but how miserable he was going to make himself over the way his father reacted. I challenged the ultimate irrational belief that one has to experience love and loving behaviors from one's parents in order to be worthwhile and even to be happy. Jack's father might never change; he might always prefer work to family involvement, but Jack learned to be less upset about this fact and to enjoy other things in his life.

Note. From "Principles of Assessment and Methods of Treatment with Children" by R. DiGiuseppe and M. Bernard, 1983, in A. Ellis and M. Bernard, Eds., *Rational-Emotive Approaches to the Problems of Childhood* (pp. 77). New York: Plenum Press.

Very little is known about the treatment of childhood depression. The dearth of definitive research is due in part to the recency of interest in this condition and in part to the fact that we are not sure what exactly it is that we are to treat. In the absence of survey data, we are not even sure what approaches are being presently used to treat depressed children. Furthermore, it is difficult to accumulate knowledge about the treatment of depressed children, many of whom are quiet and uncommunicative.

The chapter will examine the rationale, assumptions, potential uses, research base, potential limitations, and developmental goodness of fit for selected approaches to the treatment of childhood depression. It will focus on unipolar and nonpsychotic depressive conditions in children. As you will see, each of the models specifies different core symptoms and indicates treatment strategies deemed appropriate for modifying that targeted behavior. Because many authorities now view childhood depression as being similar in nature to adult depression (Clarizio, 1984), it is not surprising to see that many of the emerging therapeutic approaches to the treatment of depression in children have arisen from approaches to the treatment of depression in adults. The application of adult treatment models to children is predicated on at least two fundamental assumptions: (1) that depression is basically the same condition in adults and children and (2) that adult-oriented techniques for overcoming depression can be successfully adapted for use with childhood depressives.

Although it is still too early to have accumulated any convincing body of research evidence as to their effectiveness, many treatment models are beginning to take into account the child's cognitive developmental status in selecting intervention procedures. What follows is a review of psychoanalytic, behavioral, cognitive, familial, drug, and multimodal approaches to the treatment of childhood depression. Various models are discussed separately, but in reality, some of them overlap (e.g., behavioral and cognitive).

PSYCHOANALYTIC APPROACHES

For many years, psychoanalytic formulations dominated the psychological study of depression (Abraham, 1968; Bibring, 1965; Jacobson, 1971). Traditional psychoanalytic theorists have questioned whether depression could arise without a fairly differentiated ego and a functioning superego. Despite the debate among psychoanalytic workers as to the existence of depression in children, case studies focusing on the treatment of childhood depression are available (Cohen, 1980). Psychoanalytic theory stresses the role played by real or imagined loss in the development of depression. The suffering individual is said to have identified with the lost love object and to be ambivalent toward it. Feelings of hostility are then turned against the self rather than being directed at the appropriate object (Abraham, 1960), resulting in a drop in self-esteem, or depression. The aggressive instinct is converted into depressive affect. According to this theory, dependent persons, that is, those dependent on the love objects for maintaining self-esteem, are predisposed to depression. Even trivial disappointments are said to trigger immediate declines in self-esteem. The superego emanating from identification with the parent punishes the person. This punishment or self-bereavement is endured because atonement through punishment is a way for the narcissistic child to win love. That is, the child punishes him- or herself as a way of winning love from others (Kovacs & Beck, 1977). The object loss model, depicted by Spitz and Wolf (1946) and later by Bowlby (1960), involved separation and disruption of the attachment bond.

Bibring's (1965) ego-psychological reformulation of the original psychoanalytic model, which focuses on the individual's state of helplessness, clearly acknowledges the existence of depression in children. When the ego cannot achieve a desired goal and is simultaneously aware of its helplessness, the ego suffers a narcissistic blow and a collapse in self-esteem. According to Bibring's model, depression occurs when one cannot live up to one's ego-ideals—the desire to be worthy and to be loved, and to avoid inferiority and unworthiness; the striving to be secure, superior, strong; the aspiration to be kind, loving, and supportive, and not aggressive, hateful, or destructive. In this framework, hostility is seen as an inconsistent, secondary phenomenon brought about by object losses or objects that prevent the attainment of valued aspirations. In brief, Bibring views depression as an affect that is independent of the aggressive drive but related to the ego's awareness of helplessness. In many respects, Bibring's model is very similar to Horney's (1950) notion of anxiety as a feeling of helplessness, hopelessness, and abandonment.

In general the psychoanalytic approach to the treatment of childhood depression is very similar to that of other childhood disorders. The first phase of treatment involves the establishment of a therapeutic relationship and support of the child. The depressed child is ambivalently open to a relationship that may give a feeling of self-worth (Gilpin & Anthony, 1976). The middle phase of treatment focuses on the development of insight, and the final phase deals with termination issues and the healthy acceptance of loss (Gilpin & Anthony, 1976). Individual treatment is based on the child's age, intelligence, level of ego development, ego defenses, as well as on parent attitudes and available facilities (Toolan, 1978). Verbal expression in child analysis is generally only one of several methods used to communicate. Other methods include the use of gestures, games, and play (Cohen, 1980). In these ways, feelings can first be externalized. This helps the child to recognize and accept her or his feelings. Images that cannot be clearly expressed verbally are more easily demonstrated through the use of play. Play also is not as easily defended against as verbal expression (Wadeson, 1980). For depressed children in particular, this type of therapy encourages active involvement. Although case studies are available, no empirical studies have been conducted on the psychoanalytic treatment of depressed children.

BEHAVIORAL AND SOCIAL SKILLS APPROACHES

Whereas psychoanalytic theorists were among the first to study depression from a psychological viewpoint, behaviorists have only recently begun to study this phenomenon. There were various reasons for the behaviorists' tardiness. The early behaviorists restricted their investigation to the objective study of laboratory phenomena. Because depression referred, in part, to a subjective state, treatment of depression had to await a broadening in theoretical underpinning (Bandura, 1977), a more objective diagnostic description (e.g. Grinker, Miller, Sabshin, Nunn, & Nunnally, 1961), and utilization of behavior and symptom checklists before it could move into the mainstream of behavior modification.

Skinner (1953) presented the first attempt to link depression to the principles of positive reinforcement. His conceptualization of depression as an extinction phenomenon leading to a reduction in positively reinforced behavior has been central to all behavioral positions. Ferster (1966) furnished additional detail suggesting that such diverse variables as sudden environmental changes, punishment, and shifts in reinforcement contingencies can cause a reduced rate of behavior (depression). Depressive behavior was produced by a lack of skills, opportunity, or ability to recognize or use available reinforcers. Ferster makes a significant distinction between functional and topographical behavioral analysis, a point often overlooked by critics of behavioral approaches. Two adolescents may take too many pills while drinking (similar topographic behaviors). One wants to die whereas the other one carelessly forgets that the combination of pills and alcohol can be fatal. Thus, the function of the same behavior is different. By analyzing the functions of behavior, Ferster observed that the depressed individual (1) shows significant passivity in the face of aversive events and (2) engages in fewer positively reinforced events. Passivity is negatively reinforcing in that it succeeds in avoiding punishing interactions with others. Passivity also prevents a constructive dealing with unpleasant social events. Moreover, if a person is to adapt to life's changes and losses, she or he must be able to resist extinction of certain behaviors, and to maintain the capacity to generate new, reinforceable behavior. These skills are learned in childhood by exploration, the opposite of passivity. Unfortunately, the depressed individual is unable to achieve this satisfactorily. One reason is that many important behaviors are on continuous, predictable reinforcement schedules that show greater susceptibility to extinction.

Ferster (1966) also maintains that failures to adjust may be related to distorted perceptions of reinforcement contingencies. Specifically, the person may have (a) a limited view of the world such that he or she sulks and complains but has little insight into what behavior on his or her part would produce the required reinforcement; (b) a fear of aversive consequences, even though he or she knows what behaviors are required for reinforcement; and (c) a lack of skills. These three features lock the individual into a set of behaviors that are not positively reinforceable. Moreover, compensatory behaviors—clinging, demanding, self-blaming—often carry immediate reinforcement value. Because these compensatory behaviors are often on a variable reinforcement schedule, they are less resistant to extinction. Inadequate reinforcement not only interferes with subtle discrimination learning in interpersonal relations and complex skill building, but it produces anger which further interferes with such learning and produces hostile dependency conflicts. This anger in turn serves to reduce positive reinforcement, particularly when it is expressed through irritating, demanding ways or through explosive behavior over minor incidents.

In sum, Ferster's theory offered major insights into our understanding of depression. His functional approach, application of reinforcement schedules to depressive behaviors, analysis of the role of conditioned anger suppression, and the focus on childhood vulnerability are especially noteworthy.

Costello (1972) proposed that it is the loss of reinforcer effectiveness, rather than the loss of reinforcers per se, that gives rise to depression. As is true in many theories of depression, it is extremely difficult to establish whether lack or loss of reinforcement is primary in the etiology of depression or whether the symptoms and low response rates characteristic of depression secondarily result in lower levels of reinforcement.

The Lewinsohn group (Lewinsohn & Shaw, 1969) further hypothesized that (a) a causal link exists between the feeling of dysphoria and a low rate of response-contingent positive reinforcement; (b) the initial expression of sympathy, interest, and concern serve to maintain depressive behaviors, but the majority of people eventually find the depressive person's behavior annoying, a condition which further reduces positive reinforcement and accentuates the depression; and (c) deficiencies in social skills are important antecedents to a low rate of positive reinforcement. The therapeutic implications were straightforward: Improvement should follow from an increase in positive reinforcement. For if the loss of response-contingent reinforcement is a significant antecedent in childhood depression, then we may be able to change mood by having people engage in events they view as pleasant. To this end, the use of reinforcement surveys or pleasant event schedules designed for use with children (e.g., Children's Reinforcement Survey Schedule, Cautela, 1977; Children's Event Schedule, Garber, 1982) and adolescents (Carey, Kelley, Buss, & Scott, 1986) may well prove helpful in identifying people, places, things, and activities that lead to emotions incompatible with depression. Sample items from the Children's Reinforcement Survey Schedule and Adolescent Activities Checklist are presented in Table 4.1 and Table 4.2, respectively. The number of times a child mentions a particular reinforcer or potential mediator and the enthusiasm reflected in the child's tone of voice can be used to assess the relative strength and importance to the child of the reinforcers and mediators (Costello, 1981). This technique, of course, is predicated upon the assumption that preferred reinforcers measured through verbal reports are equivalent to preferred reinforcers assessed through observation in a natural situation. In those cases where deficiencies in social skills

Table 4.1
The Children's Reinforcement Survey Schedule: Sample Items

	Dislike	Like	Like very much
Kindergarten through 3rd grade			
Do you like playing with dogs?			
Do you like raisins?			
Do you like teaching things to other people?			
Do you like going to the library?			
Do you like to watch television?			
Grades 4 through 6			
Do you like cooking?			
Do you like to go bike riding?			
Do you like math?			
Do you like listening to music?			
Do you like camping?			
What do you think is the best thing about you?			
What do you daydream about?			
What do you do for fun?			
What would you like for your birthday?			
Do you have any collections?			

Note. From "Children's Reinforcement Survey Schedule (CRSS)" by J. Cautela, Ed., 1977, *Behavior Analysis Forms for Clinical Intervention* (pp. 53–62). Champaign, IL: Research Press.

are deemed an antecedent to childhood depression, behavioral methods may also prove of value.

According to Lewinsohn and Hoberman (1982), the feeling of dysphoria is the central feature of depression. Cognitive symptoms such as low self-esteem, pessimism, and feelings of guilt are viewed as the depressives' efforts to explain to themselves and others why they feel unhappy. Depression is assumed to result when there is either too little positive reinforcement or too much punishment. Too little reinforcement can occur under three conditions: when events contingent upon behavior are no longer reinforcing, when reinforcers become unavailable, and when the individual lacks the social skills. Conversely, punishment plays a role in depression under three conditions: when aversive events occur frequently, when the individual has a heightened sensitivity to aversive events, and when the person lacks the coping skills to terminate the punishment.

Table 4.2
Adolescent Activities Checklist: Sample Items

---

1. Having spare time.
   How often? 1__ 2__ 3__ 4__ 5__ How pleasant? 1__ 2__ 3__ 4__ 5__ 6__ 7__
2. Being told I am needed.
   How often? 1__ 2__ 3__ 4__ 5__ How pleasant? 1__ 2__ 3__ 4__ 5__ 6__ 7__
3. Shopping.
   How often? 1__ 2__ 3__ 4__ 5__ How pleasant? 1__ 2__ 3__ 4__ 5__ 6__ 7__
4. Helping someone.
   How often? 1__ 2__ 3__ 4__ 5__ How pleasant? 1__ 2__ 3__ 4__ 5__ 6__ 7__
5. Swimming.
   How often? 1__ 2__ 3__ 4__ 5__ How pleasant? 1__ 2__ 3__ 4__ 5__ 6__ 7__
6. Going to a party.
   How often? 1__ 2__ 3__ 4__ 5__ How pleasant? 1__ 2__ 3__ 4__ 5__ 6__ 7__
7. Enjoying the outdoors.
   How often? 1__ 2__ 3__ 4__ 5__ How pleasant? 1__ 2__ 3__ 4__ 5__ 6__ 7__
8. Being asked for my advice.
   How often? 1__ 2__ 3__ 4__ 5__ How pleasant? 1__ 2__ 3__ 4__ 5__ 6__ 7__
9. Talking on the phone.
   How often? 1__ 2__ 3__ 4__ 5__ How pleasant? 1__ 2__ 3__ 4__ 5__ 6__ 7__
10. Working on cars.
    How often? 1__ 2__ 3__ 4__ 5__ How pleasant? 1__ 2__ 3__ 4__ 5__ 6__ 7__

Note. From M. Carey and M. Kelley. Unpublished manuscript.

Lewinsohn's theory is not without its problems (Lewinsohn & Hoberman, 1982). First, many individuals experience a low rate of response-contingent positive reinforcement but do not experience serious depressive disorders. Second, although many studies are consistent with the view that depressed adults are less socially skillful and that they receive less reinforcement through social interactions, the specific nature of the overt behavioral deficits remains to be clearly delineated. Three of the more interesting questions center around whether these deficits will differ in accordance with (a) gender, (b) developmental status, and (c) the specific situation.

Third, because the evidence for this theory rests on correlational data, it is not clear whether participation in pleasant events caused mood improvement or whether mood improvement caused increased participation in enjoyable activities. It is very conceivable, for instance, that the number of activities pursued on any given day is caused by the person's being in a good mood. It is hardly surprising to find a positive relationship between the daily ratings of frequency of activities and daily mood ratings. Fourth, pleasant events and mood are only mildly related. Given a positive correlation of only 0.3 to 0.4, we could not expect much increase in mood as a result of participating in pleasant events. A recent study with adolescents found that individuals who engaged in more pleasant activities did not report experiencing fewer depressive symptoms (Carey et al., 1986). Fifth, it is possible that discomfort and dysphoria may be increased in children and adolescents when they attempt to engage in activities that they enjoyed in the past. Depressed youngsters may feel worse if they engage in previously enjoyable activities only to find them not rewarding. Sixth, Lewinsohn's theory is not particularly useful in explaining depressions that occur without any apparent psychological loss (e.g., negative thinking is triggered automatically).

Shortcomings aside, Lewinsohn and his colleagues have made significant contributions to the treatment of depression among adolescents. First, the publication of empirically based treatment manuals has been a plus (Clarke, Lewinsohn, & Hops, 1990a; Clarke, Lewinsohn, & Hops, 1990b). Second, this group of investigators have conducted research on treatment outcomes of this approach and the research serves as an exemplary model for other researchers in this area (Clarke et al., 1992; Lewinsohn, Clarke, Hops, & Andrews, 1990).

To date, few systematic studies of depressed children have used behavioral techniques. In one study (Frame, Matson, Sonis, Fialkor, & Kazdin, 1982), a 10-year-old male inpatient with borderline mental retardation was treated for suicidal thoughts and gestures, violent temper outbursts, and poor school performance. Several assessments were used in making the diagnosis of depression including a psychiatric interview using *DSM-III* criteria, the Children's Depression Inventory (parent rated), the Child Behavior Problem Checklist, and the Bellevue Index of Depression. The child received scores on each assessment indicating depression. The diagnosis was further verified by a rater unaware of the child's diagnosis who completed the CDI and Depression Adjective Checklist while viewing a videotaped interview of the child. Additionally, observations by hospital staff were used. The operationally defined behaviors targeted for treatment were inappropriate body position, lack of eye contact, poor speech quality, and bland affect. Interrater reliabilities showed 80%–90% agreement between two raters, both of whom were blind to the experimental conditions and viewed taped sessions in random order. Assessments were done before, after, and during treatment. Treatment was provided in 20-minute sessions held each weekday for 20 days. Treatment included instruction, modeling, role plays, and feedback. The child was instructed as to what inappropriate behaviors were and then was asked to role-play each behavior. Correct responses were praised, and incorrect responses were identified. Role play continued until responses were appropriate. The target behaviors received variable attention, starting first with body position and eye contact (six sessions), speech quality (five sessions), and affect expression (nine sessions). Follow-up reassessment was done 12 weeks after treatment. Each behavior improved with treatment and continued to remain improved after 12 weeks.

This study provides encouraging results for the use of behavioral techniques in symptom reduction because the changes in undesirable behaviors were immediate, marked, and durable. There was no proof, however, of the elimination of a depressive disorder nor any indication that the child's suicidal thoughts and gestures were in any way affected. We must also question the generalizability of the therapeutic change beyond the treatment setting. Other studies with inpatients have yielded similar results (Calpin & Cincirpini, 1978; Calpin & Kornblith, 1978; Matson, 1982; Matson et al., 1980), except that in one case (Calpin & Cincirpini, 1978) suicidal ideation cleared. The small number of subjects treated in the studies cited ($N = 11$), the fact that 9 of the 11 were boys, and the limited age range (9–11) all limit the extent to which these findings regarding the use of behavioral techniques may be generalized. The design of outcome studies should also permit analysis of the four major domains of childhood depression, namely, the affective, cognitive, somatic, and motivational realms. The inclusion of multiple outcome measures enables the researcher to ascertain if treatment in one or two domains generalizes across all four domains. The possibility of modifying several depressive behaviors by treating a correlated target behavior is an exciting one that awaits investigation.

A treatment outcome study of 68 moderately depressed middle school students examined the efficacy of various psychological interventions including cognitive-behavioral conditions, relaxation training, a self-modeling approach, and a waiting-list control group (Kahn, Kehle, Jenson, & Clark, 1990). The cognitive-behavioral approach, which focused on behavioral components consistent with Lewinsohn's model, and relaxation procedures were group administered in twelve 50-minute sessions. The self-modeling condition, which was individually administered, involved each child developing a 3-minute videotape consisting of behaviors he or she had modeled. These modeled behaviors were prosocial in nature (e.g., smiling, positive verbalizations, appropriate eye contact) and the opposite of those typically displayed by depressed youth. Based on paper-and-pencil assessments utilizing the RADS, CDI, and BID, students receiving the cognitive-behavioral and relaxation techniques tended to show the greatest gains.

An important study examined the effects of a multimodal psychoeducational intervention for unipolar depression with 59 older adolescents without comorbidity whose parents cared enough to involve themselves and their teenagers in treatment (Lewinsohn et al., 1990). Whereas previous researchers relied on self-report measures to identify subjects, Lewinsohn and his colleagues diagnosed subjects on the basis of the K-SADS to determine if they met DSM-III-R criteria for major depression or RDC criteria for current minor or intermittent depressive disorder. One group of adolescents ($N = 21$) received cognitive-behavioral treatments consisting of pleasant-activities scheduling, social skills training, cognitive restructuring, relaxation training, and a distinctive component geared to communication, negotiation, and conflict-resolution skills. Another group ($N = 19$) received cognitive-behavioral intervention plus separate group training for their parents which consisted of a discussion of the training given to adolescents on communication, negotiation, and conflict resolution. The cognitive-behavioral interventions for both adolescent groups consisted of fourteen 2-hour sessions spread over a 7-week interval. The parent training consisted of seven 2-hour sessions. A third group of adolescents ($N = 19$) comprised the wait-list control group.

Treatment outcomes were assessed using self-report and parent-report severity of depression scales and K-SADS diagnoses at posttreatment and at follow-up intervals ranging up to 2 years. Outcomes for the wait-list control group were, unfortunately, only available at the time of posttreatment assessment. Immediately following intervention, both treatment groups fared better than the control subjects. Although the adolescent–parent group tended to show greater improvement than the adolescent-only condition, the two groups differed significantly from each other on only one of numerous comparisons. Follow-up assessments showed that treatment gains were maintained. This study is distinctive in that it represents an advance over other outcome studies by its use of (a) an experimental group study of adolescents, formally diagnosed as depressed by DSM-III-R/RDC standards; (b) intense and lengthy treatment conditions (twice as long as most studies); and (c) long-term follow-up assessments.

A group-treatment study of depressed outpatients suggests that the use of interpersonal problem-solving strategies has possible therapeutic value and that social skills training alone might be psychologically beneficial (Fine, Forth, Gilbert, & Haley, 1991). The therapeutic support group sought to enhance self-concept and self-esteem by providing a supportive environment. The social skills training entailed social problem solving, conflict resolution, assertiveness development, conversational skills, and monitoring of one's own feelings as well as those of others. Before and after *within-group* comparisons showed significant changes in the CDI for only the therapeutic support condition but both groups showed significant improvement on the K-SADS. The absence of a control group and the overlap of treatment components across the two intervention conditions make interpretation of the study's mixed findings difficult.

A detailed in-depth, empirically rooted, *school-based program* for depressed youth has been reported by Stark, Brookman, and Frazier (1990). This cognitive behavioral program is based on 3 years of treatment outcome research in public schools. The core of the treatment program consists of four basic components plus consultation with teachers and principals. The four basic ingredients include cognitive procedures (cognitive restructuring, attributional retraining, and modeling), training in self-regulatory skills (self-monitoring, self-reinforcement, and self-evaluation), behavioral techniques (activity planning, social skills training, relaxation, and imagery), and parent training. See Table 4.3 for a summary of the sequencing of the child's treatment programs. Designed for implementation in a school environment, the treatment package spreads 26 sessions out over an 18-week period. During the first 2 months, sessions are held twice a week to promote assimilation of basic ideas/skills and a healthy group cohesion and identity. Groups consist of four children and two therapists. This child-to-therapist ratio enables each child to receive increased individual attention, to control disruptive behavior stemming from comorbidity, and to focus on what other members have to say.

Several noteworthy changes were made over their 3-year experience with this program to make it more developmentally sensitive. Cartoons with thought bubbles were used increasingly to illustrate fundamental concepts. Androgenous animal figures gave way to pictures of boys and girls with a variety of ethnic backgrounds. More entertaining activities, stories, and cartoons were included to cope with youngsters' intolerance of didactic presentations, a hallmark of cognitive-behavioral methods. To take advantage of children's interest in modern technology, social skills training was videotaped. Additional structure was provided to offset children's tendency to be more forgetful and less organized than adults. For instance, a "participants practice book" was used to remind them of the special homework assignments such as speaking assertively to parents when certain circumstances occurred. The first four sessions were devoted to overcoming the students' lack of trust in their peers. Children's egocentrism dictated the need for small groups with co-therapists. Last, parental cooperation was also deemed essential because children have far less control over their lives (Clarizio & McCoy, 1983). Family meetings designed to provide training and therapy are re-

Table 4.3
Sequencing of Treatment Program

Session 1	Introductions, discuss confidentiality, complete a group activity, discuss participants' perceptions of treatment.
Session 2	Introduction to treatment rationale; complete a group activity.
Sessions 3–4	Review and extend treatment rationale, complete a group activity.
Session 5	Review treatment rationale and begin training self-reinforcement.
Sessions 6–8	Review and extend training in self-reinforcement.
Session 9	Review self-reinforcement, begin training in self-monitoring of pleasant events.
Session 10	Review self-monitoring of pleasant events and add activity scheduling.
Session 11	Review self-monitoring and activity scheduling.
Session 12	Review activity scheduling and introduce relaxation training.
Session 13	Review and begin assertiveness training.
Sessions 14–15	Assertiveness training.
Sessions 16–18	Social skills training.
Session 19	Review and make social skills video.
Session 20	Introduction to cognitive restructuring and personal scientist approach (begin use of thought records).
Session 21	Review and extension of cognitive restructuring.
Session 22	Review and introduction to problem solving.
Session 23	Problem-solving mastery exercises.
Session 24	Attribution training.
Session 25	Self-evaluation training.
Session 26	Working toward self-improvement.

All subsequent sessions—Continued work toward self-improvement using all of the previously learned skills.

Note. Adapted from K. Stark, S. Brookman, & R. Frazier, R. (1990). "A Comprehensive School-Based Treatment Program," in *School Psychology Quarterly, 5,* 116.

stricted to the parents and target child. Parents meetings designed to provide training and therapy are restricted to the parents and target child. Parents meet 1½ hours each month for 3 months. The first meeting covers such topics as confidentiality, review of the treatment program, the use of positive discipline methods, and a commitment to assist their child with therapeutic homework. The second parent meeting reviews skills taught during the child's sessions, the showcasing of these skills, feedback about the child's therapeutic homework, and parental encouragement of the child's assertiveness. The third meeting again reviews previous learning and showcases the child's skills, discusses coping with the child's negativism, and teaches parental restructuring of the child's thoughts.

Research results indicate that children receiving the above outlined treatment program reported significantly less depressive symptomatology, fewer depressive symptoms, and less hopelessness than did students in the nonspecific condition (Stark et al., 1990). Two limitations of this program come to mind. First the program requires a small child-to-therapist ratio for a period of approximately 18 weeks. Many school districts might well regard this lengthy, intensive treatment program as a luxury. Second, the relationship between measures of childhood depression and various measures of school performance is generally low, suggesting that changes in one condition (depression) will not be associated with major changes in the other variable (school performance). Moreover, causal relations between depression and academic competence have not been studied. Depression may cause incompetence, incompetence may cause depression, or both may be the effects of a third variable (Rehm & Carter, 1990). Overall, these investigators are to be applauded for providing a comprehensive, developmentally sensitive treatment package that is accompanied by a highly structured therapist's manual. They have incorporated a number of therapeutic strategies in the developmentally sensitive cognitive-behavioral, multicomponent package. Such strategies include drawing and mutual story telling, fun activities to teach about emotions, and games to teach self-control. Stark and his colleagues are also to be commended for their combining cognitive-behavioral techniques with a family-systems perspective (Stark & Brookman, 1992). It may well be that target behaviors central to depression may change with age. For instance, among adolescents problems of body image may be central to depression (Teri, 1982). The close relationship between body image and depression in adolescents suggests that physical activity may be one component of an effective treatment program for some cases of adolescent depression.

Although there have been no studies involving the use of physical exercise as a treatment with depressed children or adolescents, positive changes in self-concept after participation in a variety of physical fitness programs have been documented for 7th grade males (McGowan, Jarman, & Pederson,

1974) and obese teen-age males (Collingwood & Willit, 1971). That vigorous physical activity is capable of assisting those suffering from depression is shown in at least one study using mildly depressed 18- to 30-year-olds. Using an experimental format, Greist, Klein, Eischens, and Faris (1978) assigned 13 male and 15 female patients to time-limited 10-session psychotherapy, time-unlimited psychotherapy, or individual running over a 10-week period with a leader untrained in psychotherapy. Eight young adults met with the running leader three times per week for 30- to 45-minute sessions, gradually building up to run 4 and then 5 days per week. The leader met with them less frequently, and discussion of their depression was not encouraged. The results showed that 6 of 8 patients found relief after participating in a 10-week running program, whereas those in a control group who attended traditional psychotherapy sessions did not recover from their depression as well. A follow-up study (Greist et al., 1979) found that this improvement was still evident 2 years following the running treatment. Promising as this research is, several questions remain to be answered. How can the problems of fatigue, pessimism, and hopelessness be alleviated so as to facilitate compliance with a routine of regular exercise? (Note that these difficulties are not limited solely to interventions entailing therapeutic exercises.) What facilitative role can parents play in encouraging exercise? Can other forms of vigorous physical activity such as swimming, gymnastics, or body building be equally beneficial? Is a combination of vigorous physical activity and psychotherapy more effective than either alone? Is vigorous running more effective than any other treatment that is incompatible with being depressed, such as engaging in activities that one enjoys, be they working in politics, reading poetry, or playing pool?

One of the most urgent needs is the identification of social skills, in various natural settings that are central to successful coping among both normal and depressed boys and girls at different developmental and socioeconomic levels. It would be interesting to see if there is a "g" or general factor that cuts across various social skills. Although much attention has been devoted to *how* to change (shaping procedures, modeling, direct training techniques, feedback, rehearsal, and peer pairing), little attention has been paid to *what* to change. We need to devote as much research to building the *content* of the intervention as to its mode of delivery (Conger & Keane, 1981). Also, sole reliance on social skills training might be simplistic. Depressed youth experience discomfort in social situations. Moreover, negative cognitions, our next major topic of discussion, must be addressed.

The designs of these studies do not permit analysis of the individual treatment components. This limitation may be tempered, however, by the fact that combined treatment programs are generally superior to isolated techniques in the training of social behaviors (Bellack & Hersen, 1979).

COGNITIVE APPROACHES

The cognitive approaches emphasize the role of cognitions in determining a person's feelings and behaviors. Cognitive theorists do not claim that their theories exhaust all the etiological possibilities, but distorted thinking in depression is thought to be central in the etiology of disorder with affective, motivational, and physical symptoms considered to be consequences of these cognitive distortions. According to cognitive theory, the depressed person is perceived as holding negative views of her- or himself, the world, and the future. The depressed person sees him- or herself as deficient, inadequate, and unworthy. The world appears overly demanding, and the future holds only continued suffering (Kovacs & Beck, 1977). Depressed individuals distort reality to fit their perceptions of things. They overgeneralize, minimize positives, exaggerate, misinterpret, and make absolute judgments (Emery, Bedrosian, & Garver, 1983). In therapy, individuals are taught to identify and correct distortions in thinking and the beliefs that follow. According to Kaslow and Rehm (1991), this is done through the use of the following techniques: recognizing the relationship between cognition, affect, and behavior; monitoring negative thoughts; examining the evidence for and against these thoughts; substituting more realistic interpretations for negative ones; and identifying and changing dysfunctional beliefs. In this section, we will review four cognitive theorists whose work is relevant to the treatment of depressed children. Note that cognitive-behavioral therapies do not constitute a singular approach. Rather, cognitive-behavioral treatment refers to a variety of techniques. Although they differ in regard to the specific nature of the cognitions involved, they all attribute a causal role to cognitions in the etiology of depression.

Beck's Cognitive View

According to Beck (1976), the majority of depressive symptoms stem from the depressed individual's negative and distorted thinking. That is, the signs and symptoms of the depressive syndrome are a consequence of disordered thinking. Three specific cognitive structures are seen as central in the development of depression: the cognitive triad, schemata, and cognitive errors (Beck, Rush, Shaw, & Emery, 1979).

The *cognitive triad* in depression consists of three cognitive patterns through which the depressed person experiences a pervasive negative view of *self,* the *world,* and the *future* (Kovacs & Beck, 1977). The depressed individual's cognitive structure is such that she or he sees herself or himself as inadequate, defective, and a "loser"; the world as making exorbitant demands and presenting insurmountable obstacles, and a future with unremitting suffering. The existence of *depressogenic schemata* leads to the systematic filtering or distortion of stimuli that confront people. These schemata represent stable cognitive patterns that mold incoming information in a way that is consistent with previously held ideas or beliefs (Beck et al., 1979). Beck uses this construct to explain why depressed persons cling to painful attitudes ("I am unlovable") despite objective evidence to the contrary. *Cognitive errors* leading to the depressive person's exaggerated sense of *responsibility* and *self-reproach* include magnifying or misinterpreting events, making absolute judgments, overgeneralizing from a single happening, centering on a particular detail out of context and overlooking the more obvious features of a situation, and drawing illogical inferences.

Research on adult depressives by Beck and colleagues, as well as by others, has focused on the effects of success and failure, perceptual distortion, memory distortion, and negative expectations. Although studies have provided little support for the prediction of differential effects of success and failure and for the perceptual distortion hypothesis, research generally has supported Beck's prediction of more forgetting of pleasant and less selective forgetting of unpleasant information (Lewinsohn & Hoberman, 1982). Adult depressives were also found to have higher expectancies about negative events and lower expectancies for positive events pertaining to the self but not about the world (Lewinsohn, Larson, & Munoz, 1978).

Depressive schemata may develop over many years. Various factors are believed to cause the depressive schemata to be constructed over time. These include tangible losses (e.g., loss of mother or father), expectation of loss, self-esteem-lowering events (e.g., being unwanted by parents and/or peers), and background factors (e.g., depression in a close relative). The etiological-developmental aspects of this theory remain to be detailed (e.g., how early stresses lead to distorted thinking), but the theory should prove capable of generating testable hypotheses. There are some retrospective data suggesting that depression in adult life may be related to parental rejection and control techniques such as derision, negative evaluation, and withdrawal of affection in childhood (Crook, Raskin, & Eliot, 1981). These findings are consistent with Beck's belief that thoughts of worthlessness seen in depression have their origins in early child-parent interactions. Cause-effect relationships are not clear, however. It could be that depressed patients are constitutionally different from birth and their behavior shapes the negative behavior of parents. All in all, however, an integration of Beck's theory with Piaget's cognitive developmental work may offer some promising insights into the origins and course of childhood depression.

Although Beck's cognitive approach to the treatment of depression in adults has not been used directly with children, various cognitive therapy programs for children bear a resemblance to adult cognitive therapy for depression. For instance, self-statement training may be an effective component of a treatment plan to enhance the self-esteem of depressed children. Likewise, interpersonal problem-solving therapy holds promise as a beneficial means for overcoming social inhibitions in withdrawn children many of whom may be depressed (Spivack, Platt, & Shure, 1976). Bear in mind, however, that there is disagreement as to whether the cognitive aspects of depression differ between adults and children. For example, Rie (1966) noted that hopelessness and despair, the two cardinal features of adult depression, may be absent among childhood depressives, whereas Kazdin, French, Unis, Esveldt-Dawson, and Sherick (1983) reported that hopelessness is related to depression among 8- to 13-year-old hospitalized depressives. The ability to project oneself into the future may not make its appearance until the advent of formal operational thinking. The child at the concrete operational stage might well be tied to the here-and-now of reality and unable to anticipate what the future has in store.

Research with children in grades 4 through 7 who were identified through a multiple-gait screening procedure indicated that depressed children ($N = 14$) and depressed and anxious children ($N = 18$) had a more negative view of self, view of world, and view of future than did anxious and control youngsters (Kaslow, Stark, Printz, Livingston, & Tsai, 1992). The failure to control for overall level of psychopathology among subjects leaves open the possibility that the more severe or distressed, not just depressed, the youngsters are, the more negative their view of self, world, and future. This interpretation is consistent with their data showing that the depressed and anxious group had the highest scores on the Cognitive Triad Inventory for Children, a single scale developed to assess the negative cognitive triad. (See Table 4.4.) Comorbidity (i.e., depression plus anxiety) disorder is related to severity in childhood psychopathology (Clarizio, 1990). Once the psychometric properties of this scale have been further evaluated, its use to measure progress in the application of Beck's cognitive therapy with children should be studied. Such research could aid in determining whether changes in these three cognitions are related to progress in treatment. There is a strong need to

Table 4.4
The Cognitive Triad Inventory for Children

Instructions: Circle the answer which best describes your opinion. *Choose only one answer for each idea.* Answer the items for what you are thinking **RIGHT NOW**. Remember, fill this out for how you feel today.

1.	I do well at many different things.	Yes	Maybe	No
2.	School is no fun.	Yes	Maybe	No
3.	Most people are friendly and helpful.	Yes	Maybe	No
4.	Nothing is likely to work out for me.	Yes	Maybe	No
5.	I am a failure.	Yes	Maybe	No
6.	I like to think about the good things that will happen for me in the future.	Yes	Maybe	No
7.	I do my schoolwork okay.	Yes	Maybe	No
8.	The people I know help me when I need it.	Yes	Maybe	No
9.	I think that things will be going very well for me a few years from now.	Yes	Maybe	No
10.	I have messed up almost all the best friendships I have ever had.	Yes	Maybe	No
11.	Lots of fun things will happen for me in the future.	Yes	Maybe	No
12.	The things I do every day are fun.	Yes	Maybe	No
13.	I can't do anything right.	Yes	Maybe	No
14.	People like me.	Yes	Maybe	No
15.	There is nothing left in my life to look forward to.	Yes	Maybe	No
16.	My problems and worries will never go away.	Yes	Maybe	No
17.	I am as good as other people I know.	Yes	Maybe	No
18.	The world is a very mean place.	Yes	Maybe	No
19.	There is no reason for me to think that things will get better for me.	Yes	Maybe	No
20.	The important people in my life are helpful and nice to me.	Yes	Maybe	No
21.	I hate myself.	Yes	Maybe	No
22.	I will solve my problems.	Yes	Maybe	No
23.	Bad things happen to me a lot.	Yes	Maybe	No
24.	I have a friend who is nice and helpful to me.	Yes	Maybe	No
25.	I can do a lot of things well.	Yes	Maybe	No
26.	My future is too bad to think about.	Yes	Maybe	No

Table 4.4
(Continued)

27.	My family doesn't care what happens to me.	Yes	Maybe	No
28.	Things will work out okay for me in the future.	Yes	Maybe	No
29.	I feel guilty for a lot of things.	Yes	Maybe	No
30.	No matter what I do, other people make it hard for me to get what I need.	Yes	Maybe	No
31.	I am a good person.	Yes	Maybe	No
32.	There is nothing to look forward to as I get older.	Yes	Maybe	No
33.	I like myself.	Yes	Maybe	No
34.	I am faced with many difficulties.	Yes	Maybe	No
35.	I have problems with my personality.	Yes	Maybe	No
36.	I think that I will be happy as I get older.	Yes	Maybe	No

Note. From "Cognitive Triad Inventory for Children: Development and Its Relation to Depression and Anxiety" by N. Kaslow et al., 1992, *Journal of Clinical Child Psychology, 21,* 339–347. Reprinted with permission.

tailor instruments to measure the purported central components of treatment approaches.

Cognitive therapy techniques must also be adapted in the treatment of depressed adolescents. Wilkes and Rush (1988) have identified three important differences from traditional cognitive therapy with adults. First, special care is needed to develop the therapeutic alliance because adolescents can experience a period of intense negative ambivalence toward authority figures. Second, action-oriented techniques during the session, concrete behavioral homework tasks, and cognitive restructuring must be tailored to the cognitive skills of the teenager. Finally, the family must be involved in the assessment and treatment process because the adolescent usually develops in the context of a family that has its own set of beliefs, rules, and expectations. These can perpetuate dysfunctional cognitions, behavior, and emotions.

What does objective evidence indicate about the use of Beck's cognitive therapy with depressed adolescents? In one of the few evaluative studies available, Reynolds and Coats (1986) combined elements of Beck's cognitive theory as part of a cognitive-behavioral treatment program and found that depressed adolescents went from moderate levels of depression at pretest to nondepressed levels at posttest. Gains persisted 5 weeks later at follow-up.

Seligman's Learned Helplessness

Seligman's (1975) concept of "learned helplessness" also stresses the role of learning in depression. Seligman believes that learned helplessness results when one's environment leads to a sense of having little or no control over rewards and punishments. He found that animals subjected to inescapable shock may no longer try to solve the problem confronting them and passively remain to suffer. Seligman argues that humans may also learn helplessness as a result of unsolvable traumatic encounters (failing grades, peer rejection, battering, parental death) that lead them to believe that they are unable to control the consequences of life's tragedies. Uncontrollability, and not trauma per se, was initially seen as the critical issue. The main psychological phenomena of learned helplessness include passivity, retarded learning, lack of aggressiveness and competitiveness, and weight loss and undereating. That is, motivational, emotional, and cognitive deficits arise from learned helplessness.

Early research comparing Seligman's theory of feelings of uncontrollability and ensuing helplessness with Beck's theory of self-reproach and exaggerated sense of responsibility have tended to support Beck's views (Rizley, 1978) and prompted a revision of Seligman's views (Abramson, Seligman, & Teasdale, 1978), which incorporate extensions of attribution theory. Exposure to uncontrollable events did not always lead to helplessness and depression. Furthermore, the helplessness theory did not account for the loss of self-esteem commonly seen in depressed individuals. Why should people blame themselves for events over which they have no control? In answering these objections, Seligman and his colleagues emphasized explanatory or attributional style. In other words, instead of helplessness being seen simply as a result of expectations of noncontingency, it was proposed that people's understanding of the *cause* of past or current noncontingency determined expectations of future noncontingency and ultimately led to helplessness. Depression will result if the person blames him- or herself for being helpless and sees the situation as unchangeable.

Seligman assumes that there are four sufficient but not necessary conditions for the development of depression: (1) the individual expects that a highly aversive state of affairs is likely (or a highly desired state of affairs is unlikely); (2) the individual expects that he or she will be able to do nothing about the likelihood of these states of affairs; (3) the individual possesses a maladaptive attributional style so that negative events tend to be attributed to internal, stable, and global causes, and positive events to external, unstable, and specific causes; (4) the greater the certainty of the expected aversive state of affairs and the expected uncontrollability, the greater the strength of motivational and cognitive deficits.

Although there are four main tenets of this theory, the focus is on one of these, namely, attributional style, which can be graded along three dimensions: internal-external, stable-unstable, and global-specific. The reformulated theory suggests that the depressive attributional or explanatory style (a) consists in a tendency to make internal attributions for failure but external attributions for success, (b) makes stable attributions for failure but unstable attributions for success, and (c) makes global attributions for failure but specific attributions for success (Trotter, 1987). Each dimension is linked to particular kinds of consequences for the nature of the helplessness experienced. The low self-esteem is hypothesized to result from internal attributions for personal helplessness, whereas the dysphoria results from expectation of future bad outcomes. The severity of the motivational and cognitive deficits is said to depend on the strength or certainty of expected unpleasant outcomes and the strength of uncontrollability.

Evaluation

Two recent reviews of the attribution and depression literature on adults have drawn opposite conclusions. Peterson and Seligman (1984, p. 371) concluded that "results to date support the model," whereas Coyne and Gotlib (1983, p. 500) noted "little support has been obtained for the strong claims" of the learned helplessness model. The cause of this discrepancy might well be that learned helplessness theory now generates a number of alternative predictions about the relation of attribution to depression and that attempts to evaluate the theory without articulating these predictions are destined to provide inconclusive results, according to Brewin (1985), who has outlined five specific models that bear on the hypothesized relations between attribution and depression. Following a review of the evidence, Brewin (1985) concludes that tests of the onset and vulnerability models, which derive from the reformulated learned helplessness theory of depression, do not offer any confirmation of their validity. There was some support for the symptom, recovery, and coping models, however. The lack of support is likely due in part to inherent difficulties in testing the models, but it may also be due to questionable assumptions, some of which are discussed below.

Role of events. Research has not supported the notion that the occurrence of an uncontrollable event was a necessary condition for depression, but it does suggest that cognitions bear a direct relationship with mood (Brewin, 1985). The tendency of depressed mood to correlate more highly with attributional measures involving *hypothetical* events than with measures involving *actual* events supports this conclusion (Coyne & Gotlib, 1983).

However, the reformulated model of explaining depressive onset is erroneous, perhaps because cognitions about the *triggering event* are irrelevant or because the *wrong cognitions* have been measured. Abramson et al. (1978) might have been wrong in their assumption that an analysis of recurrent triggering events in the laboratory can be generalized to explain the effects of real-life traumatic events that recur seldom if at all. Events such as death of a parent or attributions about the cause of a close friend's death tend to be nonrecurring, at least in the short run. Moreover, with this nonrecurring type of event, causal attributions are unlikely to be as closely related to future adjustment. For instance, *attributions* or *explanations* about the loss of a parent may be less relevant to adjustment than other cognitive/affective *expectations* such as one's expectations about being able to cope without the close parent. In all fairness to Abramson and her colleagues, it should be noted that some recurring traumatic events (e.g., physical and sexual child abuse) are associated with increased rates of depression. It remains for future research to establish a link between chronic child maltreatment and a subtype of depression labeled "negative cognitive depression" (Rose & Abramson, 1992). In any event, these authors are to be commended in their search for developmental precursors of negative cognitive style that would have implications for prevention, diagnosis, and treatment of hopelessness depression.

Although there is some evidence to suggest that children can learn to be helpless (Dweck, 1977) and that there is a relationship between attributional style and depressive symptoms in children (Seligman et al., 1984), we also know that adversity can result in aggressive and anxious behavior or even higher level daily functioning (Garmezy, 1983). Although the link between early loss of mother and later depression is a complex one (Brown, Harris, & Bifulco, 1986), even as traumatic an event as parental death during childhood does not appear to be an etiological factor in adult depression (Crook & Eliot, 1980). Using healthy siblings as a control group, Swedish researchers found no excess of parental loss for unipolars, bipolars, and neurotic reactive depressives (Perris, Holmgren, Von Knorring, & Perris, 1986). It is hoped that future studies will specify the conditions under which adversity leads to a sense of learned helplessness. For instance, learned helplessness may assume a more important role once adolescence is reached when there is increasing pressure from adults and peers to take responsibility for one's actions and exert control over one's environment (Dweck, 1977). There is also evidence to suggest that females develop a depressive attributional style at an earlier age than males (Craighead, Smucker, & Duchnowski, 1981) and that this attributional style is more typical of females. Further, depressed subjects manifest this attributional style only if they are also anxious (Peterson & Ebata, 1984).

Given this argument about triggering events, measuring cognitions about causal events would appear to risk irrelevance. Another possibility is that important event-related cognitions are *moral* and *self-evaluative* rather than *causal* perceptions. That is, young people may be more concerned with the adequacy of their own conduct and with violation of their own values than with the fact that their actions played some causal part leading to an uncontrollable event. Learned helplessness researchers tend to confound these two levels of self-blame judgments, overlooking that one might make an internal attribution for some negative outcome with or without feeling that one has acted foolishly, recklessly, incompetently, or immorally. Thus, for example, the socialized delinquent who has been caught and jailed for stealing might well not believe that he acted foolishly or recklessly and experience no depression even though making an internal attribution. Conversely, not studying when one had the time could lead to self-blame and depressed mood. The analyses of self-blame into moral and causal components may serve to explain why seeing events as more controllable is related to guilt and depressed mood (Weiner, Graham, & Chandler, 1982). In short, events may be important in precipitating depression for reasons other than their perceived causal properties.

Individual dimensions versus composite attributional scores. To date the vast majority of studies, almost all of which have been with adult subjects, have eschewed examination of the roles of the three individual dimensions when trying to predict depressed mood. For instance, studies almost invariably correlate internality with a general measure of depression rather than with a measure of the self-esteem component as the theory would predict. Recent research (Brewin, 1988) found self-esteem to be correlated not only with internality but also with global attributions and judgments of consensus and consistency. Attributions were less powerful predictors of self-esteem than the nonattributional cognitive variables of consensus and consistency. Moreover, most studies have failed to examine the relationships between dimensions. As a result, the amount of variance in depressed mood that is uniquely predicted by each dimension is unknown.

Other general qualifications of the work on learned helplessness among child depressives include (1) reliance on questionnaires to the exclusion of more sensitive techniques, (2) the failure to study depression as a clinical entity, (3) the absence of data on children younger than 8 or 9, (4) the lack of research showing that attributional style is specific to childhood depression as the theory argues, (5) unexplained "facts" such as the role of sex differences and helplessness in relation to an increase of depressive symptomatology at puberty, and (6) juxtaposing, rather than integrating, learned helplessness as a theory with developmental theories (Seligman & Peterson, 1986). Finally, despite the mass of theoretical and experimental papers emanating from learned helplessness theory, it has not spawned much in the way of practical therapy (Gilbert, 1984).

Future research. Future investigations need to demonstrate the superiority of attributional measures, either singularly or in composite, over other cognitive or cognitive/affective variables such as hopelessness, self-esteem, or external locus of control. If such proof is not forthcoming, then the reformulated attributional model will lose much of its theoretical and practical value. It might well be that these dimensions are not independent (Williams, 1984). For instance, effort most likely depends on the perception that one does have the necessary ability, but needs to try harder. If one believes that ability is lacking, there is no point in trying. Likewise, luck and task difficulty are also probably related. For luck attributions are more likely if the task is perceived as either unpredictable or difficult, whereas tasks judged to be predictable and easy do not lend themselves to luck attributions. The interactive nature of the dimensions might explain why global scores are most predictive.

Future studies should also address how gender impacts different kinds of stress. For example, longitudinal research by Jeanne and Jack Block (Cordes, 1984) indicates that boys and girls react differently to two kinds of stress: object loss versus change stress. Boys were more affected by object loss such as death of a loved one than were girls. And contrary to traditional thinking based on studies of clinically depressed women, girls were not only less affected by object loss but actually appeared to benefit from "change stress" such as having to adjust to new schools and peers. The roles of attitudes (e.g., "I should be loved"), anger, and pre-episode vulnerability also warrant more attention (Gilbert, 1984).

Ellis's Rational-Emotive Therapy

Rational-emotive therapy (RET) was perhaps the first cognitively oriented therapy to be used with children—a fact not commonly known, perhaps because RET remained relatively independent of other cognitive-behavior therapies (CBT) until recently. Its founder, Albert Ellis, believed that like adults, children and adolescents could achieve greater happiness if they learned to talk more sensibly to themselves. As practiced, RET is an action-oriented, education-didactic multimodal form of treatment that uses cognitive, emotive, and behavioral methods. The cognitive methods seek to get clients to give up their irrational ideas (demandingness, awfulizing, and self-rating) and to teach them how to evaluate their own thinking scientifically and logically. In its emotive aspects, RET helps clients to change their irrational ideas by dramatizing these ideas in ways that show their absurdity or phoniness (e.g., the use of humor). In its behavioral features, RET encourages the child to act in ways that contradict irrational ideas (Grieger & Boyd, 1989).

Basic Principles

Since its initial use with children in the mid-1950s, RET practitioners have become increasingly aware of the importance of taking into account the child's linguistic-cognitive development repertoire in both deciding if a problem exists as well as analyzing and treating the problem. As practiced with children, RET and CBT are virtually synonymous (Ellis & Bernard, 1983). Children are shown how they upset themselves with irrational and unrealistic beliefs and are helped to figure out more rational ways to run their lives. When applied to children and adolescents, RET uses *inelegant,* specific, problem-oriented methods (symptom removal), but the basic *elegant* goal is always to help emotionally and behaviorally disturbed youngsters to internalize a philosophy of life (cognitive strategy) that is more rational and realistic than the one they commonly abide by when they get into difficulties. That is, children are to take control of their feelings through the use of rational thinking and problem-solving skills. Cognitive restructuring approaches postulate that emotional disturbance can be best understood by analyzing the *cognitive-mediational repertoire* of the individual and that emotional and behavioral change can be brought about by modifying the mediational competence of the individual. RET accomplishes its general goal by helping children become more aware of their own emotions and thoughts and by developing a conceptual-linguistic system for expressing their emotions. They are taught to differentiate between thoughts and feelings and they are given practice in verbalizing sets of rational self-statements. Older children are taught the ABCs (Activating Event—Belief—Emotional Consequence) of RET, the difference between rational and irrational beliefs, and how to dispute irrational ideas and beliefs. See Table 4.5 for basic strategies of RET.

In tackling practical and behavioral problems, RET employs other cognitive-behavioral approaches such as interpersonal cognitive problem-solving (Spivack & Shure, 1974), self-instructional training (Meichenbaum & Burland, 1979), attributional retraining (Dweck, 1975), and stress inoculation training (Novaco, 1979).

Table 4.5
Using RET with Depressed Children

1. Have students monitor and record their self-downing thoughts such as "I'm no good," "I can't do anything right," and "I'll never be any different."
2. Challenge and dispute the irrational beliefs and substitute positive for negative self-talk.
3. Encourage students to answer the question, "Where does this negative thinking get me?"
4. Encourage children and adolescents to reward themselves each time they stop focusing on negative and begin to focus on positive or neutral material.
5. Depression is past oriented. Encourage clients to let go of the past and focus on the present.
6. Discuss the RET concept of self-acceptance, pointing out the invalidity of rating the whole person and the preferability of rating individual traits and behaviors.
7. Encourage youngsters to speak nicely to themselves, do nice things for themselves, and give themselves compliments.
8. Suggest that the student record positive accomplishments and compliments received from others and reread them when feeling depressed.
9. Use RET.
10. Suggest students use positive imagery to imagine themselves in desirable situations.
11. Teach them to ask for what they want assertively, rather than passively waiting for it to arrive on its own.
12. Encourage clients to give up the need for others' approval.
13. Point out that inertia breeds inertia. The more active they become despite their depression, the less depressed they will feel.

Note. From "Therapies for Children" by V. Waters, 1982, in C. Reynolds and T. Gutkin (Eds.), *Handbook of School Psychology* (pp. 578–579), New York: Wiley.

Evaluation

Can RET effectively and efficiently be used to overcome depression in children? Although RET procedures have been used to treat childhood depression, they have received less attention than such conditions as conduct disorders, underachievement, anxieties, and obesity (DiGiuseppe & Bernard, 1983). Although research (DiGiuseppe, Miller, & Trexler, 1977) on the use of RET procedures with children has provided support for the notion that elementary school children can acquire a knowledge of rational-emotive principles and that modification of a child's self-statement or irrational self-statements (e.g., "I did something bad and I am a bad person for having done it. I must be totally competent and loved or else I am worthless") (Grieger & Boyd, 1983) can have a positive impact on emotional adjustment and behavior, *only* case studies are offered to illustrate the use of RET techniques to treat childhood depression. The case of Penny illustrates the treatment of two common errors in thinking that can lead to depression, namely, the belief that one must always be loved and that one must be perfect. Children's negative and emotionally charged perceptions about their parents are reflected in the cases of Mike and Jack (see pp. 162, 135). These case studies illustrate how the modification of faulty thinking processes and irrational beliefs can be beneficial, but it remains for future research to delineate the benefits of RET procedures with depressed children. Given the cognitive nature of this approach and the fact that we still have a long way to go to understand the world from a child's perspective, special attention will need to be given to such subject characteristics as the child's age, cognitive maturity, language development, and attributional style (Copeland, 1981).

Penny

Penny, a 14-year-old schoolgirl with a hearing loss, was referred because her school performance had fallen off and she seemed unhappy. Penny was depressed, had lost concentration in her work, and was very flat emotionally. Assessment showed that she was under pressure at home from a perfectionistic and demanding father, and that she pressured herself to compete with and equal the very high achievements of her four older brothers. Examples of her self-verbalizations include "I'm hopeless"; "I'll never be as good as Ian." Penny described herself as nervous, lonely when her brothers were not around, and felt her childhood had been ruined because she had not done the risky and difficult things her brothers had asked her to do (such as jumping from high places). Therefore she rated herself as "gutless"—"I feel I should have done things even if it killed me."

The main focus of therapy was in teaching her rational-emotive ways of challenging her irrational beliefs and altering her causal attributions regarding her unhappiness. She acquired a new causal attribution belief: "It is possible to do something about my unhappy feelings and I am the one who can do something about them." In addition, she learned that factors under her control, namely, the learning of disputational skills and encouraging herself to make an effort, were major influences over what would happen to her in the future and how she would feel. The main irrational beliefs she learned to dispute were "I must have my brothers' love and approval at all times" and "I must perform well in my schoolwork at all times or I am a failure."

Penny was taught to distinguish between herself and her performance and learned to stop rating herself globally. Homework exercises helped her to rehearse exactly what she would say to her brothers when asked to do something she did not want to try (e.g., riding a surfboard in heavy surf). Other in-session rehearsals of rational self-talk, for dealing with schoolwork "catastrophes" worse than she had feared or imagined, reduced her exaggerated evaluations of events such as getting poor marks. Humorous exaggerations by the practitioner helped her to put her perceptions into a new perspective.

After eight sessions she was feeling happier and doing her schoolwork without rating herself globally on her performance level. Changes in Penny reported by her mother included improved self-acceptance, new positive perceptions of her teachers, and improvements in the independence and organization of her schoolwork.

Note. From *Rational-Emotive Therapy with Children* (pp. 310–311) by M. Bernard and M. Joyce, 1984. New York: Wiley.

It is especially important that we understand how the readiness of the child's critical thinking skills affects outcomes in RET. Disputing requires that therapist and child be on the same wavelength (i.e., use the same criteria of truthfulness). For many children something is true simply because they believe it, or because their parents or friends told them so. To benefit from RET, children must be able to distinguish among speculations, opinions, hypotheses, and facts if they are to discover and modify their irrational beliefs. Being logical, particularly questioning one's own beliefs and thoughts, is often difficult for adults, let alone children. Thinking about one's thinking is an abstract conceptual activity that not only may be initially foreign to children but also may be developmentally difficult, if not impossible, without creative modification of RET procedures. The proponents of RET practices with children are not unaware of these challenges but they have yet to demonstrate the efficacy of these techniques with depressed children or other children, given the fact that only about half the people ever reach the level of formal operational thinking (Niemark, 1975). Some researchers believe that cognitive therapy should focus on cognitive *deficits* rather than cognitive *errors* (Emery et al., 1983). Also, the relative contribution of behavioral components (i.e., behavioral rehearsal and written homework assignment) in RET remains to be clarified.

Mike

Mike, a 12-year-old, was referred because of depression. The school feared that he was suicidal. Mike's dad, a recovered alcoholic, experienced chronic episodes of depression. His mother felt particularly angered by these events because they greatly imposed on her life as well. The father's depression usually resulted in periods of parental arguing. Previous therapists had attempted to help Mike by focusing on the marriage and the resolution of its fights or the father's depression. But all sorts of marital therapy, family therapy, individual therapy, and chemotherapy had failed to lift the father's depression or resolve the parents' arguing. Mike was stuck with a depressed father and a mother who was angered by the depressive episodes.

The initial interview with Mike revealed that he believed it was best not to acknowledge his father's mistakes or personality failures and not to acknowledge his mother's anger. Once he did talk of these things, it was discovered that Mike believed he was destined to be depressed if his father was, that one had to be unhappy if his parents fought, and that it was awful to have both a depressed father and a fighting mother. Direct disputing of these irrational beliefs proved quite successful in a short period of time. In order to succeed, I had to agree with Mike that his dad was depressed and that his parents did fight bitterly. But he already knew that. He did not realize that fathers do not have to be perfect and are allowed to have serious problems, and that despite their serious problems they can still be nice and one can still love them. Mike learned to forgive his dad for his depression and his mom for her arguing. He also learned how to focus more on the positive aspects of both parents and how not to get upset when they put their worst foot forward.

Note. From "Principles of Assessment and Methods of Treatment with Children" by R. DiGiuseppe and M. Bernard, 1983. In A. Ellis and M. Bernard (Eds.), *Rational-Emotive Approaches to the Problems of Childhood* (pp. 76–77). New York: Plenum.

Evaluation

Is the cognitive approach to treatment of depressed children more effective than a behavioral approach? There are few studies comparing the effectiveness of these two approaches with depressed youngsters. One such study (Butler, Miezitis, Friedman, & Cole, 1980) compared a cognitive therapy approach with a social-behavioral approach using moderately depressed children in a school-based intervention program. Fifty-six 5th- and 6th-grade children—identified as depressed on the basis of their responses to a self-report depression battery—were involved in this study that compared role-play and cognitive restructuring treatments. Children were identified by using a battery of self-report measures including the Self-Esteem Scale (reduced version of the Piers-Harris Children's Self-Concept Scale), the Children's Depression Inventory, the Moyal-Miezitis Stimulus Appraisal Questionnaire, and the Nowicki-Strickland Locus of Control Scale for Children, in addition to teacher referrals.

The 56 children were placed in one of four conditions: role play, cognitive restructuring, attention-placebo, or classroom control. The role-play groups consisted of ten 1-hour sessions, focusing on problems relevant to depressed children (acceptance, rejection, success, failure, guilt, self-blame, and loneliness). Sessions involved a warm-up, review, problem, preparation, enactment, discussion, practice, second problem, summarizing discussion, and homework assignment. The objectives of the role-play condition involved sensitizing the child to the thoughts and feelings of her- or himself and others, teaching social interaction skills, and teaching a problem-solving approach.

The cognitive restructuring groups also consisted of ten 1-hour sessions, stressing the following objectives: teaching the recognition of irrational, self-deprecating automatic thoughts, and adopting more logical alternatives; enhancing listening skills; and teaching the recognition of the relationship between thoughts and feelings. Sessions included an introduction, one to three exercises, discussion, and homework. The attention-placebo groups were taught to solve problems cooperatively over the same time period. Classroom controls remained unidentified and in their regular classrooms. After their treatment sessions, all students were again given the battery of tests and evaluated by their teachers.

The role-play condition was the most successful treatment. Students' classroom behaviors improved, as reported by classroom teachers, posttest scores dropped below the cutoff scores indicating depression, and this group demonstrated the most improvement between pre- and posttests. The cognitive restructuring condition was somewhat successful, and the scores for the placebo and control conditions remained basically the same.

This study warrants replication for it appears that more than just symptoms were eliminated. Because of the lack of follow-up measurement, statements concerning the endurance of these treatment effects are not possible. More research is needed in comparing these methods of treatment with *clinically* identified children of various ages. The lack of significant success in the cognitive restructuring groups may be due to the lack of cognitive abilities in children to reason in this fashion, to the failure of the researchers to translate therapeutic interventions into terms the subjects could grasp, or to the fact that the affects felt are stronger than the reasoning statements. Also formal discussions of this type may stimulate tension in children, and the "challenge" may prove to be threatening. Children may be simply unwilling to invest their interest in this approach. Also, role playing is a more tangible method that may be more consistent with children's developmental level (i.e., modeling is a more concrete approach that shows them how to resolve the problems confronting them).

Rehm's Self-Control Model

The use of self-management techniques represents a cognitively oriented approach that emphasizes rational goal setting, planning, and self-instruction (Meichenbaum & Burland, 1979). Rehm (1977) has postulated a self-control model of depression in which negative self-evaluations, low rates of self-reinforcement, and high rates of self-punishment are seen as leading to behavior typical of depressed individuals. Building on Kanfer's (1971) concept of self-control, Rehm (1977) notes that individuals can have deficits in three processes: self-monitoring, self-evaluation, and self-reinforcement. (1) Kaslow and Rehm (1983) note two types of *self-monitoring* problems: attending to negative events while ignoring positive events, and focusing on the immediate rather than the later consequences of behavior. Maladaptive self-monitoring is believed to result in a negative view of self, the world, and the future. (2) The two maladaptive difficulties in *self-evaluation* usually entail setting unrealistically stringent self-standards (high standards for positive self-evaluation and low standards for negative self-evaluation), and inaccurate attributions of success or failure. Strict evaluation criteria are assumed to cause lowered self-esteem and feelings of helplessness. (3) Deficits in the area of *self-reinforcement* can be evidenced in extreme self-punishment and inadequate self-reinforcement. A lack of self-reward is associated with low activity levels and a lack of initiative, whereas excessive self-punishment is thought to be reflected in self-critical comments and other forms of self-directed hostility. The therapy program is didactic, involves homework assignments, and is typically conducted in a group format. It attempts to remedy the self-monitoring, self-evaluation, self-attribution, and self-reinforcement deficits characteristic of depressed youth. An illustrative therapeutic program is presented in Table 4.6.

Evaluation

Rehm's self-control therapy, which involves reversing the problems in self-monitoring, self-evaluation, and self-reinforcement behaviors, has yielded mixed results in reducing and eliminating depression in adults (Lewinsohn & Hoberman, 1982). Self-control methods have been used with depressed children (Stark, Reynolds, & Kaslow, 1987) and adolescents (Reynolds & Coats, 1986).

The Reynolds and Coats study (1986) involved the direct treatment by a school psychologist of 30 moderately and severely depressed adolescents in a school setting. The subjects were randomly assigned to either a cognitive-behavioral intervention that combined elements of Beck's, Lewinsohn's, and Rehm's models; a relaxation approach a la Jacobsen; or a wait list control group. Each treatment consisted of ten 1-hour sessions spread over a 6-week interval. The scores on various self-report measures indicated meaningful gains for both treatment groups at the time of intervention and at a 4-week follow-up. The wait list control group did not change over the course of the experiment. These findings are encouraging in that both treatment groups went from depressed to nondepressed levels. Replication of these results using adolescents who are referred for their depression and subsequently diagnosed as clinically depressed using *DSM-III-R* criteria would be even more encouraging.

There is no question but that self-control strategies offer potential advantages over other techniques. Cole and Kazdin (1980) have delineated three pluses for self-management training: (1) It can interrupt or inhibit a sequence of thoughts or actions; (2) verbal self-instruction draws upon a natural developmental process whereby children use their verbal behavior to regulate thoughts and actions; (3) it provides general coping skills rather than situation-specific responses.

Self-control training is not without its limitations, however. First, we need further research in laboratory and natural settings to document that clinically depressed children are deficient in various self-control skills. A basic tenet in self-control and cognitive theory is that depressives attend to negative

Table 4.6
Self-Control Therapy

Session 1. Clients are taught that mood in general is related to one's behavior and to their accompanying self-statements. The clients are also made aware that they frequently overlook positive cognitions and activities that occur in their lives but instead focus on negative events. The homework assignment is to monitor daily positive and negative events and to make a daily mood rating.

Session 2. Depressed youth graph their mood and events for each day, noting the relationship between the two. They are asked to identify those behaviors that appear most related to mood. For homework, they must not only monitor their mood, but are encouraged to increase the positive events in their lives.

Session 3. Discriminating between the immediate and long-term effects of their behavior constitutes the focus of the third visit. Homework consists in continued self-monitoring plus the listing of a positive delayed effect—of at least one positive behavior each day.

Session 4. Attributional retraining now occupies the center of attention. Clients are helped to make more realistic self-statements about their successes and failures. In addition to monitoring positive events and moods, participants are asked to include a minimum of one positive self-statement about a failure.

Sessions 5 and 6. The goal is to teach realistic self-evaluation and goal setting. Participants are encouraged to establish subgoals as a series of small steps en route to their ultimate goal. The goals and subgoals must be operationally defined, positive, attainable, and under their control.

Sessions 7 and 8. These sessions stress the significance of overt and covert reinforcement. Reward menus are encouraged with the rewards ranging from small to large and consisting of activities, tangibles, or self-statements. In addition to continued self-monitoring, the homework consists in self-reinforcement contingent upon successful completion of a subgoal.

Sessions 9 and 10. The final sessions consist of review.

Note. From "Conceptualization, Assessment and Treatment of Depression in Children" by N. Kaslow and L. Rehm (1985). In P. Bornstein and A. Kazdin (Eds.), *Handbook of Clinical Behavior Therapy* (pp. 635–636). Homewood, IL: Dorsey.

information and thus receive a distorted view of the world. A competing alternative view is that nondepressed individuals are unduly optimistic and that the apparent pessimism of the depressive is just how they see the world (Williams, 1984). There is increasing evidence that both adult and school-aged depressives are accurate in their judgments about the external environment (Seligman & Peterson, 1986). At this time, the fundamental tenet that depressed people distort the world seems in doubt. Nondepressed adults on a variety of cognitive tasks (1) see themselves as having more control than they actually have; (2) believe that they are more socially skilled than judges rate them; (3) are less accurate in remembering the number of successes and failures; and (4) show an optimistic "lopsidedness" in attributions for success versus failure. Nondepressed children showed the same lopsided attributional style that nondepressed adults do (Seligman & Peterson, 1986). The depressed individual may need a buffer for reality in order to develop "delusions" of adequacy. It might be that cognitive distortions are not cognitive distortions at all, but the natural consequences or rational forecasts of a person's specific learning history (Gilbert, 1984).

Second, there is a need for standardized methodologies to evaluate systematically self-control deficiencies in depressed children particularly in the areas of self-monitoring or self-reinforcement (Kaslow & Rehm, 1983). Relatedly, scales assessing self-control skills must be developed and employed at various points throughout the treatment process in an effort to show that therapeutic gains made in the treatment program actually produce changes in self-control skills. Presently there is a conspicuous absence of such scales.

Third, we need carefully executed studies demonstrating that the reversal of specific self-control problems does indeed overcome depression in children. For example, it might well prove difficult for depressed children to monitor their own moods (Emery et al., 1983). Teaching depressed youngsters to identify their feelings along a continuum or having them respond to pictures reflecting different feeling states may render self-monitoring of mood a more concrete and less elusive task. It is also critical to show that children can be trained to alter their own evaluations vis-à-vis opposite frequent evaluations that are made by significant others (parents, teachers). We also need to know which depressed symptoms will be eliminated in self-control approaches. For instance, will somatic complaints be cleared up by use of these strategies?

Fourth, self-control models have not yet shown their superiority over methods relying on external controls in correcting a wide variety of problem behaviors in children (Ledwidge, 1978). A meta-analysis of self-statement modification with childhood disorders showed that the efficacy of this technique is less impressive than its popularity (Dush, Hirt, & Schroeder, 1983).

Fifth, the concept of self-control may have already outlived its usefulness (Coates & Thorensen, 1979). Instead of focusing on either/or models wherein self-control theory stresses the controlling functions of the person and operant theory stresses the controlling function of the environment, we need to move ahead with a reciprocal-influence model that better reflects the complexity of children's development. The reciprocal-influence model would not preclude the use of self-regulatory procedures but may, in fact, encourage them as one component of the model.

DRUG THERAPY

Depressed children often require a variety of interventions, and altering the internal physiology or biochemical systems appears to be one critical component of a total therapeutic regimen (Petti, 1983a,b,c). Indeed, the treatment approach for depressive children that, if not the most common, has received the most attention is the use of drugs (Pearce, 1981; Staton, Wilson, & Brumback, 1981), particularly by pediatricians. Given the established effectiveness of various antidepressant medications in adult affective disorder and that the clinical picture of major affective disorder in childhood and adolescence is highly similar to that of adult depression (Cantwell & Baker, 1991), it would seem reasonable to expect that antidepressants would be effective with younger people.

In contrast to the burgeoning field of adult psychopharmacology, there has been a relative paucity of well-controlled empirical studies evaluating the efficacy and safety of most psychotropic drugs in the treatment of child and adolescent psychopathology, with the exception of stimulants for attention-deficit hyperactivity disorder (Biederman, 1992). Fortunately, the effectiveness of psychopharmacological interventions has become a research priority in pediatric drug research in the 1990s (Keltner, 1991). In their efforts to discover whether the practice of treating depressed youth with antidepressants is well advised, researchers have four kinds of research studies available to them: promising clinical case reports, open studies, confirmation in controlled double-blind studies, and replication of controlled trials at various centers to deal with issues such as small sample size and diagnostic heterogeneity. Following this ideal path from case reports to replication at multisites allows for increased confidence in the generalizability of findings.

The discussion of psychopharmacological studies is organized around the medications used to treat depressive disorders in young people, namely, tricyclic antidepressants (TCA), monoamine oxidase inhibitors (MAOI), and lithium. See Table 4.7 for an overview of commonly used medications in the treatment of depression in children or adolescents.

Antidepressant Medications

Is the practice of treating children and adolescents with antidepressants well advised? Is it the treatment of choice? The first open trials generated considerable optimism that a new treatment was available for depressed children. For example, in a study involving children seen at an educational diagnostic center, Weinberg and colleagues (1973) reported moderate to marked improvement in 18 of 19 children receiving antidepressant drugs. However, even though the diagnostic criteria were reasonably explicit, this study lacked objective assessment of symptoms. Further treatment groups were neither blind nor systematically assigned, and no placebo group was included. *Open trials* of antidepressants with adolescents have also been conducted but with fewer reported successful outcomes. For instance, in one study of the outcomes of imipramine (IMI) with 35 adolescent inpatients who were relatively free of psychiatric comorbidity and characterized by endogenomorphic features believed responsive to tricyclic antidepressant response, only 30% of these adolescents showed a favorable response (Strober, Freeman, & Rigali, 1990). In general, open trials of antidepressants, especially the tricyclic antidepressants, appear to have been more effective in preadolescents than in adolescents. Favorable response rates, as judged from findings of open trials, are in the 50% to 100% range for preadolescents and in the 30% to 40% range in adolescents (Pliszka, 1991).

Controlled experiments of antidepressants have rarely, if ever, shown these drugs to be superior to placebos with children or adolescents (Gadow, 1992; Pliszka, 1991). In double-blind placebo-controlled trials of IMI, Hughes and colleagues (1990), for instance, examined outcomes among two groups of children ages 6 to 12 with depressive disorder. One group also had a conduct or oppositional disorder. The other group had depressive disorder alone or with a concomitant anxiety disorder. The placebo response rate among the comorbid conduct disorder group was 67%. Those with a major affective disorder showed a 57% response to IMI and only a 20% response rate to placebo. Thus, comorbidity might well be a significant factor in forecasting response to antidepressants. In summarizing the literature on antidepressant drugs in children and adolescents, Pliszka (1991) concludes that (a) the placebo response rate may be as high as 60% in both age groups, and (b) the data do not support the belief that antidepressants are clearly effective for either children or adolescents. Based on these findings, the practitioner might well wait through 4 weeks of nonpharmacological help (e.g.,

Table 4.7
Common Psychopharmacologic Medications Used with Depressed Children or Adolescents

Type (Trade name & Dosage*)	Indication	Therapeutic Effects	Side Effects	Other Considerations
Tricyclics: Imipramine (Tofranil®) 10–175 mg 75–225 mg	Unipolar in children Unipolar in adolescents	Improvement in vegetative symptoms at first, followed by improvement in mood some 3 or 4 weeks later.	Dry mouth, drowsiness (especially Elavil®), blurred vision, constipation, cardiac arrhythmias (EKG monitoring is essential and overdose in suicidal patients becomes a concern).	After offset of 1 month, discontinue gradually over 3 or more months (withdrawal symptoms mimic depression). Has been used to treat separation anxiety, hyperactivity, enuresis.
Amytriptyline (Elavil®) 45–110 mg	Unipolar in adolescents (little research with children)			
Lithium Carbonate (Lithonate) 450–1800 mg	Bipolar in adolescents and occasionally in multiple episodes of unipolar.	Improvement in symptoms in 4–10 days, with most of effect within first 2 weeks: "smooths" rather than eliminates	Nausea, drowsiness, thirst, frequent urination, hand tremors, possible cardiac or kidney problems.	Small dose added to tricyclic medication during withdrawal as long-term prophylaxis against recurrence. Has

Monoamine Oxidase Inhibitors 30–60 mg	Atypical depression in adolescents.	Gradual improvement over 1- to 3-week period.	Nausea, dizziness, fainting, sleep disturbance, and possible fatal reactions upon ingestion of certain cheese or yeast products.	Used primarily in intractable conditions refractory to other drugs.
Carbamazepine (Tegretol®) 30–60 mg	Bipolar in adolescents, especially rapid-cycling.	Relatively more rapid onset of improvement.	Nausea, drowsiness, weight loss, ataxia, in instances, and possible toxic reactions with lithium.	Primarily a seizure medication but has been used in lithium-resistant depression.
Fluoxetine Hydrochloride (Prozac®) 20–80 mg	Unipolar depression in adolescents.	Gradual improvement over 5–6 weeks (long-term effects have not been systematically studied).	Anxiety, nervousness, insomnia, weight loss, hypomania or mania, and seizures.	Prozac® has not been systematically studied for its potential for abuse, tolerance, or physical dependence.

*These are doses in what have generally been considered as optimum levels and, in most cases, are determined on a mg/kg ratio based on body weight. Dosage levels vary widely, so these ranges should be considered with caution.

Note. From "Depression in Children and Adolescents: Identification, Assessment, and Treatment" by J. Maag and S. Forness, 1991, *Focus on Exceptional Children 24*, p. 14. Reprinted with permission.

reassurance or psychotherapy) before recommending antidepressants for those young people whose depression was of *moderate* severity. For example, Geller and associates (1992) found that a third of their group improved during a 2-week placebo washout period. After waiting up to 4 weeks, antidepressant drugs may be prescribed, for there may be a small subset of depressed young people, as yet undetected through current research, who do respond favorably to those drugs.

Certain cautions should be noted regarding the use of antidepressants. First, the TCAs have a narrow therapeutic window. That is, the difference between a therapeutic dose and a lethal dose is small. Thus, strict adherence to the prescribed dose is critical and the drug must be kept out of the youngster's control (Keltner, 1991). If drug overdose is suspected, hospitalization is *required*. Second, the anticholinergic side effects (the drying up of body secretions) must be treated. For example, overheating, particularly in hot weather, must be guarded against because of decreased sweating.

Monoamine Oxidase Inhibitor (MAOI) Drugs

MAO is an enzyme distributed widely throughout the body that catalyzes the chemical turnover of the brain's neurotransmitters such as dopamine and serotonin. MAOI drugs inhibit this enzyme but are only weak inhibitors of presynaptic uptake of norepinephrine. The MAOI drugs have lacked the popularity of other antidepressants, in part because of dietary restrictions (e.g., cheese on pizza). Compared with the literature on tricyclic antidepressants, there are relatively few reports on the treatment of childhood depression with MAOI inhibitors.

In an open study of MAOI medication, Ryan and colleagues (1986) reported a 44% response rate among 23 adolescents. Based on clinical judgment, 17 were said to respond well. Unfortunately the report is not clear as to which adolescents took MAOI in combination with tricyclic medication and those who took it alone. In a double-blind, cross-over study, Frommer (1967) divided a heterogeneous group of "depressed" children into a phobic and mood disorder group (weeping, irritable, temper outbursts, and serious antisocial behavior). She reported significantly greater improvement while the children were receiving phenelzine or chlordiazepoxide than while taking phenobarbitone with a placebo. Unfortunately, there was no objective assessment of specific symptoms.

Lithium

Lithium carbonate is used primarily to treat bipolar disorder, especially the manic episodes. Although the extent to which lithium is used to treat bipolar disorder is unknown, its use is probably not as widespread as tricyclics simply because manic disorder is rare and/or difficult to diagnose among children and adolescents (Bowring & Kovacs, 1992). The absence of approval from the Food and Drug Administration for the use of lithium with children under the age of 12 might also limit its use in the treatment of manic episodes and nonresponsiveness to other antidepressant medications.

The issue of lithium's frequency of usage is separate from the issue of its effectiveness. In a follow-up study of 196 children and adolescents treated with lithium over a 10-year period 66% (39 of 59 subjects with manic-depressive disorder) responded favorably (DeLong & Andershof, 1987). Its effectiveness with unipolar major depressive disorder only was more limited as only 17% responded favorably. In general, reports of lithium's efficacy have relied largely on single-subject case description methods or open trial designs.

A recent study of 11 hospitalized children examined behavioral and cognitive improvements stemming from lithium treatment for a maximum of 8 weeks. Among the 7 youngsters studied with a double-blind crossover design, improvements were maintained on placebo. Only 3 of the 11 children improved sufficiently to permit discharge (Carlson, Rapport, Kelly, & Pataki, 1992).

Cautions regarding lithium's use stem from the paucity of well-controlled outcome studies and its potential harmful side effects (renal and endocrine effects, impairment in concentration, learning, and memory) (Jefferson, 1982). Lithium has a low therapeutic index. Thus, the child's blood level is to be checked daily. There is no pharmacologic antidote for lithium poisoning (Keltner, 1991). Whether lithium will prove as effective with children and adolescents as it has with adults remains for further research to ascertain.

Evaluation

Research on psychopharmacological intervention with depressed children has been methodologically flawed by (1) the absence of explicit diagnostic criteria, (2) lack of control groups, (3) failure to use a double-blind procedure, (4) failure to study possible age-related differences in drug response, (5) small sample size, (6) reliance on parent or self-report as criteria of progress, (7) failure to control for comorbidity, (8) variation in other treatments used in conjunction with antidepressant medication, and (9) differences in how treatment outcome is assessed. A probable placebo response rate of 60% among outpatient neurotic children (Eisenberg, Cytryn, & Molling, 1961) is also seen among depressed children (Pliszka, 1991; Weise,

O'Reilly, & Hersbacker, 1972) and highlights the need for controlled studies of drug effectiveness. Although many placebo responders later relapse, suggesting that this type of spontaneous improvement is short-lived (Gadow, 1992), anecdotal reports (Cytryn & McKnew, 1972) suggest that many cases unexpectedly show marked improvement and maintain their improvements over a 5-year follow-up period. Further, the responsiveness of dysphoria to antidepressant drugs is no indication of the presence of depression in children, for those drugs also reduce enuresis (Doleys, Schwartz, & Ciminero, 1981). Although effective treatment may validate a diagnosis in the medical fields, it is not a sound way to validate diagnoses of psychological problems. Furthermore, because childhood depression is usually reactive to external events, consideration must be given to family relationships and other environmental stress factors (Pearce, 1981). In future studies, specific attention should be given to such factors as the types of depression treated, how the diagnosis was arrived at, the compliance rates in taking the medication, the index of improvement, the intensity and duration of therapy, drug dosages, and long-term effects. It will be interesting to see if the use of antidepressant drugs with depressed children affects certain symptoms more than others. For example, will drugs help more with the vegetative symptoms (appetite, sleep disturbance, and somatic complaints) than with social functioning as is the case with adults (Cantwell, 1982)? What impact, if any, will they have on the child's academic learning and behavior in school? Despite the increasing interest of school personnel in the effects of medications on students, next to nothing is known about the impact of antidepressants on school performance (Maag & Forness, 1991). Finally, it will be helpful to know if the effects of antidepressant drugs add to any benefits accruing from psychotherapy.

Despite the limitations of current knowledge, the use of such drugs will most likely continue to be an important component in a total treatment program given their ease of administration and their purported ability to promote rapid alleviation of symptoms. Research in the next decade should provide an increased scientific basis for psychopharmacological treatment of depressed youth.

FAMILY THERAPY

The value of family therapy is illustrated in the case study (Emery et al., 1983) of a 16-year-old female who attempted suicide. The girl was adopted at age 9 after being abandoned by her biological mother as a toddler and being shuttled between a series of unhappy, sometimes physically and sexually abusive, foster homes. The adoptive mother tried to help the daughter resolve numerous scholastic, social, and personal difficulties but the mother's over-involvement seemed to reinforce the 16-year-old's sense of helplessness and worthlessness. Family treatment sought to disengage mother and daughter, to have the father alert the mother when she made excessive demands on their daughter, and to promote a stronger alliance between father and mother. Once the overt conflict in the home was at a more manageable level, the therapist focused more intently upon the daughter's dysfunctional cognitions. Experienced therapists recognize the need for family involvement to reduce scapegoating in the family or to restructure parental expectations. Without such interventions, children have difficulty securing approval, enhancing self-esteem, and achieving happiness.

There has been a dearth of research activity in the realm of family-based therapy for depressed youth. The application of adult models of depression to children might well partially explain this void. For the most part, adult models attribute unipolar, nonpsychotic depression to intrapsychic essentially cognitive disturbances and bipolar and endogenous depressions to biological and intrapsychic disturbances (Stark & Brookman, 1992). In brief, the use of adult models which provided a basis for treating children with depressive disorders had no family component. Gradually, the growing awareness that depression in young people is also an interpersonal phenomenon has led theorists, researchers, and clinicians to include the family context in explaining the etiology and course of the disorder as well as implementing corrective procedures.

There are at least two assumptions underlying family therapy. One is the belief that noxious family relationships cause affective problems in children. The other is the belief that the affective problems of any one member are determined and maintained by the problems of the relationships within the family. Hence, the mother, father, and children must be treated as a total unit.

Parental depression constitutes an environmental as well as a genetic risk factor for the children and the risk is for nondepressive as well as depressive disorders in the offspring (Quinton & Rutter, 1985). Research has addressed the likelihood that children with depressive parents will have children who are depressed. The findings indicate that the chances of any single child's being depressed are significantly increased if one or both parents are depressed. If one parent has a major depression or if there is a family history of a major depression, there would be about a 15% risk that any single child would develop depression. If both parents have had a major depression, the risk rises to 40% for any given child (Goodwin, 1982). Indeed, depressed mothers were rated, by a reviewer "blind" to specific maternal diagnosis, as showing the greatest conflict in their children's adjustment and as less satisfactory than within groups of schizophrenic mothers and their children (Cohler, Gallant, Grunebaum, & Kaufman, 1983). Children of depressed parents are not only at greater risk for major depression but also for anxiety disorders, other psychiatric disorders, and suicide attempts. Moreover, they were reported to have more learning disabilities and more need for special education services (Weissman et al., 1986). Having a depressed parent is, of course, not the only route to childhood depression. Nondepressed parents can also have depressed children.

What contributes to the development of a depressed youngster within the family context? To answer this question, various types of research methodology have been employed—clinical observations/inferences, retrospective studies, prospective studies, and family-systems guided research. From an etiological standpoint, there appear to be four major dynamics that contribute to the level of expressed depressive pathology in a family. In addition to a family history from both a genetic-biochemical and an emotional stand, there are such factors as previous handling of past traumatic events (e.g., family violence, parental divorce, parental mental illness), the quality of family boundaries and structures (e.g., limited differentiation between generations leading to limited development of autonomy, privacy, and outside relationships as family loyalty is all-consuming), and the family's ability to express and process emotions (e.g., denial of conflict stemming from difficulty in expressing and dealing with emotions) (Oster & Caro, 1990). Of course, depressive symptomatology can arise from a combination of family pressures and tensions with individual influences (e.g., social-skill weakness).

Oster and Caro (1990) have identified three outpatient strategies in working with families with depressed youth. The first of these strategies, which are not mutually exclusive, entails strengthening the parental role. The objective is to help the parents feel more comfortable with their role as parents in executing directions, limits, and support. Strengthening the parental role is achieved through a twofold approach: (1) empowering the parents (e.g., "Bill, I want to trust you but you've been taking advantage of us lately, so now you have to prove yourself again by getting in on time") and (2) positively affirming a future in which problems are solved. Concentrating on an adolescent's positive behaviors is one way in which the focus can be shifted from demoralization to hopefulness.

The second major strategy centers around restructuring the family hierarchy. Problems with the parental hierarchy are often brought on by a crisis or series of crises (such as death of a family member or parental loss of employment). At these times, the family may reorganize hoping to forestall the negative impact of the crises on the family. Illustratively, in the case of divorce, a parent may use the adolescent as a confidant in an effort to minimize the loss of the partner (e.g., a good listener) and to maintain some connectedness via the teenager with the estranged spouse (e.g., finding out about her ex's new girlfriend). By placing the youth in more of a caregiving role, his or her energy is depleted or deflected from accomplishment of typical adolescent developmental tasks. When intervening, the clinician must be respectful of the family's reorganization. By presenting the family's pattern of relating as an outgrowth of mutual caring, the practitioner's task of reorienting that caring in a more positive context is more readily accomplished.

The third major strategy involves helping families to share affectively. Because an adolescent's depression may be based on modeling the parent's mood disturbance, it is wise to explore the possibility that depression is pervasive rather than confined to one member. Also, because grief reactions may be delayed, it is important to take a full family history. By openly discussing the difficulty, the teenager no longer needs to be burdened by the adult's pain (e.g., sometime following a husband's death both the mother and her son are experiencing negative affect over the thought of his leaving home to go to college).

No one denies the significance of the home situation on the child's affective development. Yet, it is difficult to come to a general conclusion about the specificity of the "depressogenic environment" (Eisenburgh, 1983). Because those studies are correlational in nature, the causal links remain unclear. But we are not sure to what specifically the child is reacting in a family scene that is so chaotic that happiness is impossible for the child. Are the parents modeling depressive behavior? Are the parents reinforcing depressive behavior in their children? Are their expectations too high to result in an adequate sense of self-esteem in their offspring? Further research is also needed to see if the child's vulnerability is related to developmental level. We must also remember that even if both parents are depressed, the odds against any single child's being depressed are 60%. To date, no systematic studies have compared the outcomes of various types of family therapy with depressed youngsters. It is quite possible that the different therapeutic approaches might postulate different criteria to indicate the need for family intervention. Finally, it is important to study the means by which children of depressed mothers remain invulnerable to psychopathology rather than to focus only on those who are adversely affected.

MULTIMODAL THERAPY

Multimodal treatment addresses the various contributing factors to the development and maintenance of depression in children: home, school, community, intrapsychic, physiological, and cognitive (Petti, 1983a). A multimodal treatment package is said to be warranted because (a) this disorder has multiple roots and (b) depressed children often have problems in more than one area. For instance, consider the multiple etiology of childhood depression. Family factors affect the development, course, and intensity of the depression through such mechanisms as modeling of depressive, helpless behavior and through separations, psychological abandonment, rejection, and possible genetic vulnerability. Likewise, the child plays a major role in this process, with the outcome depending on such factors as developmental level, individual temperament, internal physiological changes, adaptation to chronic stress, and goals the child sets (Petti, 1983b). This approach would seem well suited to depressed children with multiple problems (e.g., depressed children who are also hyperactive or depressed children with learning disabilities). In brief, multimodal therapy involves several methods such as individual psychotherapy, academic remediation, and antidepressive drug therapy, depending on the results of a comprehensive assessment of the child's problem(s).

Case Studies in Multimodal Therapy

The first case involved a 10½-year-old African-American girl suffering from depression. The child's history was remarkable, indicating a premature birth, alcoholic parents, school failure, and possible child abuse. At the time of admission the child was living with a foster care family. The child was assessed using the Bellevue Index of Depression, a psychiatric interview, physical and lab exams, hospital ward behaviors, and the WISC-R.

The multimodal treatment involved a stepwise progression of interventions, some of which overlapped. Treatment began with individual psychotherapy, which focused on the understanding of feelings and improved self-image. The second intervention was a psychoeducational program aimed at the individualized treatment of cognitive deficits and inappropriate school behaviors. A creative dramatics group was used to provide an opportunity for peer interactions. In addition, family therapy was provided to the foster parents and her biological mother to help improve home environment. At the end of the fourth week, little improvement was seen as demonstrated by the Children's Behavior Inventory, Scale of School Age Depression, and observations. At this time imipramine administration was initiated. A marked improvement was noted through observations and the readministration of the above scales. The final phase of treatment provided for social skills training, which involved instruction in appropriate verbal and nonverbal behaviors through the use of modeling, behavioral rehearsal, and feedback. The specific skills attended to were eye contact, smiles, duration of speech in response to compliments, and deficits in appropriate requests for new behavior in response to unreasonable demands. All behaviors improved as compared to baseline data, and spontaneous use of new skills was observed in other settings. At the time of a 6-week follow-up, improvement was reported by the child, foster mother, and the school (Petti, Bornstrong, Delemater, & Conners, 1980).

Note. From "Evaluation and Multi-Modality Treatment of a Depressed Prepubertal Girl" by T. Petti, M. Bornstein, A. Delemater, and C. Conners (1980). *Journal of the American Academy of Child Psychiatry, 18,* p. 690.

IMPLICATIONS FOR PRACTICE

Which Target?

One of the first issues that the psychologist must resolve is defining what is meant by the condition of depression. One must decide whether it is a symptom, a syndrome, a disorder, or a disease that is to be treated. Some psychologists will focus on a given depressive symptom (e.g., looking sad), whereas others will view depression as a syndrome consisting of different behaviors that covary. Others will focus on behaviors to alter, and others will stress cognitions. Others might concentrate on a combination of behaviors and cognitions, but vary among themselves in their emphasis (e.g., RET encourages children to engage in behaviors to refute irrational beliefs). Still others view depression as a biological condition and prefer drug-based interventions. Confusion will most likely reign for the foreseeable future about the nature of this condition and as to which features are essential and which are secondary.

Which Psychological Techniques?

Once a decision has been made as to what it is that one hopes to treat, the clinician must decide what approach to use in treating the child's depression. Again there are no easy answers. The choice is dictated, in part, by the choice of target behaviors to be altered. For those who view dysphoria as capturing the essence of depression, behavioral methods that increase response-contingent reinforcement might well be the methods of choice. If the child does not engage in reinforcing activities because of lack of social skills, then social skills training is warranted. If social skills are present, but the depressed child is frightened, then desensitization techniques are in order.

When cognitions are perceived as the root of the problem, the psychologist can choose among the four cognitive approaches discussed earlier.

At present, there is little research to guide practicing psychologists in the selection of treatment. Clinical practice with depressed youth does indicate a need for modification of interventions with depressed youth. Prominent among such changes are the need for entertaining sessions, increased structure, concrete concepts, shortened sessions along with an increased number of sessions, a co-therapist, reinforcement of completed homework assignments, attributional retraining, increased social skills training, assertiveness training, and relaxation training (Kaslow, 1986). We will welcome the time when treatment approaches are grounded in research. Meanwhile, in evaluating therapeutic outcomes, attention should be devoted not only to therapeutic effectiveness and cost effectiveness, but also to the acceptability of the methods used to children, parents, and teachers and treatment integrity (the extent to which a given model was actually implemented). To date, the few available research studies have concentrated on the effectiveness issue (does it work?), but have largely ignored the other evaluative concerns. It is heartening to note that many professionals in this area of childhood depression are data-oriented persons who are inclined to evaluate the effectiveness of their intervention efforts. It is probably not unreasonable to assume that the majority of clinicians are using an eclectic approach to the psychological treatment of childhood depression with some blend of cognitive-behavioral training perhaps being the most common treatment model. Hopefully within the next decade an empirically supported selective eclecticism (as contrasted with "sloppy" eclecticism) will be available.

Meanwhile, in the absence of empirically based guidelines to aid in the choice of intervention strategies, psychologists will have to rely on a rational evaluation of treatment models by giving careful attention to what is known about cognitive development of children. We have only begun to scratch the surface in understanding the child's conception of the world, but consideration of the child's stage of cognitive development can help to avoid therapeutic pitfalls and to better appreciate limitations of therapeutic interventions. A recent meta-analysis indicates that the cognitive developmental level of dysfunctional children, rather than age per se, is related to treatment outcomes of cognitive-behavior modification (Durlak, Fuhrman, & Lampman, 1991). The treatment effect size for children in the cognitive stage of formal operations (ages 11–13) was almost twice the magnitude of the effect obtained for children in less advanced cognitive stages (ages 5 to 7 or ages 8 to 11). Although this meta-analysis did not single out depressed children for study, cognitive-behavioral training was equally effective for all types and severities of child problems regardless of the components that comprised the intervention (Durlak et al., 1991). Thus, cognitive-behavioral training might be best suited for children who have reached the age of formal operations. In brief, practitioners must not only be conversant with a variety of therapeutic approaches but they need a sound foundation in child development, particularly in the area of social cognition.

Can Drugs Help?

Although psychologists will be inclined more toward behavioral and/or cognitive approaches than toward psychopharmacologic studies in the treatment of childhood depression, they should recognize the potential value of chemical manipulations. Antidepressant drugs may have more immediate response than nondrug therapies with children (Elkins & Rapoport, 1983). The rapid response to drugs may prevent a prolonged period of poor school performance that could adversely affect expectations and attitudes for an extended period of time (Trad, 1987). Moreover, antidepressant drugs are warranted in cases where suicidal ideation accompanies the depression. Parental guilt may also be reduced when the focus of treatment is shifted from their behavior to their child's organic condition (Trad, 1987). Drug therapies never constitute a total treatment program, but their value should not be overlooked as one component in a treatment package.

It is clear that much remains to be learned about the treatment of depressed children and adolescents. Yet, it is equally clear that psychologists will be more involved than ever before in the treatment of depressed youngsters. Whether it is more effective and/or efficient for psychologists to provide direct treatment or indirect treatment via consultation to parents and teachers of depressed students remains to be seen.

Can Schools Help?

What evidence is there that the treatment of childhood and adolescent depression can be conducted successfully within a school setting? Preliminary evidence indicates that direct treatment of childhood and adolescent depression can be implemented successfully in a school setting (Reynolds & Coats, 1986; Stark et al., 1987).

A different school-based approach offered school psychological services through teacher-mediated intervention at the elementary school level. This consultation process involved three phases: assessment, intervention, and follow-up (Butler & Miezitis, 1980). In the assessment phase, the consultant interviews the teacher about the depressed child. The interview is then followed by classroom observations of the child's functioning in various academic and social situations (large group and small group lessons, individual seatwork activity, recess, and gym). As the consultant and teacher reach agreement about the child's behavior, both formulate their objectives and negotiate a plan of action. Of the utmost importance is that the teacher feels competent to implement the strategies and the behavioral changes anticipated. The teacher is free to call upon the consultant to provide additional information, resources, and support. In the follow-up phase, the consultant remains in contact with the teacher and provides feedback regarding the child's behavior effects on other students in the class and on the teacher's classroom styles. Research findings indicate that this consultation approach is helpful in modifying the depressive behaviors of elementary school children (Butler & Miezitis, 1981). The investigators of this project have also developed a handbook for elementary school teachers and consultants detailing practical ways to cope with depressed children in the classroom (Butler & Miezitis, 1980). Table 4.8 illustrates the use of cognitive strategies to deal with such depressive behaviors as low self-esteem, withdrawal, self-deprecating remarks, helplessness/hopelessness, and fatigue. The question whether the consultation approach as implemented in this model is more cost effective than traditional, direct intervention approaches with depressed students is not answered by their research, but their work does indicate the feasibility of treating depressed children through a consultation model in public school settings.

SUMMARY

Whereas there has been a recent surge in research on assessment of depression in young people, there are only a handful of studies on psychological interventions with depressed youth. By and large, adult-oriented techniques have been adapted for use with depressed children and adolescents. Although the amount of research with depressed youth has been scant in comparison to that with depressed adults, preliminary findings have been supportive of cognitive-behavioral approaches but not supportive of antidepressant medications. Given the absence of a broad research base, and prompted perhaps by our own biases, practitioners have turned to a number of treatment models (psychoanalytic, behavioral, cognitive, familial, psychopharmacological, and multimodal). The choice of treatment approaches is dictated, in part, by the objective of therapy. Some therapists, for instance, prefer to modify behavior whereas others attempt to change the individual's cognitions. The more biologically oriented therapists often seek to change the youngster's

Table 4.8
Strategies for Dealing with Depressive Behaviors

Low self-esteem
   If the depressed child is reasonably competent, arrange for him or her to be a peer tutor for a child in a lower grade.

Withdrawn, uncommunicative behavior
   Assign a special task or responsibility to the depressed youngster and a peer of the same sex as "partners," explaining they are to complete the assignment cooperatively.

Self-deprecating remarks
   Discuss personality differences with the class, noting that differences make us interesting. Assign a composition in which each child describes his or her best characteristics and those he or she would like to change. Volunteers can read their compositions, or unsigned papers can be passed around the class. Realizing that other students perceive weaknesses and faults in themselves is invaluable to the depressed child.

Helpless/hopeless behavior
   Have the depressed child generate as many potential solutions to a stressful situation as possible. They can ask others to help. Then arrange the potential solutions hierarchically, with the most probable solution at the top. Next, have the child try the solutions. Point out that some problem situations can't be changed but the "solution" will be how the individual can best live with the stressor.

Note.   From *Releasing Children from Depression* (pp. 12–16) by L. Butler and S. Miezitis, 1980, Toronto: Ontario Institute for the Study of Education.

biochemistry. Following the choice of *what* to treat, the practitioner must decide on which methods to use. Behaviorists will commonly use response-contingent reinforcement. Others will seek to develop social skills. Desensitization and/or modeling techniques might be used in instances where the depressed youngster has the necessary social skills but does not use them. When cognitions are seen as causative, a choice can be made among Beck's cognitive approach, Seligman's attributional retraining approach, Ellis' rational-emotive therapy, or Rehm's self-management techniques. Or one might choose to combine various approaches as in multimodal therapy. According to research, school personnel can also play an effective role in direct and indirect interventions with moderately depressed youth.

   Overall, a number of controlled group outcome studies suggest that cognitive-behavioral techniques originally designed for use with adults can be adapted successfully for use with children and adolescents. Despite generally favorable outcomes, one third to one half of adolescents treated have not recovered from their initial episode by the end of treatment. Attempts to identify why some adolescents do better than others, although somewhat frustrating, have indicated that we obtain very different results when continuous (self-report measures of depression) and dichotomous (diagnostic classification) approaches to defining recovery are used (Clarke et al., 1992b).

REFERENCES

Abraham, K. (1960). Notes on the psychoanalytic investigation and treatment of manic-depressive insanity and allied conditions. In *Selected papers in psychoanalysis*. New York: Basic Books.

Abraham, K. (1968). Notes on the psychoanalytic investigation and treatment of manic-depressive insanity and allied conditions. In W. Gaylin (Ed.), *The meaning of despair* (pp. 26–49) New York: Science House.

Abramson, L., Seligman, M., & Teasdale, J. (1978). Learned helplessness in humans: Critique and reformulation. *Journal of Abnormal Psychology, 87*, 49–74.

Bandura, A. (1977). *Social learning theory*. Englewood Cliffs, NJ: Prentice-Hall.

Beck, A. (1976). *Cognitive therapy and emotional disorders*. New York: International Universities Press.

Beck, A., Rush, A., Shaw, B., & Emery, G. (1979). *Cognitive therapy of depression*. New York: Guilford Press.

Bellack, A. S., & Hersen M. (Eds.), (1979). *Research and practice in social skills training*. New York: Plenum Press.

Bernard, M., & Joyce, M. (1984). *Rational-emotive therapy with children*. New York: Wiley.

Bibring, E. (1965). The mechanism of depression. In P. Greenacre (Ed.), *Affective disorders* (pp. 13–48). New York: International Universities Press.

Biederman, J. (1992). New developments in pediatric psychopharmacology. *Journal of the American Academy of Child and Adolescent Psychiatry, 31*, 14–15.

Bowlby, J. (1960). Grief and mourning in infancy and early childhood. *Psychoanalytic Study of the Child, 15*, 9–52.

Bowring, M., & Kovacs, M. (1992). Difficulties in diagnosing manic disorders among children and adolescents. *Journal of the American Academy of Child and Adolescent Psychiatry, 31*, 611–614.

Brewin, C. R. (1985). Depression and causal attributions: What is their relation? *Psychological Bulletin, 98*, 297–309.

Brewin, C. R. (1988). *Cognitive foundations of clinical psychology*. Hillsdale, NJ: Lawrence Erlbaum.

Brown, G. W., Harris, T. O., & Bifulco, A. (1986). Long-term effects of early loss of parent. In M. Rutter, C. E. Izard, & P. B. Read (Eds.), *Depression in young people: Developmental and clinical perspectives* (pp. 251–296). New York: Guilford Press.

Butler, L., & Miezitis, S. (1980). *Releasing children from depression.* Toronto: Ontario Institute for the Study of Education.

Butler, L., Miezitis, S., Friedman, R., & Cole, E. (1980). The effect of two school-based intervention programs on depressive symptoms in pre-adolescents. *American Educational Research Journal, 17,* 111–119.

Calpin, J., & Cincirpini, P. (1978, May). *A multiple baseline analysis of social skills training in children.* Paper presented at Midwestern Association for Behavioral Analysis, Chicago.

Calpin, J., & Kornblith, S. (1978, November). *Training of aggressive children in conflict resolution skills.* Paper presented at Midwestern Association for Behavioral Analysis, Chicago.

Cantwell, D. (1982). Childhood depression: A review of current research. In B. Lahey, & A. Kazdin (Eds.), *Advances in clinical child psychology* (Vol. 5, pp. 39–93). New York: Plenum.

Cantwell, D., & Baker, L. (1991). Manifestations of depressive affect in adolescence. *Journal of Youth and Adolescence, 20,* 121–133.

Carey, M., & Kelley, M. *Adolescent Activities Checklist.* Unpublished manuscript.

Carey, M., Kelley, M., Buss, R., & Scott, W. (1986). Relationship of activity to depression in adolescents: Development of the Adolescent Activities Checklist. *Journal of Consulting and Clinical Psychology, 54,* 320–322.

Carlson, G., Rapport, M., Kelly, K., & Pataki, C. (1992). Lithium in hospitalized children at 4 and 8 weeks: Mood, behavior and cognitive effects. *Journal of Child Psychology and Psychiatry and Allied Disciplines, 33,* 411–425.

Cautela, J. (1977). Children's Reinforcement Survey Schedule (CRSS). In J. Cautela (Ed.), *Behavior analysis forms for clinical intervention* (pp. 53–62). Champaign, IL: Research Press.

Clarizio, H. (1984). Childhood depression: Diagnostic considerations. *Psychology in the Schools, 21,* 181–197.

Clarizio, H. (1990). Assessing severity of behavior disorders: Empirically based criteria. *Psychology in the Schools, 27,* 5–14.

Clarizio, H., & McCoy, G. (1983). *Behavior disorders in children.* New York: Harper-Collins.

Clarke, G., Hops, H., Lewinsohn, P., Andrews, J., Seeley, J., & Williams, J. (1992). Cognitive-behavioral group treatment of adolescent depression: Prediction of outcome. *Behavior Therapy, 23,* 341–359.

Clarke, G., Lewinsohn, P., & Hops, H. (1990a). *Leader's manual for adolescent groups: Adolescent coping with depression course.* Eugene, OR: Castalia.

Clarke, G., Lewinsohn, P., & Hops, H. (1990b). *Student workbook: Adolescent groups: Adolescent coping with depression course.* Eugene, OR: Castalia.

Coates, T., & Thorensen, C. (1979). Behavioral self-control and educational practice or do we really need self-control? In D. Berliner (Ed.), *Review of research in education* (Vol. 7, pp. 3–45). New York: AERA.

Cohen, D. (1980). Constructive and reconstructive activities in the analysis of a depressed child. In A. Solnit, R. Eissler, A. Freud, M. Kris, & P. Neubauer

(Eds.), *The psychoanalytic study of the child* (Vol. 35, pp. 237–266), New Haven: Yale University Press.

Cohler, B., Gallant, D., Grunebaum, H., & Kaufman, C. (1983). Schizophrenic, depressed, and well mothers. In H. Morrison (Ed.), *Children of depressed parents: Risk identification and intervention* (pp. 65–98). New York: Grune & Stratton.

Cole, P., & Kazdin, A. (1980). Critical issues in self-instruction training with children. *Child Behavior Therapy, 2,* 1–21.

Collingwood, T. R., & Willett, L. (1971). The effects of physical training upon self-concept and body attitudes. *Journal of Clinical Psychology, 27,* 411–412.

Conger, J., & Keane, S. (1981). Social skills training. *Psychological Bulletin, 90,* 478–495.

Copeland, A. (1981). The relevance of subject variables in cognitive self-instructional programs for impulsive children. *Behevior Therapy, 12,* 520–529.

Cordes, C. (1984). The triumph and tragedy of longitudinal research. *APA Monitor, 15,* 318.

Costello, G. (1972). Depression: Loss of reinforcers or loss of reinforcer effectiveness. *Behavior Therapy, 3,* 240–247.

Costello, G. (1981). Childhood depression. In J. Mash & L. Terdal (Eds.), *Behavioral assessment of childhood disorders* (pp. 305–346). New York: Guilford Press.

Coyne, J. C., & Gotlib, I. H. (1983). The role of cognition in depression: A critical appraisal. *Psychological Bulletin, 94,* 472–505.

Craighead, W. E., Smucker, M. R., & Duchnowski, A. (1981). *Childhood and adolescent depression and attributional style.* Paper presented at the meeting of the American Psychological Association, Los Angeles.

Crook, T., & Eliot, J. (1980). Parental death during childhood and adult depression: A critical review of the literature. *Psychological Bulletin, 87,* 252–259.

Crook, T., Raskin, A., & Eliot, J. (1981). Parent-child relationships and adult depression. *Child Development, 52,* 950–957.

Cytryn, L., & McKnew, D., Jr. (1972). Proposed classification of childhood depression. *American Journal of Psychiatry, 129,* 149–155.

DeLong, G., & Andershof, A. (1987). Long-term experience with lithium treatment in children: Correlation with clinical diagnosis. *Journal of the American Academy of Child and Adolescent Psychiatry, 26,* 389–394.

DiGiuseppe R., & Bernard, M. (1983). Principles of assessment and methods of treatment with children, In A. Ellis & M. Bernard (Eds.), *Rational-emotive approaches to the problems of childhood* (pp. 45–88). New York: Plenum Press.

DiGiuseppe, R., Miller, N., & Trexler, L. (1977). A review of rational-emotive psychotherapy outcome studies. *Counseling Psychologist, 7,* 64–72.

Doleys, D., Schwartz, M., & Ciminero, A. (1981). Elimination problems: Enuresis and encopresis. In E. Mash & L. Terdal (Eds.), *Behavioral assessment of childhood disorders* (pp. 679–710). New York: Guilford Press.

Durlak, J., Fuhrman, T., & Lampman, C. (1991). Effectiveness of cognitive-behavior therapy for maladapting children: A meta-analysis. *Psychological Bulletin, 110,* 204–214.

Dush, D., Hirt, M., & Schroeder, H. (1983). A meta-analysis of the effectiveness of self-statement modification with childhood disorders. *Psychological Bulletin, 94,* 408–422.

Dweck, C. S. (1975). The role of expectations and attributions in the alleviation of learned helplessness. *Journal of Personality and Social Psychology, 31,* 674–685.

Dweck, C. S. (1977). Learned helplessness: A developmental approach. In J. Schultervrandt & A. Raskin (Eds.), *Depression in childhood* (pp. 127–130). New York: Raven Press.

Eisenberg, L., Cytryn, L., & Molling, P. (1961). The effectiveness of psychotherapy alone and in conjunction with perphenazine or placebo in the treatment of neurotic and hyperkinetic children. *American Journal of Psychiatry, 17,* 1088–1093.

Eisenbruch, M. (1983). Affective disorders in parents: Impact upon children. In D. Cantwell & G. Carlson (Eds.), *Affective disorders in childhood and adolescence* (pp. 279–334). Jamaica, NY: Spectrum.

Elkins, R., & Rapoport, J. (1983). Psychopharmacology of adult and childhood depression. In D. Cantwell & G. Carlson (Eds.), *Affective disorders in childhood and adolescence* (pp. 363–374). New York: Spectrum.

Ellis, A., & Bernard, M. (1983). *Rational-emotive approaches to the problems of childhood.* New York: Plenum Press.

Emery, S., Bedrosian, R., & Garber, J. (1983). Cognitive therapy with depressed children and adolescents. In D. Cantwell & G. Carlson (Eds.), *Affective disorders in childhood and adolescence: An update* (pp. 445–472). New York: Spectrum.

Ferster, C. (1966). Animal behavior and mental illness. *Psychological Record, 16,* 345–356.

Fine, S., Forth, A., Gilbert, M., & Haley, G. (1991). Group therapy for adolescent depressive disorder: A comparison of social skills and therapeutic support. *Journal of the American Academy of Child and Adolescent Psychiatry, 30,* 79–85.

Frame, D., Matson, J., Sonis, W., Fialkor, M., & Kazdin, A. (1982). Behavioral treatment of depression in a prepubertal child. *Journal of Behavior Therapy and Experimental Psychiatry, 13,* 239.

Frommer, E. (1967). Treatment of childhood depression with antidepressant drugs. *British Medical Journal, 1,* 729–732.

Gadow, K. (1992). Pediatric psychopharmacology: A recent review. *Journal of Child Psychology and Psychiatry and Allied Disciplines, 33,* 153–195.

Garber, J. (1982). *The Children's Event Schedule.* Unpublished manuscript. University of Minnesota.

Garmezy, N. (1983). Stressors of childhood. In N. Garmezy & M. Rutter (Eds.), *Stress, coping, and development in children* (pp. 43–84). New York: McGraw-Hill.

Geller, B., Cooper, T., Graham, D., Fetner, H., Marsteller, F., & Wells, J. (1992). Pharmacokinetically designed double-blind placebo-controlled study of nortriptyline in a 6-to-12-year-old with major depressive disorder. *Journal of the American Academy of Child and Adolescent Psychiatry, 31,* 34–44.

Gilbert, P. (1984). *Depression: From psychology to brain state.* Hillsdale, NJ: Lawrence Erlbaum.

Gilpin, D., & Anthony, J. (1976). *Three clinical faces of childhood.* New York: Spectrum.

Goodwin, F. (1982). *Depression and manic-depressive illness.* Bethesda, MD: National Institutes of Health.

Grieger, R., & Boyd, J. (1989). Rational-emotive approaches. In D. Brown & H. Prout (Eds.), *Counseling and psychotherapy with children and adolescents* (pp. 301–362). Brandon, VT: Clinical Psychology Publishing Company.

Griest, J., Klein, M., Eischens, R., & Farris, J. (1978). Antidepressant running. *Behavioral Medicine, 5,* 23–27.

Griest, J., Klein, M., Eichens, R., Farris, J., Gurman, A., & Morgan, W. (1979). Running as a treatment for depression. *Comprehensive Psychiatry, 20,* 41–54.

Grinker, R., Miller, J., Sabshin, M., Nunn, R., & Nunnally, J. (1961). *The phenomena of depressions.* New York: Paul B. Hoeber.

Horney, K. (1950). *Neurosis and human growth.* New York: Norton.

Hughes, C., Preskorn, S., Weller, E., Weller, R., Hassanein, R., & Tucker, S. (1990). The effect of concomitant disorders in childhood depression on predicting treatment response. *Psychopharmacology Bulletin, 26,* 235–238.

Jacobson, E. (1971). *Depression-comparative studies of normal neurotic, and psychotic conditions.* New York: International Universities Press.

Jefferson, J. (1982). The use of lithium in childhood and adolescence: An overview. *Journal of Clinical Psychiatry, 43*(5), 174–177.

Kahn, J., Kehle, T., Jenson, W., & Clark, E. (1990). Comparison of cognitive-behavioral relaxation, and self-modeling interventions for depression among middle-school students. *School Psychology Review, 19,* 196–211.

Kanfer, F. H. (1971). The maintenance of behavior by self-generated stimuli and reinforcement. In A. Jacobs & L. Sachs (Eds.), *The psychology of private events: Perspectives on covert response systems* (pp. 39–59). New York: Academic Presss.

Kaslow, N. (1986, August). *Symposium on childhood depression.* Presented at the annual meeting of the American Psychological Association, New York.

Kaslow, N., & Rehm, L. (1983). Conceptualization, assessment, and treatment of depression in children. In P. Bornstein & A. Kazdin (Eds.), *Handbook of clinical behavior therapy* (pp. 599–657). Homewood, IL: Dorsey.

Kaslow, N., & Rehm, L. (1991). Childhood depression. In R. Morris & T. Kratochwill (Eds.), *The practice of child therapy* (pp. 43–75). New York: Pergamon.

Kaslow, N., Stark, K., Printz, B., Livingston, R., & Tsai, S. (1992). Cognitive Triad Inventory for Children: Development and relation to depression and anxiety. *Journal of Clinical Child Psychology, 21,* 339–347.

Kazdin, A. E., French, N. H., Unis, A. S., Esveldt-Dawson, K., & Sherick, R. B. (1983). Hopelessness, depression and suicidal intent among psychiatrically disturbed inpatient children. *Journal of Consulting and Clinical Psychology, 51,* 504–510.

Keltner, N. (1991). Psychopharmacology. In P. Clunn (Ed.), *Child psychiatric nursing* (pp. 380–395). St. Louis: Mosby.

Kovacs, M., & Beck, A. T. (1977). An empirical-clinical approach toward a definition of childhood depression. In J. Schulterbrant & A. Raskin (Eds.), *Depression in childhood: Diagnosis, treatment, and conceptual models* (pp. 1–25). New York: Raven Press.

Ledwidge, B. (1978). Cognitive behavior modification: A step in the wrong direction? *Psychological Bulletin, 85,* 3653–375.

Lewinsohn, P., Clarke, G., Hops, H., & Andrews, J. (1990). Cognitive-behavioral treatment for depressed adolescents. *Behavior Therapy, 21,* 385–401.

Lewinsohn, P., & Hoberman, H. (1982). Depression. In A. Bellack, M. Hersen, & A. Kazdin (Eds.), *International handbook of behavior modification and therapy* (pp. 397–431). New York: Plenum.

Lewinsohn, P., Larson, D., & Munoz, R. (1978, November). *The measurement of expectancies and other cognitions in depressed individuals.* Paper presented at the Association for Advancement of Behavior Therapy, Chicago.

Lewinsohn, P., & Shaw, D. (1969). Feedback about interpersonal behavior as an agent of behavior change: A case study in the treatment of depression. *Psychotherapy and Psychosomatics, 17,* 82–88.

Maag, J., & Forness, S. (1991). Depression in children and adolescents: Identification, assessment and treatment. *Focus on Exceptional Children, 24,* 1–19.

Matson, J. (1982). The treatment of behavioral characteristics of depression in the mentally retarded. *Behavior Therapy, 13,* 209.

Matson, J., Esveldt-Dawson, K., Andrasik, M., Allendick, T., Petti, T., & Hersen, M. (1980). Observation and generalization effects of social skills training with emotionally distrubed children. *Behavior Therapy, 11,* 522–531.

McGowan, R., Jarman, B., & Pederson, D. (1974). Effects of a competitive endurance training program on self-concept and peer approval. *Journal of Psychology, 86,* 57–60.

Meichenbaum, D., & Burland, S. (1979). Cognitive behavior modification with children. *School Psychology Digest, VIII,* 425–433.

Niemark, E. (1975). Intellectual development during adolescence. In F. Horowitz (Ed.), *Review of child development research* (Vol. 4, pp. 541–594). Chicago: University of Chicago Press.

Novaco, R. (1979). The cognitive regulation of anger and stress. In P. Kendall & S. Hollon (Eds.), *Cognitive-behavioral interventions: Theory, research, and procedures* (pp. 241–286). New York: Academic Press.

Oster, G., & Caro, J. (1990). *Understanding and treating depressed adolescents and their families.* New York: Wiley.

Pearce, J. B. (1981). Drug treatment of depression in children. *Acta Paedopsychiatrica, 46*(5–6), 317–328.

Perris, C. Holmgren, S., Von Knorring, L., & Perris, H. (1986). Parental loss by death in the early childhood of depressed patients and healthy siblings. *British Journal of Psychiatry, 148,* 165–169.

Petersen, A., & Ebata, A. (1984). *Psychopathology in adolescence: Does development play a role?* Invited address presented at the annual meeting of the American Psychological Association, Toronto.

Peterson, C., & Seligman, M. E. (1984). Causal explanations as a risk factor for depression: Theory and evidence. *Psychological Review, 91,* 347–374.

Petti, T. A. (1983a). Future trends in the study and treatment of depression in young children. *Journal of Children in Contemporary Society, 2,* 87–95.

Petti, T. A. (1983b). Behavioral approaches in the treatment of depressed children. In D. Cantwell & G. Carlson (Eds.), *Affective disorders in childhood and adolescence: An update* (pp. 417–443). New York: Spectrum.

Petti, T. A. (1983c). Imipramine in the treatment of depressed children. In D. Cantwell & G. Carlson (Eds.), *Affective disorders in childhood and adolescence: An update* (pp. 375–415). New York: Spectrum.

Petti, T., Bornstein, M., Delemater, A., & Conners, C. (1980). Evaluation and multimodality treatment of a depressed pre-pubertal girl. *Journal of the American Academy of Child Psychiatry, 18,* 690.

Petti, T. A., & Wells, K. (1980). Crisis treatment of a preadolescent who accidently killed his twin. *American Journal of Psychotherapy, 34,* 434.

Pliszka, S. (1991). Antidepressants in the treatment of child and adolescent psychopathology. *Journal of Clinical Child Psychology, 20,* 313–320.

Quinton, D., & Rutter, M., (1985). Family pathology and child psychiatric disorder: A four-year prospective study. In A. Nicol (Ed.), *Longitudinal studies in child psychology and psychiatry: Practical lessons from research experience* (pp. 91–134). Chichester: Wiley.

Rehm, L. (1977). A self-control model of depression. *Behavior Therapy, 8,* 787–804.

Rehm, L., & Carter, A. (1990). Cognitive components of depression. In M. Lewis & S. Miller (Eds.), *Handbook of developmental psychopathology* (pp. 341–351). New York: Plenum.

Reynolds, W., & Coats, K. (1986). A comparison of cognitive-behavioral and relaxation therapies for depression with adolescents. *Journal of Consulting and Clinical Psychology, 54,* 653–660.

Rie, H. E. (1966). Depression in childhood: A survey of some pertinent contributions. *Journal of the American Academy of Child Psychiatry, 5,* 653–685.

Rizley, R. (1978). Depression and distortion in the attribution of causality. *Journal of Abnormal Psychology, 87,* 32–48.

Rose, D., & Abramson, L. (1992). Developmental predictors of depressive cognitive style: Research and theory. In D. Cicchetti & S. Toth (Eds.), *Developmental perspectives on depression* (pp. 323–349). Rochester, NY: University of Rochester Press.

Ryan, N., Puig-Antich, J., Cooper, T., Rabinovich, A., Ambrosini, P., Davies, M., King, J., Torres, D., & Fried, J. (1986). Imipramine in adolescent major depression: Plasma level and clinical response. *Acta Psychiatrica Scandinavia, 73,* 275–288.

Seligman, M. E. P. (1975). *Helplessness: On depression, development and death.* San Francisco: Freeman.

Seligman, M. E. P., & Peterson, C. (1986). A learned helplessness perspective on childhood depression. In M. Rutter, C. Izard, & P. Read (Eds.), *Depression in young people: Developmental and clinical perspectives* (pp. 223–250). New York: Guilford.

Seligman, M. E. P., Peterson, C., Kaslow, N. J., Tannenbaum, R. L., Alloy, L. B., & Abramson, L. Y. (1984). Attributional style and depressive symptoms among children. *Journal of Abnormal Psychology, 93,* 235–238.

Skinner, B. F. (1953). *Science and human behavior.* New York: Free Press.

Spitz, R., & Wolf, K. (1946). Anaclitic depression: An inquiry into the genesis of psychiatric conditions in early childhood. *Psychoanalytic Study of the Child, 2,* 313–342.

Spivack, G., Platt, J., & Shure, M. (1976). *The problem-solving approach to adjustment.* San Francisco: Jossey-Bass.

Spivack, G., & Shure, M. (1974). *Social adjustment of young children: A cognitive approach to solving real-life problems.* San Francisco: Jossey-Bass.

Stark, K., & Brookman, C. (1992). Family-school intervention: A family system perspective. In M. Fine & C. Carlson (Eds.), *The handbook of family-school intervention: A systems perspective.* (288–301). Boston: Allyn & Bacon.

Stark, K., Brookman, C., & Frazier, R. (1990). A comprehensive school-based program for depressed children. *School Psychology Quarterly, 5,* 111–140.

Stark, K., Reynolds, W., & Kaslow, N. (1987). A comparison of the relative efficacy of self-control therapy and a behavioral problem-solving therapy for depression in children. *Journal of Abnormal Child Psychology, 15,* 91–113.

Staton, R. D., Wilson, H., & Brumbach, R. A. (1981). Cognitive improvement associated with tricyclic antidepressant treatment of childhood major depressive illness. *Perceptual and Motor Skills, 53,* 219–234.

Strober, M., Freeman, R., & Rigali, J. (1990). The pharmacotherapy of depressive illness in adolescence: An open label trial of imipramine. *Psychopharmacology Bulletin, 26,* 80–83.

Teri, L. (1982). Depression in adolescence: Its relationship to assertion and various aspects of self-image. *Journal of Clinical Child Psychology, 11,* 101–106.

Toolan, J. M. (1978). Therapy of depressed and suicidal children. *American Journal of Psychotherapy, 32,* 243.

Trad, P. (1987). *Infant and childhood depression: Developmental factors.* New York: Wiley.

Trotter, R. (1987, February). Stop blaming yourself. *Psychology Today, 21,* pp. 31–39.

Wadeson, H. (1980). *Art psychotherapy.* New York: John Wiley and Sons.

Waters, V. (1982). Therapies for children: Rational-emotive therapy. In C. Reynolds & T. Gutkin (Eds.), *Handbook of school psychology* (pp. 578–579). New York: Wiley.

Weinberg, W., Rutman, J., Sullivan, L., Penick, E., & Dietz, S. (1973). Depression in children referred to an educational diagnostic center: Diagnosis and treatment. *Pediatrics, 83,* 1065–1072.

Weiner, B., Graham, S., & Chandler, C. (1982). Pity, anger and guilt. An attributional analysis. *Personality and Social Psychology Bulletin, 8,* 226–232.

Weise, C., O'Reilly, P., & Hersbacker, P. (1972). Perphenazine-amitriptyline in neurotic underachieving students: A controlled study. *Disorders of the Nervous System, 5,* 318–325.

Weissman, M., John, K., Merikangas, K., Prusoff, B., Wickramaratne, P., Gammon, D., Angold, A., & Warner, V. (1986). Depressed parents and their children. *American Journal of Diseases of Children, 140,* 801–805.

Wilkes, T. C., & Rush, J. (1988). Adaptations of cognitive therapy for depressed adolescents. *Journal of the American Academy of Child and Adolescent Psychiatry, 27,* 381–386.

Williams, J. M. (1984). *The psychological treatment of depression.* New York: Basic Books.

5 SUICIDE IN SCHOOL-AGED YOUTH

Danny, a 13-year-old, killed himself to help solve the financial problems confronting his family. Before his death, he told his mother, "If there was one less mouth to feed, things would be better." Prior to his death, Danny collected cans for a penny apiece to help buy food for his sister and two brothers. His death was caused by an overdose of analgesics.

Craig was a happy-go-lucky 17-year-old and a top-notch student. He was described by school authorities as "just a straight-arrow, neat kid, well respected by students and staff." In addition to his heavy class schedule, which included advanced algebra, advanced English composition, chemistry, and a seventh-hour computer course, he worked 3 days a week in a supermarket. He also found time to work out regularly with weights. Although the teacher of the advanced algebra course was fairly certain that the answer key to the final exam had been passed around, Craig did very well when given a different math final. At 2:30 p.m. that same day he talked, laughed, and joked with his mother for several minutes on the phone. By 3:30, his brother found him dead in his room. He had hanged himself with a rope.

Larry, a 15-year-old, was found dead in his bathtub at 9:55 a.m. He was a quiet teenager who divided his free time between managing the high school basketball team and working part-time at a pizza parlor. He had cut his right wrist and inner elbow with a razor and shot himself in the mouth with a twelve-gauge shotgun. A friend said that Larry "had mentioned suicide" in the past week. He was apparently upset over the breakup with his girlfriend.

Suicide is a symptom that cuts across diagnostic categories. It continues to be a disquieting problem, particularly among children and adolescents. Self-induced death is especially disturbing in that it terminates a life at a time when the life cycle has scarcely begun. It is perhaps ironic that only members of the highest level species, humans, voluntarily commit self-destructive acts (Frederick, 1985). This chapter will address what we know about the prevalence of suicide in young people, factors that place youth at risk for suicide, how we predict suicide, how we assess suicidal tendencies, and how suicide can be treated or prevented. Empirical data, clinical experience, and a developmental perspective will be combined in the search for a fuller understanding of this devastating problem.

Before delving into the topic of suicide, the reader should be aware of the problems encountered in studying self-destructive behavior and the ensuing limitations placed on the certitude of the information gleaned. The first difficulty, and a very significant source of confusion in the literature, is the definition of suicide. For instance, making appropriate judgments about whether self-destructive behaviors such as self-biting, wrist cutting, anorexia, running into traffic, and the ingestion of toxic substances are suicidal requires clarification about the cause of the behavior, the meaning the child attaches to it, and the resultant extent of injury produced by the behavior (Pfeffer, 1986). Second, distinguishing between accidents and intentional self-destruction can sometimes be a challenging task. For instance, knowing whether the child fell out of the window because he jumped or was dizzy from medication, whether his car went off the dark road because he missed the curve or drove off intentionally, whether she darted in front of an on-rushing car without looking or to willfully hurt herself, and whether he stabbed himself while playing "cowboys and Indians" or on purpose, are difficult judgment calls. The higher percentage of accidental deaths that occur in the younger age groups suggests that coroners are prone to label such deaths as accidents rather than suicides (Shaffer, 1974). Third, the phrase "suicidal behavior" is often used to include completed suicide, attempted suicide, suicidal gestures, suicidal threats, and suicidal ideation. Undifferentiated use of this phrase is a source of confusion in the literature as debate continues as to the value of studying nonfatal suicidal behavior as a means to further understanding completed suicide. Fourth, even if definitional difficulties are resolved, the problem of underreporting remains. Figures are not reported as a cause of death by the National Center for Health Statistics. Because developmental theory suggests children do not understand the finality of death until around age 10, there is a reluctance to classify preadolescents as suicidal (Frederick, 1978). The net result is that we know very little about suicidal behavior in young children although documented evidence of suicides exists even among preschoolers (Rosenthal & Rosenthal, 1984). Finally, what little we know about suicide completions and suicide attempts is often based on retrospective studies (psychological autopsies) that rely on unrecorded data, records lacking in detailed information, and unwilling informants. Given the above methodological shortcomings, many of the inferences drawn from the research literature must be regarded as tentative.

PREVALENCE

Suicide, a symptom with a wide variety of etiologies, does occur in children below the age of 10, but it is extremely uncommon. Compared to the general population rate of 12 per 100,000, suicide in children under 15 is a low-frequency phenomenon. In 1984, for example, the rate was effectively zero as only 7 suicides were reported among 5- to 9-year-olds in the entire United States, according to the National Center for Health Statistics ("Children's Suicide," 1987). In 1988—the latest data available—the rate among 10- to 14-year-olds was 1.4 per 100,000, Neergaard (1993). The suicide rate increases significantly, however, in the 15- to 19-year age group, climbing to 9 per 100,000. It peaks by the late teenage years 18 to 20, followed by a plateau for the remainder of the young adult years, 20 to 24 (Garfinkel & Golombek, 1983).

The suicide rate has almost doubled in the past 10 years. In 1985, over 5,000 teens took their own lives (National Center for Health Statistics, 1986). Also disquieting are the 50 to 100 estimated suicide attempts for every adolescent who commits suicide (Otto, 1966). Yet, suicide is underrepresented in this age range in that the rate is lower than expected, based on the percentage of this age group in the general population. Whereas the 15- to 19-year-old age group accounted for 9.1% of the general population, they accounted for only 5.9% of the total number of suicides (National Center for Health Statistics, 1980). With the exception of children, the adolescent suicide rate is the lowest in the life cycle (Offer & Schonert-Reichl, 1992).

Reliability of Suicide Figures

The reliability of suicide statistics has been questioned by many authorities, especially in the case of young people. Misreporting can take two forms. One is bias stemming from variations in investigative and recording procedures. This form of misreporting does not appear to be a significant source of error. For instance, the incidence of suicide within a given coroner's district is unaffected either by change in coroner or by personnel changes among police officers, pathologists, or others involved (Shaffer, 1986). Underreporting, on the other hand, does appear to be a sizable problem. A number of suicides are categorized as "undetermined" whether death is accidental or purposefully inflicted. The ratio of undetermined to suicidal judgment seems to be greater among children and adolescents (McClure, 1984). The category most likely subject to misclassification is death by poisoning. Adelstein and Mardon (1975) found considerable variation in the percentages that were reported as "accidents," "suicides," or "open verdicts." The actual suicide rate may be two or three times greater than the recorded rate (Wilkins, 1970).

Several factors may be associated with the underreporting of suicide among children and youth (Hawton & Osborn, 1984; Husain & Vandiver, 1984). These factors include (1) a belief in the relative rarity of the event, which may render those responsible for determining the cause of death prone to consider the death as accidental; (2) the desire to protect parents or institutions from the distress that a verdict of suicide may produce (e.g., a diagnosis of "accidental poisoning" is socially acceptable); (3) religious beliefs (e.g., Catholicism's view that suicide is a mortal sin leading to eternal damnation may make officials less likely to believe that a young person has intentionally taken his or her own life); (4) the training of the assessor (e.g., legal versus medical) may influence how evidence is appraised; (5) the inability of young children to prepare a suicide note; (6) the methods used by younger children (e.g., running into traffic); and (7) the fact that insurance companies will pay in the event of accidental death but not for the taking of one's own life. Despite the presence of a number of factors that might lead to our underestimating the number of self-induced deaths, suicide has been among the top three causes of death for young people for several decades (Frederick, 1985).

Demographic Factors

Age, gender, and race are all demographic factors associated with suicide. The rate of suicide is correlated with age (Garfinkel, Froese, & Hood, 1982). No national data are kept on preschoolers. The youngest group for whom national suicide data are recorded is for 5–9-year-olds. The rate for this group consistently per 100,000 is 0.0 (Smith, 1992). Those under 10 years of age are at the least risk for suicide. Indeed, only a few suicides (5 to 7) are recorded annually in the 5- to 9-year-old group. Suicidal behavior in this age range consists primarily of suicidal ideation and threats, as opposed to attempts and completions. No gender or race differences are discernible in this age group. The suicide rate is still low in the 10–14-year-old age range (e.g., 250 per 100,000 in 1986). The suicide rate increases again in the 15-to 19-year-old group.

Why is completed suicide a rare event for those under the age of 10? Among the more obvious explanations for the underrepresentation of children in the suicide rates are their putative lack of comprehension of the finality of death, their limited exposure to suicide as a means of problem solving, and their inability to carry out a successful plan (Carlson, Asarnow, & Orbach, 1987). Two additional hypotheses centering around the role of family factors and developmental variables have been advanced by Shaffer (1986). One possibility is that childhood is a period of life when there are rich, multiple support systems (home, relatives, school) that provide guidance, support, direction, and problem resolution when needed. Successful suicides often occur in a context of social isolation. Increasing self-consciousness in the older adolescent and the drive for independence may weaken support systems. Interestingly, the suicide rate peaks among young people at a time during which they are leaving high school, leaving home for college, or seeking a job for the first time. A second major hypothesis is that cognitive changes coincide with the increase in suicide rates. It may be that despair stemming from a sense of hopelessness requires an ability to reflect upon one's existence, to choose between various abstract life alternatives, and to conclude that none is a satisfactory solution to problems in the future. Cognitions of this nature do not appear until the period of adolescence.

Suicide is also strongly related to gender and race. Males continue to dominate with respect to committed suicide throughout all age ranges by at least a 3-to-1 ratio. Moreover, the sex ratio for committed suicide increased from 3.2 to 1 in 1968 to 4.3 to 1 in 1978 (Frederick, 1985). Data based on an eight-state sample of 469 junior and senior high school students who indicated a history of one or more suicide attempts showed that 65% of the attempters were female and 35% male (Reynolds & Mazza, 1992a). Similarly, Andrews and Lewinsohn (1992), in their community-based study of 1,710 older adolescents, found that being female is a significant risk factor.

Research has consistently noted age and sex differences in suicide, but psychological explanations differ, necessitating further research. For example, one study of 46 adolescent suicide attempters (Triolo, McKenry, Tishler, & Blyth, 1984) found that the suicidal attempt of the younger adolescent is more likely to be directly related to parent-child relationships, whereas the suicidal attempt of the older adolescent is more likely to be mediated by social circumstances outside the family that may serve to exacerbate a poor parent-child relationship. Also, the adolescent's perceived relationship with the mother is much more predictive in female adolescent suicide attempts than in male attempts.

Suicide rates among Whites continue to exceed that of persons in most other racial groups. For example, the suicide rate among White persons 15 through 19 years old in both sexes is almost double that of all other racial groups. It is important to note, however, that among all racial groups, there has been a steady increase in suicide rates that requires the attention of concerned professionals (Seiden, 1972). For instance, native Americans kill themselves at about twice the rate of non-Indian adolescents and they kill themselves at a younger age (Harras, 1987). There is great variability across tribes, however (Garland & Zigler, 1993).

Surprisingly, there is little information on socioeconomic status as it relates to adolescent suicide (Husain & Vandiver, 1984). Garfinkel (1986) notes that middle- to upper-class youth have a higher suicide rate than children of lower socioeconomic status, but Carlson et al. (1987) report that lower socioeconomic children have a higher rate of suicidal behavior. More definitive research is needed before the role of socioeconomic factors in suicide is clearly understood.

IDENTIFICATION AND PREDICTION OF YOUTH AT RISK

There are many factors that place youth at risk for suicide. In some instances, identification and prediction of youth at risk for suicidal behavior are a relatively easy matter. For example, a teenager may talk with his parents about "wanting to die." On other occasions, the suicidal youngster may tell a friend who, in turn, alerts the school counselor. On various other occasions, many of the parties who knew the suicidal youth did not recognize his vulnerability to self-injury despite subtle whispers for help (e.g., "My life is empty"). Under these circumstances, suicide comes as an unexpected, unexplainable catastrophe. In this section, predictive factors are reviewed together with considerations that render these pursuits problematic. Although this discussion focuses on psychiatric conditions, biological and cognitive factors, demographic variables, the role of specific environmental stresses, and the concept of base rates, other significant predictors of suicide are presented in Table 5.1. A cautionary note needs to be sounded before discussing risk factors for completed suicides; namely, that the risk factors for completers and attempters are significantly different. Whereas the present discussion centers around suicide completers, the reader should be aware of the risk factors for attempted suicide. (See Table 5.2.)

Table 5.1
Indicators of Suicidal Risk

Predicting who will and who will not commit suicide is difficult, but the following indicators of suicidal risk should prove helpful:
1. Loss of family members through death or family dissolution.
2. Social isolation.
3. A family history of affective disorders.
4. Interpersonal problems with peers, especially those of a heterosexual nature.
5. Sexual identity problems.
6. Abuse and/or neglect by parents.
7. Suicides committed by peers, loved ones, and role models.
8. Previous suicide attempts.
9. Expressing suicidal thoughts or threats.
10. Physical illness or injury.
11. The number of stressors.
    School-based problems
    Peer-based difficulties
    Family-based conflicts
12. Maladaptive coping strategies.
    Recent acting-out behavior
    Passive withdrawal
    Avoidant behavior
    Deteriorating schoolwork

Note. Adapted from "Major Affective Disorders in Children and Adolescents" by B. Garfinkel, 1986, paper presented at the Conference on Suicide and Depression in Children and Adolescents, Minneapolis, MN, and from *Suicide and Attempted Suicide Among Children and Adolescents* (p. 126) by K. Hawton, 1986, Beverly Hills, CA: Sage.

Factors are complex, highly interrelated, and only partially understood. We have already noted that gender (being male), age, and race can place one at greater risk. In this section, other considerations such as psychiatric status, biological factors, and intellectual factors are examined.

Psychiatric Factors

The prevalence of suicidal ideas, threats, attempts, and completed suicides is relatively common among psychiatric outpatients and inpatients (Cohen-Sandler, Berman, & King, 1982; Pfeffer, Solomon, Plutchik, Mizru-

Table 5.2
Selected Characteristics of Suicide Completers Versus Attempters

Characteristics	Completers	Attempters
Gender	Mostly males	Mostly females
Mean age	20	15
Method of choice	Guns	Drugs
Anticipation	Unexpected	Seldom completely unexpected
Interpersonal relationships	Stable	Unstable
Pursuit of educational and vocational goals	Stable	Unstable
Antecedent illness	Severe psychiatric	Physical
School performance	Success	Failure

Note. Adapted from "Suicidal Behavior" by B. Garfinkel and H. Golembek, 1983, in H. Golembek and B. Garfinkel (Eds.), *The Adolescent and Mood Disturbance* (p. 208), New York: International Universities Press.

chi, & Weiner, 1982). Of course, not all young people who attempt or commit suicide have a diagnosed psychiatric disorder, but the suicide rate for people with affective disorders is 25 times greater than that of the general population (Blumenthal & Hirschfeld, 1984).

Depression is the most important risk factor for suicide (Blumenthal & Hirschfeld, 1984; Carlson & Cantwell, 1982; McGuire, 1983). Major depressive and dysthymic disorders are significantly related to higher rates of suicidal behavior than are nondepressive psychiatric disorders and adjustment disorders with depressed mood (Kovacs, Goldston, & Gatsonis, 1993). Fifteen percent of patients with either primary major depression or schizophrenia will commit suicide (Blumenthal & Hirschfeld, 1984). Nonetheless, it should be noted that depressed children are not necessarily suicidal. One study (Cohen-Sandler et al., 1982) showed that whereas 65% of suicidal children were diagnosed as depressed, only 38% of depressed children engaged in suicidal behavior. Conversely, 35% of all suicidal children were not diagnosed as depressed. Later research (e.g., Myers et al., 1991) also shows that there is not a one-to-one correspondence between depression and suicide. Reynolds (1991) reports that about 20% to 30% of students endorsing a clinical level of suicidal thoughts do not show a clinical level of symptomatology. Thus, although depressed affect is related to suicidal behavior, it does not specifically indicate that a person will take his or her own life. Its use as a diagnostic indicator would lead to unacceptably high false positive (the percent predicted to commit suicide but who did not) and false negative rates (the percent predicted not to commit suicide but who did). In investigating the relationship between depression in youth and suicidal behavior, one must also keep in mind the fact that diagnostic criteria and scales of depression commonly vary across studies (Clarizio, 1984). Moreover, for some investigators, the definition of suicidal behavior is restricted to actual suicidal behavior—generally attempters (Cohen-Sandler et al., 1982)—whereas others use the term more inclusively to cover suicidal ideas, gestures, threats, and attempts (Pfeffer et al., 1982). The importance of this latter distinction is demonstrated in Carlson and Cantwell's (1982) finding that the intensity of suicidal ideation was related to a child's severity of depression, but that many youngsters who thought about suicide were not depressed at all. Still other authorities argue that although depressed individuals often harbor suicidal thoughts, suicidal behavior is not associated with any particular syndrome for either boys or girls (Achenbach & Edelbrock, 1979). Likewise, Hawton and Osborn (1984) point out that relatively few (about one in five) younger suicidal attempters appear to suffer from psychiatric disorders. The conclusion most warranted is that depression plays a facilitory role but it is neither a necessary nor sufficient condition in suicidal behavior. The major advantage of depression among potentially serious suicidal persons is that professionals' sensitivity to this condition has been heightened and depression among young people is taken more seriously these days. If suicidal behavior is only imperfectly related to clinical depression, what other factors are related to this self-destructive act?

Alcohol, drug abuse, and chemical dependency increase suicidal risk. As many as 80% of those who attempt suicide have been drinking at the time (National Institute on Alcohol and Alcoholism, 1983). Furthermore, alcoholics commit suicide from 6 to 15 times more frequently than the general population. Suicide victims who use firearms are almost five times more likely to have been drinking than were those who used other methods of suicide (Brent, Perper, & Allman, 1987). In light of these data, the early detection and treatment of young people with serious affective disorders and chemical dependence constitute important prevention strategies. Acting out antisocial behavior, which has been reported to be associated with depression and/or suicidal behavior in children and adolescents (Blumenthal & Hirschfeld, 1984; Mattson, Seese, & Hawkins, 1969; Reynolds & Mazza, 1992b; Shaffer, 1974), also appears to be descriptive of psychiatrically hospitalized children in general. Behaviors such as fire-setting, truancy, stealing, destructiveness, disobedience, running away, fighting, temper tantrums, and impulsivity not only failed to differentiate suicidal from depressed children, but also did not differentiate these groups from a psychiatric control group. Similarly, in contrast to the high frequency of school adjustment problems reported for depressed and suicidal youngsters (Garfinkel & Golombek, 1974; Toolan, 1978), items such as school refusal, poor concentration, truancy, and poor schoolwork failed to discriminate among suicidal, depressed, and otherwise psychiatrically disturbed children (Cohen-Sandler et al., 1982).

Use of symptomatology does not appear to differentiate the suicidal child from other disturbed children. Developmental changes in depression and antisocial behavior could account for the rising incidence of suicide from childhood through adolescence (Shaffer, 1986). Although antisocial behavior is evident from an early age (West & Farrington, 1977), the social consequences attached to that deviant behavior such as expulsion from school and arrest become more severe with increasing age.

Life-history data might provide a sounder basis for discriminating suicidal youngsters from other disturbed youth. In one study, 40 adolescent attenders at a community mental health clinic who committed suicide up to 30 years later were matched on age, sex, and year of first registration at the clinic with those who had not killed themselves. The findings revealed that suicide completers had experienced a greater amount of personal and social disruption in their lives, including fathers with alcoholism and mothers who had committed suicide (Pettifor, Perry, Plowman, & Pitcher, 1983). Other investigators have also reported significantly greater amounts of life stress, particularly during the year prior to their inpatient status (Cohen-Sandler et al., 1982). Suicidal attempts and completions might be explained in part as a last-ditch coping effort to counteract a sense of hopelessness and produce changes in an intolerable situation (Garfinkel & Golembek, 1974).

Biological Factors

Biochemical investigations of suicidal attempters and victims have reported deterioration in the function of serotonin, a neurotransmitter in the brain. The most promising line of brain biochemistry research has focused on neurotransmitter monoamine metabolites, notably serotonin metabolite 5-hydroxyindoleacetic acid (Berman & Jobes, 1991). Reduced serotonergic activity, which has also been noted in association with other psychiatric impairments, and violent suicide attempts may increase the risk of completed suicide twenty-fold at 1-year follow-up (Blumenthal & Hirschfeld, 1984). Research on neuroendocrine factors holds promise for increased prediction of suicide, new psychopharmacologic treatment, and ultimately prevention of suicide.

Genetic contributions may also constitute a risk factor for suicide. Blumenthal and Hirschfeld (1984) report that (1) half of the persons with a family history of suicide have attempted suicide themselves, (2) over half of all the parents with a family history of suicide had a primary diagnosis of affective disorder, (3) a high concordance rate occurs in identical twins for suicide, and (4) that biological relatives have a six-times greater increase in suicide than do adoptive relatives. These findings suggest a genetic factor in both affective disorders and suicide. Environmental factors could also play a role, however (Hawton, 1986). Living with depressed relatives may involve a lack of affection and feelings of rejection. Having a parent or older sibling who models a marked or hopeless attitude can also predispose one to affective disorder. Finally, living with a parent or sibling with a psychiatric problem can prove intolerable. Regardless of etiology, a family history of suicide is one of the strongest predictors of a serious suicidal attempt in children and adolescents (Dabbagh, 1977).

Another biological factor related to suicide completions is height. Children aged 12–14 who committed suicide were tall for their age (Shaffer, 1974). Because height is closely related to puberty, those few who commit suicide tend to be physically precocious. Only 10% of the 20 who committed suicide were below the 50th percentile in height.

Cognitive Factors

There have been few studies of the intellectual level of young people who commit suicide. Moreover, the limited evidence is mixed. Seiden (1966), in a study conducted at the University of California at Berkeley, discovered that two thirds of students committing suicide had above-average grades although the difference was not statistically significant. Garfinkel and Golombek (1983) reported that adolescents who commit suicide are more intelligent than suicide attempters. Moreover, Sargent (1984), following the analysis of 15 suicide completions, noted that better students made the most severe attempts at ending their lives. Estimates of intelligence that were available for 28 of 30 twelve- to fourteen-year-olds who committed suicide indicated that 30% had IQs in the 115–129 range, whereas another 10% were over 130 IQ (Shaffer, 1974).

Webb, Meekstroth, and Tolon (1982) suggest three reasons why gifted youngsters may be more prone to depression, the most common emotional concomitant of suicide. First, their desire to achieve very high or impossibly high standards can predispose them to depression. Second, because gifted youngsters are by definition statistically rare, they often feel alienated and cut-off from their classmates. Their acceptance is for being a "brain," not for themselves as people. Third, they worry more about fundamental moral issues (e.g., justice, world peace) and the meaning of life. They precociously seek answers to questions about life at a time when their adolescent idealism far outstrips their experiential and emotional backgrounds. Their ability to perceive problems far exceeds their ability to influence outcomes. Thus, there is always a genuine danger that their idealism may be prematurely dashed. Without hope, they experience an "existential depression" and possibly despair, as is seen in the case of Peter.

Many professionals are concerned about suicidal behavior among gifted young people (Delisle, 1992). Clinicians who work with adolescents are familiar with a high-risk adolescent group of either gender who are high achieving and narcissistically oriented. These include honor-roll students, star athletes, cheerleaders, and yearbook editors who experience a severe humiliation (e.g., caught cheating, jailed for drunk driving) and find their faults painfully exposed and impossible to bear (Smith, 1992). These students often have families whose parents are good, well-meaning, but personally preoccupied (Orbach, 1988). This group has been overlooked by researchers who focus primarily on attempters, a group in which this student is rare (Smith, 1992).

Most investigators have attempted to assess intelligence subjectively after the fact. Cognizant that Terman's longitudinal study provided data on 1,528 children identified as gifted by virtue of their scores (IQ 140 and above) on a standardized measure of intelligence, Schneidman (1971) analyzed the suicide rate for this precocious group. His analysis did not reveal a higher suicide rate for this very bright group. It is possible that society takes greater note of suicides in gifted youth than in average youngsters. Witness, for instance, the attention given to Dallas Egbert, a 16-year-old computer genius whose disappearance from the Michigan State University campus prompted a national search. Shortly after his reappearance, he shot himself in the head in his Ohio home. His case was discussed on the *Phil Donahue Show* and continues to be mentioned in the professional literature (Delisle, 1986). His case would not have received national and continual attention except for his giftedness. In sum, further research will be needed to clarify the relationship between intellectual precocity and suicide, but it is already clear that as much attention and care should be devoted to the noncognitive facets of gifted children's development as to their intellectual capabilities.

Peter

April 14

Hello everyone. My name is Peter Walker, I'm presently 15 years old, and I'm dead. Yes, dead. I'm trying to figure out how long I've been dead. I think now it's been about 6 or 7 years. Actually, if you looked at me you wouldn't notice anything strange about me. I certainly wouldn't look like a dead person. But I'm convinced that I'm dead. I'm sure that I'm not alive, so I'm either in a state of unbalance or I'm dead. One thing for sure. I am not alive.

When I said I was dead, what I really meant was that I don't know what I am, where I am, now and going, what I'm doing here, and in other words, I don't know anything. I'm just one crazy mixed up kid who hasn't got the foggiest idea of what is going on. I don't understand life, love, anything. I just keep asking questions and getting nothing for answers. And it's driving me crazy. I'm not content to live when I don't know what it is to live. I must know all the answers. I will not be satisfied until I know all the answers.

April 20

I don't even know who I am. Something must have created me. But who and why? I am really an agnostic in this area. I say there must have been a creator or supreme being, but then again, did there really have to be one? And I think a creator of something would have control over what he has created. God is supposed to be so kind and right. But what kind of creator would allow such things he has created to kill each other and be so cruel to each other? The situation on earth has gotten out of control and I want to get off.

Dec. 6

To everybody:

Please don't misinterpret what I have done. I want no one person to take the blame. It was my decision, and I am not sad that I did what I did. There are very many reasons why I did this. First, and this may seem strange, I am very curious as to what happens after death. Sorry, Mom, but I can't take what the Bible says as the Gospel Truth (*heh!*). I really am an agnostic.

Second, everyone will die sooner or later by old age or an atomic war, so why not sooner.

Third, the pressures of schoolwork and homework were just too much. With six big projects going at the same time I knew I just couldn't take it. And if it's this bad now it sure won't get any better in university.

Fourth, sorry Mom and Dad, but you must admit we didn't have very good relationships. You drove me nuts sometimes, Mom, and I probably did the same to you.

Fifth, I see the world turning into an evil place. There is too much corruption, exploitation, misery, and pain. If people say, "Oh, it's too bad he's dead, and I'm happy to be alive and living and well," then the situation might change. I am hopeful.

Sixth, I am really screwed up in so many areas. I have so many questions about life and no answers. It really got to me. I think I really said this in my poems. My poems and my short story will tell you everything you want to know. The Beatles played the biggest part in my "life." They really helped to relax me. They really did more for me than anything else. Oh, how they would make my body and soul float in the air. And I always cried when I realized that they are no longer producing music together.

I believe that pure Marxism is the best possible society. No class distinction. Everybody at the same level. That's beautiful. So I guess I am like Joan and Craig and am dying for peace and love.

I thought having a religion was important. Mine was a mixture of Buddhism and Christianity, but I could not take all the stuff in the Bible about miracles, etc., which don't seem to be possible. Buddhism tries to eliminate the thought of "I." It appeals to me because it stresses the finding of truth within your own mind.

Dad, I thought you were an okay person. You really tried to get things right for the Indian. I hope you continue and that you are successful. You really amazed me in that you always had a joke for the situation. I think you may come up short this time. You treated me well, and I thank you for what you have done for me.

Arlene, you were a beautiful person and I hope you continue in that path. You were very close to me and I know this will affect you in many ways. I thought you would answer my poems and was very disappointed when you didn't. I really felt a love between us and it was nice. I loved you in many ways. You always amazed me with your strict belief in God. I will remember you and my mind will think of you often. Remember me. Love, Peter.

Jim, you were a very close friend and I enjoyed your companionship. Try to remember what I have taught you. Try to pick up where I left off. Above all, keep going and fight for betterment. Remember me, Peter.

I want to say thank you to all my teachers over the years. I'm sorry it did not work out better.

"Many times I've been alone and many times I've cried; anyway you'll never know the many ways I've tried." (Beatles)

"Living is easy with eyes closed, misunderstanding all you see. It's getting hard to be someone but it all works out. No one I think is in my tree. I mean it must be high or low." (Beatles)

"All the lonely people, where do they all come from? All the lonely people, where do they all belong?" (Beatles)

Please don't hassle my friends about this. They knew all right, but they sure tried to talk me out of it. My last request is to play *Strawberry Fields Forever*, and *A Day in the Life*, in that order, at my funeral. Please don't deny me that much. Keep trying for peace and love.

Peter Walker

Note. From *Growing Up Dead* (pp. 109–111, 123-125) by B. Rabkin, 1979, Nashville, Tennessee: Abingdon.

Demographic Variables

Research evidence (Triolo et al., 1984) and theoretical rationales (Glasser, 1965; Kashani & Simonds, 1979) suggest that predictors of youth suicide may vary with gender and age or developmental status. Indeed, age has been a confounding variable in most studies of child and adolescent suicide (Triolo et al., 1984). Differences between subgroups warrant serious consideration in future prediction studies. For instance, factors contributing to suicide in preadolescents seemed to stem from poor parent-child relationships whereas such relationships were not the crucial determinant in older adolescents (Triolo et al., 1984). The implication is that all youth not be lumped together to arrive at a common profile. Rather, distinguishing features associated with different age and gender groups should be identified in an empirical manner.

Specific Events

As Cytryn and McKnew (1979) note, clinical evidence indicates that suicidal behavior is often a response to frustrations, interpersonal difficulties, developmental crises, and the dissolution of love affairs. In a similar vein, Hawton and Osborn (1984) reported that 64% of overdoses appeared to have been precipitated by a tangible event in the 48 hours preceding the act. In half of the cases, the event entailed a description of a relationship with parent(s), and, in a few cases, a quarrel had occurred with an adolescent peer. Other specific events cited are arrests, moving to a different neighborhood, death of a pet, public revelation of homosexuality (Grob, Klein, & Eisen, 1983; Tishler, 1983), and suicide of a friend (Robbins & Conroy, 1983). Many of the above events involve psychological losses, disciplinary crises, and humiliation (e.g., an honor student being caught cheating). In short, several reports have suggested that the majority of adolescent suicide attempts are related to adjustment reactions or adolescent crises (Mattson et al., 1969; White, 1974). It is quite possible that a specific event might trigger an already suicidal youngster. As Garfinkel and Golombek (1983) note, "Suicidal behavior most likely represents an impulsive reaction to crisis, superimposed on pre-existing recurrent depression" (p. 208). The role that specific situational factors play in precipitating suicidal behavior undoubtedly deserves careful consideration in the prediction process. Interestingly, unwanted pregnancy is only rarely a factor in adolescent suicide attempts (Otto, 1972; White, 1974).

Base Rates

Consideration of the child's age, sex, and psychopathology, together with the role of specific events involving loss, should help in the development of more adequate scales to assess suicidal behavior. Yet at least one other major factor must be considered in forecasting suicidal behavior, namely, base rates. The concept of base rates is, by no means, a new idea (Meehl & Rosen, 1955), but it is one that psychologists have been relatively slow to accept into their clinical work as a major factor in predicting suicide. This concept refers to the frequency of a given event. If we are forced to predict rare events with scales that at best have only moderate validity, then we will make an unacceptably high rate of diagnostic errors. This situation—forecasting rare events with psychometrically deficient techniques—occurs in the case of predicting suicide in young persons. Indeed, according to figures from the National Center for Health Statistics for 1985, suicide in children under 15 years of age is a low-frequency phenomenon, being less than 1 per 100,000 ("Children's Suicide," 1987). The rates for those in the 15- to 19-year age range are higher, but are still statistically too infrequent—less than 9 per 100,000 ("Children's Suicide," 1987)—to permit valid prognostication. For example, assume we had a scale whose cutoff score would correctly identify 95% of suicide completers and attempters. Further, assume that there would be 20 completed suicides and 2,000 attempts per 100,000 adolescents at risk in any given year. The 5% incorrectly identified would translate into 4,899 false positives as needing intervention (Rosen, 1959). In addition to the problem of predicting infrequent events, assessment and prediction of suicidal behavior is hindered because suicidal urges and behaviors are largely temporally and situationally specific (Berman & Jobes, 1991). As a result, the prediction of suicide or assigning a probability estimate that an individual will commit suicide is neither a viable nor reasonable outcome for a measure of suicidal behaviors. Note, however, that the base rates for suicidal behavior will vary in relation to most of the factors discussed earlier—age, gender, psychopathology, and the individual's status (inpatient, outpatient, general population)— possibly resulting in an overall incidence of suicidal behavior (gestures, ideation, threats) that may be high enough to permit improved predictive preciseness. For example, Pfeffer and colleagues (1982) reported that 33% of children referred to an outpatient clinic exhibited suicidal behavior. The rate for suicidal ideation and gestures reached 78.5% for inpatients (Pfeffer et al., 1982). The closer the base rate is to a 50/50 division in the population, the less difficulty there is in prediction. Moreover, as the psychometric properties of predictive scales are enhanced, the problem of base rates might diminish. Also, altering the cutoff score on a test can result in a larger proportion of correct predictions than would result from using the base rate.

Although the high-risk suicide group includes a large number of false positives—people who, despite their suicide-prone characteristics, do not commit suicide—the identification of that group remains imperative because of the finality of suicide. We cannot allow the price paid for false positives— the alarming of parents, teachers, and friends—to immobilize us in our quest to find those who are seriously considering suicide.

ASSESSING THE SUICIDAL ADOLESCENT

Problems in Assessment

Once suicidal acts, gestures, or thoughts become evident, a thorough assessment must be conducted before intervention plans can be established. Unfortunately, assessment can have its problems as Hawton (1986) has noted. First, the young person may be ashamed or feel guilty. Second, the clinician may be seen as an authority figure who represents the parents' point of view. Third, the adolescent may feel uncomfortable and frightened by hospital or clinic surroundings and procedures. Fourth, some hospital staff are unsympathetic to suicide attempters. The initial assessment may be hurried and superficial, carried out by overworked (harried) and sometimes unsympathetic emergency room staff (Ramon, Bancroft, & Skrimshire, 1975), whose primary concern is to deal with the physical aspects of the suicide attempt. Finally, immediate offers of help may be rejected, perhaps because the suicide attempt often is intended to influence the attitudes and behavior of other people rather than to obtain outside help to modify the attempter's own behavior. All of these factors can hinder the development of open communication necessary for adequate assessment.

Difficulties are also common in the evaluation of parents. Family members are often puzzled by the suicide attempt. Anger, sympathy, and guilt are commonly part of the confusing mixture of emotions. Parents frequently attempt to "play down" their youngster's attempt, partly to minimize their role in this act. Parents can be helped to realize the seriousness of the attempt by pointing out that the self-injury represents an attempt to cope with stressful circumstances.

Factors to Be Assessed

The detailed assessment should address several factors (Hawton, 1986).

Events preceding the attempt. Asking for details of events leading up to the attempt, such as major conflicts or humiliations, can shed light on precipitating factors.

Extent of suicidal intent. A serious suicidal intent is indicated if carried out in isolation, timed so that intervention is unlikely, precautions are made against discovery, final acts are made in anticipation of death (e.g., giving away of favorite albums), an unequivocal communication of intent is made to others beforehand, a suicide note is left, and extensive preparation is made (Beck, Schuyler, & Herman, 1974).

Reasons for attempt. In exploring motivations, special attention should be paid to obtaining relief from a terrible state of mind, escaping from an overwhelming situation, making others understand your desperation, eliciting regret from others for the way they mistreated you or seeking revenge, influencing others to change their mind or ways, expressing love for another, seeing if someone really loved you or not, and seeking help from someone.

The person's current problems. At times the individual's present difficulties may be obvious. On other occasions, it may be necessary to investigate problems with parents, school, work, boyfriend or girlfriend, siblings, social life, sex life, peer relationships, alcohol/drugs, physical health, the legal system, and finances.

Psychological disorder. Because depression is a common psychiatric disorder preceding suicidal behavior, the clinician must be alert to cognitive, affective, motivational, and physical symptoms of depressive disorders. In addition, the various aspects of the child's mental status warrant examination. These include appearance, speech (amount, flow, content), thought processes (speed, structure, and content), cognitive functioning (concentration, memory, orientation), perceptual distortions (hallucinations), manner and appearance, and insight.

Family and personal history. Because depression and suicidal behavior run in families, the clinician must inquire about any family history of psychopathology. Further, information covering developmental milestones, family relationships, peer relationships, and school performance must be gathered from family members.

The adolescent's strengths. Planning a treatment program entails assessment of the individual's strengths as well as personal shortcomings. Ascertaining which of the previous methods of coping worked well is essential. Second, the adolescent's suggestions for resolving the current crisis need to be considered. Third, the availability of supportive relationships must be determined.

Risk of further suicidal behavior. As noted earlier, forecasting suicidal behavior is no easy task. Yet we do know that risk is greater among boys than girls, among older teenagers than younger teenagers, and among those who use more dangerous methods in their efforts to impose self-inflicted injuries. In addition, repeat attempts are probably related to alcohol and drug abuse, psychological disorder, not living with parents, social isolation, poor school record, and depressive disorders.

Attitudes toward help. As already noted, young attempters are often not motivated to enter into a therapeutic relationship. Parents, too, would just as soon put the episode out of mind. Given this reluctance, it is best to recommend, at least initially, brief therapy and modest treatment goals. Examples of specific assessment questions to ask parents and children are presented in Table 5.3.

TREATMENT

Treatment is the final step in helping a young suicidal person. Despite its crucial role, there is little literature on this problem. The guidelines for treating suicidal youth are essentially the same as those for working with disburbed youth in general (Motto, 1984). Whereas there are perhaps few special techniques, there are three major questions that must be addressed regarding therapy: Is therapy necessary? Where should it take place? and What form should it take (Hawton, 1986)?

It should not be assumed that psychotherapy is always necessary. About one third of suicide attempters may require no special after-care arrangements. To assist in answering the often-difficult question of whether therapy

Table 5.3
Interview Questions for Children and Parents

Questions for child
—It seems that you've had some bad times lately. Your parents and/or teachers have said _____. Most children your age would feel upset about that.
—Have you felt upset, maybe some sad or angry feelings you've had trouble talking about? Maybe I could help you talk about these feelings and thoughts.
—Do you feel like things will get better or just stay the same or get worse? (Look for feelings of hopelessness or "magical" solutions.)
—Some children who feel that sad and/or angry think that things would be better if they were dead. Have you ever thought that? What were your thoughts?
—What would it feel like to be dead?
—How would your father and mother feel? What do you think would happen to them if you were dead?
—Has anyone that you know of attempted to kill himself or herself? Do you know why?
—Have you thought about how you might make yourself die? Do you know how you would do it?
—Do you have (the means) at home?
—Have you ever tried to kill yourself before?
—What has made you feel so unhappy?

Questions for parents
—Has any serious change occurred in your child's or your family's life during the last year?
—Has your child experienced a particular loss lately?
—Has your child had any accidents or illnesses without a recognizable physical basis? (stomachaches, headaches, etc.)
—Has your child experienced difficulty in sports, school, peer relations, or other areas?
—Has your child been very self-critical or have you or his/her teachers been very critical lately?
—Has your child made any unusual statements to you or others about death or dying? Any unusual questions or jokes about death or dying?
—Have there been any changes that you've noticed in your child's mood or behavior over the last few months?
—Has your child ever threatened or attempted suicide before?
—Have any of his or her friends or family, including yourselves, ever threatened or attempted suicide?

Table 5.3
(Continued)

—How have these last few months been for you? How have you reacted to your child?

Note. Adapted from "Recognizing Suicidal Behavior in Children" (pp. 255–305) by B. Corder and Haizlip, 1982, September, *Medical Times.*

is needed, it is helpful to divide attempters into three groups: acute, chronic, and chronic with behavior disturbance. For the acute cases, the problems often resolve themselves as a result of the attempt. These adolescents are usually well adjusted, and their attempt represents a reaction to an acute stress. The chronic cases form the largest group of attempters and commonly require active psychological treatment to overcome their depressive symptoms, isolation, and long-standing conflicts with their families. The chronic adolescent with behavioral disturbances commonly requires continuing care by social and welfare agencies because of his or her antisocial nature and the lack of family support.

As to the type of treatment, individual therapy, family therapy, group therapy, and psychopharmacological treatment are all possibilities. In certain cases, a number of these might be used with the same individual. More typically, however, no more than two approaches are used. Whereas antidepressants might be prescribed if a biologically based depression (insomnia, weight loss, loss of appetite) were clearly in evidence, and major tranquilizers if schizophrenia were present, minor tranquilizers are generally unsuitable. Generally speaking, most attempters do not need medication. All agree that medications cannot be substituted for psychological treatment (Motto, 1984). Moreover, antidepressants must be given cautiously as they can easily be used for an overdose. By and large, family and individual therapy are the methods of choice for young attempters.

Family Therapy

Family therapy is often the method of choice because of the etiological significance of family interactions. Examination of family communication patterns leads to the conclusion that "suicide is not an individual act, but a part of a collusive communication system that involves an entire family and social network" (Richman, 1986, p. 147). Yet, family resistance and the shortage of "trained" family therapists result in less frequent use of family therapy than might be considered ideal. As is true of family therapy in general, the main aim is to modify family interactions, particularly communication patterns. See Table 5.4 for eight major ground rules for governing

Table 5.4
Ground Rules for Family Meetings

1. Agreement is reached (often in the family assessment session) as to the number of meetings.
2. Achieve agreement on goals. A most basic goal is to facilitate the family's becoming a self-help group wherein each one helps the other.
3. Ask each family member to read, discuss, and agree to a no-suicide contract.
4. Each family member is free to express himself or herself. To encourage expression, each party must agree that whatever is said during the therapy session cannot be used against the individual outside of therapy.
5. Each family member is also free not to speak.
6. Each person is given equal time to speak.
7. One person cannot speak for another. Individuals are asked to make "I" rather than "you" or "we" statements. This simple intervention is designed to avoid a courtroom-like scapegoating atmosphere in which one relative assumes the role of prosecuting attorney. If a Jack Webb-type interrogation occurs, the therapist must gently remind the family member that this is a family meeting, not a court of law, and ask what the family situation has been like for him or her.
8. The rule of reciprocity reigns. What one member does to another during the session, so it shall be done to him or her. If you give advice, you receive advice. Giving advice not only communicates that the suicidal individual is weak and incompetent but hinders development of a mutual relationship characterized by genuine human intimacy.

Note. From *Family Therapy for Suicidal People* (pp. 74–75) by J. Richman, 1986, New York: Springer.

communication and behavior during family sessions. Additionally, family therapists seek to plan alternative ways to deal with disagreement between parent and child, to achieve a tolerance for change while establishing or maintaining a consistent, stable family atmosphere, to promote autonomous functioning to decrease tendencies toward impulsive and extremely aggressive behaviors in both parents and child, and to diminish fears of separation between family and child (Pfeffer, 1986). Given the likelihood of resistance, it is important that the therapist emphasize the strengths of the family and its individual members rather than dwelling upon negative features. Hawton

(1986) recommends the use of a clear therapeutic contract that delineates the specific goals of therapy, who will attend, where treatment will occur, the number of sessions (typically six), and the duration of sessions. As therapy proceeds, discussions must include the attempt itself and its meaning, a topic that is often neglected. Such discussion can decrease the chance of a repeat attempt. It is imperative that the therapist point out the seriousness of the attempt, even if death was not the intended outcome. The parents must understand that the attempt represented an escape from an intolerable situation. Therapy does not try to force family members to change their explanation of the attempt. Rather, it assists the parties to recognize and accept each other's view of the incident and to lay plans for resolution and prevention of conditions likely to produce similar behavior. A family check-up is recommended 2 to 3 months after treatment has ended to review the consolidation of progress.

Family therapy is not for every attempter. The family may no longer be intact, may lack adequate motivation, may pose problems regarding confidentiality, and may not be the best means of addressing stressful situations arising from other sources. Family members may be very unsympathetic to the adolescent's present crisis, in part because they have had to cope with long-standing earlier problems. They may be quite rejecting and uncooperative, conveying a "he's expendable, we've given up" attitude (Garfinkel, 1986). Motto (1984) notes that inclusion of the father is essential. For an extended dicussion of family treatment, the reader is referred to Richman's (1986) *Family Therapy for Suicidal People*.

Individual Therapy

The nature of individual, outpatient psychotherapy with the suicidal child has been thoughtfully addressed by Pfeffer (1986). She notes that individual psychotherapy with the suicidal child consists of three phases, each of which has its specific goals and interventions as shown in Table 5.5.

Individual therapy is often indicated for older adolescents and not uncommonly follows the principles of crisis intervention. Accordingly, the sessions are limited in number, varying between one and ten; intensive, with very short intervals between sessions; and centered on current problems. Even in the crisis-oriented individual treatment, therapy needs to occur within a network. The therapist cannot work alone. One to 2 hours with the therapist may not be enough at the time of crisis. The therapist must involve members from various organizations such as legal agencies, mental health clinics, churches, 4-H groups, parent groups, and schools. The latter's im-

Table 5.5
Phases, Goals, and Selected Interventions in Individual Psychotherapy with Suicidal Youth

Beginning phase

Goal 1. Form therapeutic alliance
   Interventions:
   A. State that therapy can help.
   B. State that therapist and child work together to resolve difficulties.
Goal 2. Protect child from harm
   Interventions:
   A. Stress dangerousness of suicidal behavior.
   B. Urge the child to inform therapist of the child's suicidal tedencies.
   C. Emphasize that suicidal behavior is not an effective way to deal with problems.

Middle phase

Goal 1. Decrease suicidal tendencies
   Interventions:
   A. Consider alternative solutions to problems.
   B. Discuss why child feels he or she cannot gratify his or her wishes and how compromise gratifications can be achieved.
Goal 2. Decrease depression
   Interventions:
   A. Discuss positive aspects of the child's circumstances.
   B. Discuss ways to form new supportive relationships to replace lost ones.
   C. Help structure the child's day to ensure proper eating and sleeping.
Goal 3. Enhance self-esteem
   Interventions:
   A. Compliment child's achievements, skills, and appropriate autonomous behaviors.
   B. Suggest ways to act independently and successfully.
   C. Reinforce child's efforts to develop friendships.
   D. Assist the child to accept shortcomings and disabilities.
Goal 4. Alter aggressive responses
   Interventions:
   A. Point out other ways to respond to frustration.
   B. Help child accept disappointment and achieve satisfaction in other ways.

Table 5.5
(Continued)

  C. Remind child that his or her feeling angry does not justify hurting others.

End Phase

Goal: Cope with feelings of loss and separation
  Interventions:
  A. Discuss feelings of loneliness, anger, relief, and happiness about ending therapy.
  B. Discuss ways to establish new relationships.
  C. Discuss warning signs of suicidal behaviors.
  D. Form an agreement that child will reenter therapy if signs of suicidal tendencies arise.

Note. From *The Suicidal Child* (pp. 224–225) by C. Pfeffer, 1986, New York: Guilford.

portance is underscored by the finding that three of the top ten stressors among adolescent suicide attempters were school-based involving trouble with teachers, failing grades, and changing schools (Garfinkel, 1986). The therapist should arrange to have someone in the school talk with the adolescent once a day, if necessary. Thus, the therapist must also be a consultant to and coordinator of professionals and other emotionally important people who are available to the adolescent in every sphere of his or her activity. The functions of the environmental support team include recognizing suicidal tendencies in young people, augmenting the treatment plan, carrying out the therapist's recommendations regarding early interaction and management, providing feedback to the therapist, and communicating the nature of the child's functioning to his or her parents. For school personnel who are members of the support team, additional roles include promptly referring suicidal children for comprehensive psychological evaluation, allowing opportunities for these youth to talk about stressful experiences and suicidal tendencies, and educating children about alternative ways to cope with stress (Pfeffer, 1986). Because crisis intervention with suicide attempters is very taxing, the therapist may not handle more than one or two cases simultaneously.

In this type of problem-solving therapy, the therapist forms a supportive relationship with the adolescent and they work together collaboratively to resolve the problem. Also, the therapist is more verbally active and direct. For example, direct compliments may be given to bolster losses in self-esteem stemming from a failing grade. Direct interpretation may also be given. For example, the therapist might note, "Your feeling down now may be related to the stress from your learning disability in reading." Reestablishing a sense of autonomy or control over the environment is a common first step in therapy. Target problems are generally of two kinds: a choice between alternatives (Should I continue to work after school and stay in my advanced placement classes or should I make some adjustments in my school/work schedule?) and the seeking of specific goals (How can I get over the breakup with my girlfriend?). Brief homework assignments are given, and the next therapy session examines how things went. If successful, then the reasons are explored and encouragement is given regarding use of the same approach again on an alternative position. Other therapeutic strategies that can be incorporated in crisis intervention include cognitive techniques such as recognizing and reevaluating negative cognitions, explicitly defining and clarifying, giving specific advice, using contracts, and providing information. Table 5.6 summarizes the steps involved in crisis intervention.

Table 5.6
Components of Crisis Intervention for Suicide Attempters

1. Establish a link to an adult to counteract negative peer dependency.
2. Form a network involving professionals and nonprofessionals to provide emotional support.
3. Assign homework that is reviewed at next session.
4. Involve parents and other significant family members.
5. Rank order here-and-now problems.
6. Prioritize solutions.
7. Develop a contract guaranteeing not to commit suicide and to work on solutions within the time limits of the agreement.
8. Schedule a mandated follow-up session.

Note. Adapted from *Attempted Suicide: A Practical Guide to Its Nature and Management* (pp. 68–83) by K. Hawton and J. Catalan, 1982, Oxford: Oxford University Press.

The use of a no-suicide contract is strongly recommended (McBrien, 1983). A contract of this type offers the impulsive adolescent the control that he or she needs. Drye, Goulding, and Goulding (1973) report that not one of about 600 patients over a 5-year span who had made no-suicide contracts committed suicide. Unfortunately, because the demographic characteristics of these patients were not reported, it is not clear how many were adolescents. Twiname (1981) suggested the following contract: "No matter what happens, I will not kill myself accidentally or on purpose, at any time." The contract should also require the youth to contact someone should (s)he feel suicidal. The therapist should be cautious about any modifications suggested by the adolescent such as "I'll try." Lack of a firm commitment on the client's part should alert the therapist to consider hospitalizing the adolescent. Ideally, the contract includes (Hawton & Catalan, 1982):

1. Which of the client's problems will be treated;
2. The types of changes in the problems that will be attempted;
3. Who else, if anyone, will be involved in therapy and whom the therapist will keep informed about the client's progress;
4. Practical arrangements including the projected number of sessions, duration of sessions, their timing and location, and any open access arrangement to the therapist;
5. Client responsibilities including attending therapy sessions, working actively on problems, and being frank about progress;
6. Therapist responsibilities including keeping arrangements made, ensuring confidentiality, and helping the client to find solutions to problems.

No-suicide contracts have several advantages. First, they appear to be effective in preventing suicide. Second, they can be used by nonprofessionals as well as by professionals. Third, they reduce or eliminate the adolescent's ambivalence, thereby making him or her feel better. Once a decision is reached, the conflict is resolved, at least temporarily, and a heavy burden has been lifted from the teenager. A sample contract is provided in Table 5.7.

Group Therapy

Group therapy involving peer interaction constitutes another form of environmental support. There are no written reports of group therapy with suicidal youth. Yet, group participation seems to have certain advantages that are not offered in other forms of treatment. The tasks of group therapy with suicidal children include decreasing loneliness and isolation, understanding how peers view the suicidal child, expressing self-perceptions with peers, discussing values and methods of coping with stress and conflict, providing a forum for sharing common experiences, and enhancing relationships with peers in the community who are not members of the therapy group (Pfeffer, 1986).

Table 5.7
No-Suicide Contract

1. I, _____, agree not to kill myself, attempt to kill myself, or cause any harm to myself during the period from _____ to _____, the time of my next appointment.
2. I agree to get enough sleep and to eat well.
3. I agree to get rid of things I could use to kill myself—my guns and the pills.
4. I agree that if I have a bad time and feel that I might hurt myself, I will call _____, my counselor, immediately, at ; _____ or the Crisis Center (or Suicide Prevention Center) at # _____.
5. I agree that these conditions are part of my counseling contract with _____.

Signed _____
Witnessed _____
Date _____

Note. From *Brief Counseling with Suicidal Persons* (p. 269) by W. Getz, D. Allen, R. Myers, and K. Lindner, 1983, Lexington, Massachusetts: D. C. Heath.

Outcomes of Treatment

The effectiveness of treatment methods remains to be established as there have been no systematic controlled treatment studies of the efficacy of treatment for suicidal children or adolescents (Pfeffer, Peskin, & Siefker, 1992). Indeed, case reports have been the primary source of information on the treatment of suicidal youngsters (Pfeffer, 1986). One problem warranting special attention is nonattendance at outpatient sessions, with nonattendance rates ranging from 21% (White, 1974) to 44% (Taylor & Stansfield, 1984). Motto (1984) noted that only 8 of 30 suicidal youth continued after the first inverview, and most quit after only 3 to 4 sessions. Attendance is positively associated with (1) severe psychological symptoms like depression, loss of appetite, and insomnia; (2) a definite psychiatric disorder; (3) an overdose taken with suicidal intent in response to family arguments; and (4) positive parental attitudes toward psychological help (Taylor & Stansfield, 1984). Attendance can be facilitated by ensuring the relevance of treatment, focusing on here-and-now concerns, tailoring the therapeutic time schedule to fit the patient's circumstances, and by keeping intervention as brief as possible (Hawton, 1986).

What is the fate of suicide attempters? Despite the attention devoted to the topic of suicide, there has been a paucity of follow-up studies of suicide attempters. Some tentative conclusions are possible, however. The social and psychological adjustment of attempters is found to be relatively good within a month of the attempt in the majority of cases. The outlook is better for subjects in the acute group, with 90% improved within 1 month after overdose, and only 10% making a repeat attempt in the following year. For those in the chronic group, the figures for improvement and subsequent attempts were 75% and 0%, respectively. For those in the chronic group with behavior disturbance, the prognosis was bleakest with the figures for improvement and subsequent attempts being 25% and 50%, respectively (Hawton, Cole, O'Grady, & Osborn, 1982). Thus, the majority of attempters make a reasonably adequate adjustment, although a substantial minority continue to experience problems in adjustment. In general, studies based on small samples of adolescent suicide attempters suggest that about 1 in 10 will make further attempts requiring hospital referral within a year after the first attempt (Haldane & Haider, 1967; Hawton et al., 1982). A 6- to 8-year follow-up study of 53 suicidal preadolescent and young adolescent psychiatric inpatients showed that 20 attempted suicide again during this period and that 55% of those 20 individuals were in treatment at the time of the attempt (Pfeffer, et al., 1992). In general, higher repetition rates are found among older male teenagers, those with psychological problems, and those from families with extensive psychopathology and alcoholism (Choquet, Facy, & Davidson, 1980; Goldacre & Hawton, 1985). Surprisingly, studies of eventual death by suicide among attempters are rare. Evidence from Otto's well-known 10- to 15-year follow-up study in Sweden of 1,547 suicide attempters reported that 67 (4.3%) committed suicide during that period. The rate was far higher among boys (10%) than among girls (2.9%). Goldacre and Hawton (1985) found only 6 (.24%) probable suicides approximately 3 years after the initial attempt among 2,492 adolescent self-poisoners in the United Kingdom, however. The discrepancy between the suicide rates in those two studies may be attributed to the inclusion of adolescents who injured themselves as well as took overdoses in the Swedish study, rather than just overdosers, who have lower suicide rates. Also, the length of follow-up (10 to 15 years vs. under 3 years) may have contributed to the discrepant findings. Clearly, this is an area in need of further longitudinal research.

STRATEGIES FOR PREVENTION

Limiting Lethal Means

Will denying one violent method of killing oneself simply result in the finding of another lethal method? For instance, will gun control laws reduce the number of suicides by handguns or will they merely cause people to seek other means of suicide such as hanging or jumping in front of trains? The evidence is mixed. A 4-year study based on data from the coroner's office in Toronto following the passage of a stringent gun control law suggested that the rate of suicide by guns among men dropped from 29% to 13%. But the overall rate of suicide remained about the same as there were more suicides by other easily accessible violent means (Swartz, 1987). Although the passage of strict gun laws may be a valuable long-term goal in suicide prevention, more immediate, less controversial steps could be taken in gun management and education (e.g., storing guns and ammunition separately) (Garland & Zigler, 1993).

Yet, other studies suggest that reducing the availability of lethal means of self-destruction is a preventive method deserving of serious consideration. Although the means used in suicidal acts are so readily available that efforts to reduce their availability might seem futile, both logic and research evidence might suggest otherwise. From a rational standpoint, Eisenberg (1980) has observed that (a) many suicidal acts are done impulsively and depend on the immediate availability of a means; (b) one method may be acceptable while others are not, even among those with serious suicidal intentions; and (c) many attempters have mixed feelings about following through with the suicidal act. From an empirical standpoint Khuri and Akiskal (1983) noted various ways in which reducing lethal means has lowered suicide rates. For instance, as a result of the transition from the use of coal gas to that of a much less toxic gas in domestic supplies in Great Britain in the early sixties, suicide via domestic gas poisoning became negligible and the annual rate of completed suicides dropped by a third. Comparable results were found in Vienna and Brisbane following detoxifying measures. In a similar vein, the gradual shift from barbiturates to the use of less lethal psychoactive agents (e.g., benzodiazepines) may have contributed to a modest decrease in the mortality of suicidal behavior. Although the prescribing of lethal drugs needs to be done cautiously, attention needs to be focused on nonprescribed drugs such as analgesics because adolescents commonly overdose on these. Selling such products in small amounts and wrapping the tablets individually might limit the number of suicides by impulsive individuals. Jumping from high places, although not a common means of suicide, is also preventable through the restriction of access. All in all, despite its apparent simplicity, limiting access to deadly means is a method worthy of consideration. It is not a substitute, however, for careful monitoring of a suicidal individual. For whereas availability of a lethal agent may be the most important determinant of the lethality of *impulsive* attempts, suicidal intent and severity of psychopathology may be the most important determinants of the lethality of attempts by hopeless, dysphoric individuals (Brent, 1987).

Media Influence and Suicide Clusters

Publicity regarding suicides may elicit life-threatening behavior on the part of others. Indeed there is serious concern on the part of mental health specialists about media-related contagion effects as the ripple effect might well be a factor in cluster suicides. For example, in Plano, Texas, seven suicides occurred among 15- to 18-year-olds within a 6-month period. Some of these suicides were clearly linked. Two of the boys were friends, and one was found to have newspaper clippings on two of the suicides pinned up in his room. In Chappaqua, New York, a small offbeat suburban community of 15,800 inhabitants, the high school with a population of 1,300 reported two deaths from suicide separated by 3 months, followed by five attempts within 7 weeks of the second death. These cases occurred among a group of students who not only related to each other in school but who also visited each other at the time of hospitalization for treatment of their suicidal behavior. During the same period 1 year earlier, there were no admissions for suicidal attempts from the same high school (Robbins & Conroy, 1983). In Westchester County, New York, five young people committed suicide in less than a 3-week period. In the close-knit community of Bergenfield, New Jersey, four teenagers put $3 worth of gas into their car, drove into the garage, closed the door, and let the carbon monoxide end their lives. Just 9 days later, 10 more teenagers were dead in apparent copycat suicides ("Opinion," 1987). The explanation of cluster phenomena is consistent with other evidence indicating that media publicity surrounding suicides contributes to self-destructive behavior (Bollen & Phillips, 1982). The media have a professional responsibility to see that they do not promote greater acceptance of suicide as an option.

Do fictional television films about suicide aired on national TV increase the number of suicides and suicide attempts? To answer this question, Gould and Shaffer (1986) studied the influence on suicide rates in the New York City area of four fictional films about suicide aired during a 25-week period during the 1984–85 season. The number of completed suicides (13) by teenagers 19 years of age or younger during the 2-week periods following three of the movies was greater than the number of expected suicides if they were randomly distributed over the 25-week study period (7.5). The total number of teenage suicides following the fourth movie (which focused on family survivors rather than the suicide victim) was not greater than expected. The number of suicide attempts (88) by teenagers following the movies was also greater than expected (70).

We have seen that movies dealing with suicide that are made for television increase suicidal behavior. What about less emotional presentations on suicide? Data based on 12,585 suicides by youth ages 10 to 19 from 1973 to 1979 showed that there is an increase in the number of suicides following national television news broadcasts about suicide (Phillips & Carstensen, 1986). The observed number of suicides exceeded the expected suicide rates for the 7-year period by 110 for the 7-day period following broadcasts of 38 news reports about suicides. In other words, there were an average of three excess suicides per news story. Curiously, females were more susceptible than males (14% vs. 5%). This is particularly surprising because male teens evidence a much higher suicide rate than females despite the fact that girls make more attempts. There was no comparable excess of suicides for adults, males or females, following the same TV news broadcasts. The authors concluded that any television attention to suicide, no matter how nonsensational or matter-of-fact, has a lethal impact on teenagers, especially females.

In contrast to widely publicized earlier reports, subsequent studies have found no evidence of imitative effects of television presentations on suicide (Berman & Jobes, 1991). For instance, Davidson and Gould (1989) conducted the first systematic, matched case-control investigation of both direct and indirect exposure in two clusters of teenage suicides in Texas in the 1980s. In the case of direct exposure, the subsequent suicidal teenager actually knew the suicide victim. In indirect exposure, the adolescent knew of the suicide victim only through word of mouth news, or fictional accounts. Surprisingly, neither direct nor indirect exposure to suicide was associated with these suicidal deaths. Case subjects did have much in common, however. They suffered the recent loss of a friend, were easily hurt, experienced hospitalization for a mental disorder and had made prior suicidal threats or attempts.

Three explanations have been advanced to explain the relationship between exposure to suicide and subsequent risk for suicidal behavior. The most commonly cited mechanism by which exposure influences subsequent suicidal behavior is through modeling or imitation. A second explanation involves the concept of pathological bereavement which is most likely to occur in close friends of adolescent suicide victims. Pathological bereavement is most apt to occur in those with a personal or family history of psychiatric disorder, particularly affective disorder. Another pathway by which exposure to suicide might produce harmful effects involves the trauma associated with finding the body of the suicide victim. This experience could lead to posttraumatic stress disorder. To test this possibility, friends and acquaintances of 10 adolescent suicide victims were interviewed 6 months after the death of the victims. Compared to a matched unexposed control group, the exposed group did not differ in their rate of suicide attempts but they did show a higher rate of new major depressive disorder. The findings were most consistent with the pathological grief explanation (Brent et al., 1992).

Do these studies mean that we shouldn't talk about suicide to public audiences that include teenagers until after we are able to distinguish between the beneficial and harmful component of educational messages and prevention programs? It is evident that good intentions and expert consultants are not per se an adequate safeguard against a lethal impact. It does appear that television and newspaper coverage of this topic is a complex and more provocative enterprise than imagined. Heightened caution is warranted. The public learns many undesirable things from the media such as methods for killing oneself, reasons for killing oneself (e.g., for love of each other), and the location to kill oneself (e.g., a familiar place like home). In short, media can teach the how, why, and where of suicidal behavior. At present, there is no evidence that "live" educational programs run a similar risk of precipitating self-destructive behavior.

Suicide Prevention Centers

Suicide prevention centers expanded rapidly between 1967 and 1973, from 58 centers to 403 centers, reflecting the considerable support for suicide and crisis intervention centers during the 1960s and 1970s. There continues to be both enthusiasm and pessimism regarding these centers. Particular controversy has surrounded the issue of their effectiveness in preventing suicides to any significant degree. Researchers have found no evidence of any preventive impact of these centers in California where the best organized suicide prevention centers exist (Khuri & Akiskal, 1983). Relatedly, similar negative results have been found in studies carried out in other parts of the United States and abroad (Dew, Bromet, Brent, & Greenhouse, 1987; Ettlinger, 1973). Research on the Samaritan organization, which has been active since 1953 in Great Britain, has also failed to provide any convincing evidence one way or the other as to the effectiveness of their suicide prevention role. It might well be that those patients most likely to kill themselves do not usually call suicide prevention centers. Those who call such centers are more apt to resemble suicide attempters in that they tend to be young females. A more positive note is sounded in a recent study (Miller, Coombs, Leeper, & Barton, 1984). The suicide rates between counties with and without crisis intervention centers did not differ overall. A significant difference in suicide rates for young females was noted, however, in the two types of counties, with a 55% decrease in counties with centers and an 85% increase in counties without centers. More impressive was the ability to replicate this finding in a different set of counties for a different time span. Moreover, the credibility of this finding is enhanced by the fact that young White females constitute by far the most frequent callers to such centers. Miller and colleagues estimated that in excess of 600 lives per year might be saved if suicide prevention centers were available throughout the United States.

Contacts with Caretakers

Many suicidal youngsters have contacts with various community caretakers or caregivers within a month prior to inflicting self-injury. For example, in one study half of adolescent self-poisoners had seen their family doctor within a month of overdose, and about one fourth within one week (Hawton et al., 1982). The findings also indicated a noticeable age difference with older adolescents (16–18 years) being more likely to have consulted their physician than younger adolescents (13–15 years). Smaller percentages of adolescent self-poisoners had been in touch with either social agencies (24%) or psychiatric agencies (12%) within a month prior to their overdose. Although the prediction of suicide is plagued with problems, as noted earlier, the threat of suicide is never to be taken lightly, particularly when depression, poor child–parent relations, alcoholism/drug abuse, public humiliation, and losses of friends occur among older adolescent males. The provision of a reliable, supportive person who can be readily available throughout this stressful period constitutes an important preventive measure. Table 5.8 summarizes the steps that the mature adult can take with the suicidal youngster.

Additional suggestions for dealing with a person in a suicidal crisis include: building trust but not lying or making false reassurances; not believing that the adolescent has recovered after only one session; notifying a relative or guardian and perhaps even initiating an involuntary commitment procedure if voluntary help is refused; avoiding philosophical discussions about the "right-to-die" as they cannot be won, pointing out instead that there is nothing to be lost by trying to resolve the situation with your help; making the environment as safe and provocation free as possible, giving reassurances that depressed feelings are temporary and will pass with time but that suicide is a permanent solution to a temporary problem; eliciting from the individual possible deterrents to committing suicide (for example, failing and ending up paralyzed for life); and arranging for a receptive person to stay with the youth during the acute crisis.

Table 5.8
Preventive Steps

Step 1: Listen.
The first thing a person in a mental crisis needs is someone who will listen and really hear what he or she is saying. Every effort should be made to understand the feelings behind the words.

Step 2: Evaluate the seriousness of the youngster's thoughts and feelings. If the person has made clear self-destructive plans, however, the problem is apt to be more acute than when his or her thinking is less definite.

Step 3: Evaluate the intensity or severity of the emotional disturbance. It is possible that the youngster may be extremely upset but not suicidal. If a person has been depressed and then becomes agitated and moves about restlessly, it is usually cause for alarm.

Step 4: Take every complaint and feeling the patient expresses seriously. Do not dismiss or undervalue what the person is saying. In some instances, the person may express his or her difficulty in a low key, but beneath this seeming calm may be profoundly distressed feelings. *All* suicidal talk should be taken seriously.

Step 5: Do not be afraid to ask directly if the individual has entertained thoughts of suicide. Suicide may be suggested but not openly mentioned in the crisis period. Experience shows that harm is rarely done by inquiring directly into such thoughts at an appropriate time. As a matter of fact, the individual frequently welcomes the query and is glad to have the opportunity to open up and bring it out.

Step 6: Do not be misled by the youngster's comments that he or she is past the emotional crisis. Often the youth will feel initial relief after talking of suicide, but the same thinking will recur later. Follow-up is crucial to insure a good treatment effort.

Step 7: Be affirmative but supportive. Strong, stable guideposts are essential in the life of a distressed individual. Provide emotional strength by giving the impression that you know what you are doing and that everything possible will be done to prevent the young person from taking his or her life.

Step 8: Evaluate the resources available. The individual may have both inner psychological resources, including various mechanisms for rationalization and intellectualization that can be strengthened and supported, and outer resources in the environment, such as ministers, relatives, and friends, whom one can contact. If these are absent, the problem is much more serious. Continuing observation and support are vital.

Table 5.8
(Continued)

Step 9: Act specifically. Do something tangible; that is, give the youngster something definite to hang onto, such as arranging to see him or her later or subsequently contacting another person. Nothing is more frustrating to the person than to feel as though he or she has received nothing from the meeting.

Step 10: Do not avoid asking for assistance and consultation. Call upon whomever is needed, depending upon the severity of the case. Do not try to handle everything alone. Convey an attitude of firmness and composure to the person so that he or she will feel something realistic and appropriate is being done to help.

Note. From "Trends in Mental Health: Self-Destructive Behavior Among Younger Age Groups" by C. Frederick, 1976, *Keynote, 4*, pp. 3–5.

The need to enlist the aid of friends is compelling in that they are the persons most likely to be the recipients of a suicidal message. In one survey of 120 high school students, 91% selected "Friend" as the first choice of individuals to be contacted (Ross, 1985). Adults were viewed as unable to understand but able to interfere. Friends, however, were seen as showing a common bond of needs, offering greater empathy, more likely not to interfere, and showing greater respect for maintaining a confidence. Reviews of psychological autopsies have also revealed that, in many cases, a friend of the suicidal adolescent knew of his or her intent but did not betray the confidence (Ross, 1985).

A sound educational program on suicide should attempt to involve peers as potential sources of identification. However valuable a resource that friends constitute in the identification of those contemplating suicide, some of the very qualities that make them confidants also make them impotent as identifiers and rescuers. Their disinclination to intervene actively, their inability to evaluate the seriousness of the message, and their lack of knowledge as to what they should do render them an uncertain asset in the identification process (Ross, 1985). Any sound educational program on suicide education must attempt to deal with the confidant's ambivalence. Inaction stemming from their conflicted loyalties can be offset by their understanding that "if you keep a secret, you may lose a friend." Also, advocating the notion of "selective communication," or "secret sharing" with a trusted adult who respects their friend's need for privacy but enables them to explore alternatives, is an essential message in mobilizing peers as a resource. The use of peers in identification and prediction also assumes that all suicidal youngsters have friends. In reality many suicidal youth may be socially isolated.

HELPING A FRIEND

Mary: Hi, Pat . . . gee, you're looking really down. What's the matter?

Pat: Oh, nothing much, I guess.

Mary: Come to think of it, Pat you've been down a lot lately. Is something bothering you?

Pat: Just the usual . . . you know, I feel so lonely since I broke up with Tony. And now he's dating Serena . . . I saw them in the cafeteria today and he just looked at me and grinned. I felt like killing him . . . or killing myself.

Mary: That's really tough, Pat. You feel really bad about you and Tony breaking up.

Pat: What we had was so special . . . and I know I'll never feel like that about somebody again. And no one will ever love me again.

Mary: You feel like no one really loves you and you're all alone.

Pat: Yeah, even my parents don't care about me. All they ever do is fight about money and work all the time.

Mary: You feel like even your own parents don't love you. You feel all alone.

Pat: Yeah, I might as well be dead for all they'd care.

Mary: Gee, Pat, it really scares me when you say things like that. And you've mentioned a couple of times that you'd like to kill yourself or you'd be better off dead. Pat . . . are you thinking of killing yourself?

Pat: I don't know . . . maybe. I think about it sometimes . . . in fact, I went to the drug store and bought a whole bunch of bottles of different pills. But I'm not sure which kind are strong enough . . . you know, what would really work and how many to take. Ugh . . . I'd hate to wake up getting my stomach pumped! But I'm such a failure, that's probably what would happen.

Mary: Pat, I care about you. I don't want you to do any crazy thing like that.

Pat: Yeah, I know, Mary. You're my friend. . . . Listen, you won't tell anybody about this, will you? When I go, it's going to be dramatic. Then Tony will be sorry he did this to me!

Mary: Pat . . . if you took those pills, you wouldn't be around to find out how Tony was feeling. Pat, I want you to see Mrs. Wyman, the school counselor.

Pat: Oh, forget it! I'm not talking to that old bat . . . she'd just tell my parents. Mary, don't tell anybody about this!

Mary: Pat, I can't do that. You've got to talk this over with somebody. How about Mr. Clawson in English? He's pretty neat.

Pat: Well . . . maybe. He's okay. But Tony's in his second period class and I don't want him to know we broke up. . . . Mary, I don't even know what to say, how I'd start a conversation with him.

Mary: I'll tell you what, Pat . . . I'll go with you. I have Mr. Clawson for American Lit. and he and I get along pretty well. C'mon, let's go find him now.

Note. From *Teacher's Guide for Secondary School Unit on Youth Suicide Prevention*, (pp. 60–61) by L. Hunter and D. Lloyd-Kolkin, 1985, Los Angeles, CA: Youth Suicide Prevention Program.

School-Oriented Measures

Given that children and adolescents have contacts with school personnel over extended periods of years, it is not surprising that schools should be accorded a central role in the prevention of suicidal behavior. Garfinkel (1986) has identified the following nine essential components of school-based prevention programs.

1. Early Identification and Screening. This aspect consists of the examination of three general areas. First, there is the identification of depression in students and the recognition of risk factors (older adolescent, male, previous attempts, chemical dependency in the family, family breakdown, deteriorating school performance, recent antisocial behavior involving rage, aggression and impulsivity, living away from home, and a history of depression). The multistage screening model described in Chapter 3 illustrates how early identification might be undertaken.

Second, school personnel must recognize the stressors of school performance. The 10 stressors reported most often by attempters centered around breaking up with boyfriend or girlfriend, trouble with siblings, change in parents' financial status, parental divorce, losing a close friend, trouble with a teacher, shifting to another school, personal injury or other physical problems, failing grades, and increased arguments with parents. The key to recognizing school-related stressors is a network of informed and concerned school personnel and peer groups who keep school mental health specialists informed about students who are experiencing severe life crises known to be danger signals.

Third, attention must be focused on the adolescent's methods of dealing with difficult problems. Coping strategies of attempters to stressful situations often alienate adults and are characterized by passive problem solving (drinking, drug usage, and smoking); angry, explosive outbursts (yelling, complaining, crying, saying mean things); avoidant behavior (deteriorating schoolwork, not doing things with family, hypersomnia); recent antisocial behavior (fighting, stealing, vandalism); and visits to family doctors regarding depression. Again, knowledgeable and caring school personnel and fellow students play a critical role in alerting school mental health specialists about students whose adjustment styles suggest risk for suicide. Teachers and classmates are not expected to be psychotherapists, but they can learn to be more sensitive to suicide symptomatology and knowledgeable about proper referral procedures. Examination of the above three areas will enhance the identification of those in need of a comprehensive evaluation.

2. Comprehensive Evaluation. The comprehensive assessment should entail a structured psychiatric interview (self, teacher, parent, and clinician), rating scales, and psychometric tests. Evaluation must pinpoint cognitive as well as affective disorders, because learning disabled and brain dysfunctional youth have a high rate of depression, and severe depression may have marked cognitive changes that can impair school performance. It is also essential that the evaluation rule out any psychopathological disorder because suicidal behavior often arises from psychiatric disturbance when no psychosocial stressors are apparent.

Reynolds (1991) has described a school-based procedure for the identification of adolescents at risk for suicidal behaviors. Because screening for depression will miss roughly 30% of suicidal youth who are not depressed, schoolwide screening of adolescents is necessary to identify those adolescents who are thinking of killing themselves. Reynolds recommends a two stage process. Stage one consists of the Suicidal Ideation Questionnaire (SIR) (Reynolds, 1988), a 15-minute paper-and-pencil self-report measure. Some 9% to 11% of adolescents are typically identified as scoring above the cutoff score. In stage two, the Suicidal Behavior Interview (SBI) (Reynolds, 1992), a semistructured clinical interview, is administered. Using a conservative cutoff score of 30 on the SIQ resulted in a 100% level of clinical sensitivity but a specificity rate of only 49% (Reynolds, 1991). That is, the SIQ cutoff score of 30 did not miss anyone at risk as judged by the SBI but did overidentify many as at risk when this was not the case.

3. Crisis Intervention. As noted earlier, an eight-step crisis intervention model has been recommended by Hawton and Catalan (1982). This model emphasizes brief, collaborative problem solving designed to provide rapid resumption of control over one's environment. Although the crisis intervention team includes various community members, it also commonly includes such school members as the school psychologist, school social worker, school

counselor, nurse, principal, coach, speech pathologist, and special education teacher.

4. Programs Following a Suicide. Educators face the difficult task of managing and counseling peers, classmates, and relatives of the young person who committed suicide. Two major principles underlie this work. First, there is the charge to prevent negative modeling from occurring. Second, there is the need to prevent negative feelings of guilt, anger, and responsibility from overwhelming the survivors. At least one third of the student body will have heard about the suicide. In discussing the suicide, stress should be placed on the individual's psychopathology in an effort to demystify the suicide and to render identification with the dead person less likely. Also, unique stressors such as gender identity problems or physical illness should be identified and discussed with classmates, again in an effort to make identification with the deceased more difficult. Efforts should also be made to limit memorialization. If there is a eulogy, it should be brief. Admittedly, the above points run counter to the natural grieving process but are needed to forestall contagion effects. Media attention should be minimal because widespread publicity serves only destructive ends. It is probably best not to talk to members of the media, informing them that they may be liable to a law suit if additional suicides follow their publicity. Finally, discussion is needed to help survivors come to grips with the sense of loss and abandonment. Special attention must be given to the permanent and volitional aspects of the deceased's actions in dealing with feelings of guilt, anger, and responsibility.

5. Educational Programs. Several educational programs are now available for students and educators that are designed to deal with issues surrounding suicide. The basic components of various programs include coping skills, prevention, intervention, and postvention. The effectiveness of those programs is unknown. Moreover, it is not clear if those programs have unintended adverse outcomes by inadvertently idealizing suicide. Any evaluative efforts must address potentially deleterious effects as well as positive ones. A pilot study by Garfinkel (1986) examining suicide educational programs in rural Minnesota found these nonstandardized programs did not correlate with either the suicide attempt rate or with the occurrence or severity of depression recorded. Neither the speaker's area of expertise nor whether the speaker was an outside or in-house person had any effect on suicide rate or severity of depression.

Perhaps the most successful programs focus on coping skills and stress management instead of the topic of suicide. At present it is not known whether it would be more beneficial to emphasize coping skills, communication skills (e.g., listening, trust, openness) and problem-solving skills (e.g., avoidance of self-blame, logical/rational judgment) or to discuss the topic of suicide directly. It is hoped that future studies will clarify this issue. From a rational standpoint, emphases on the examination of effective/ineffective coping styles, networking including adult guidance, and assertive, clear communication would appear to be worthwhile ingredients of an educational program dealing with suicide.

6. Community Linkage and Networking. The school suicide prevention team must form a community link to other schools, districts, community health centers, hospitals, churches, law enforcement agencies, recreational facilities, and the media. This linkage can afford both prevention, crisis intervention, as well as a research base for enhancing of scientific and clinical knowledge about suicide in young people.

7. Research. Extensive networking enables researchers to collect data that would otherwise not be available. In addition to data on program effectiveness, information can be collected on such topics as prevalence, demographic characteristics of attempters, stressful life events, coping skills, and identification tools.

8. Monitoring and Follow-up. Given that children attend schools all day, 5 days a week, for several years, the school prevention team is in an advantageous position to monitor and follow up those most prone to commit suicide. Moreover, school personnel have within broad limits a culturally sanctioned obligation to meddle in students' lives insofar as events impact student performance and adjustment. Relatedly, this team is in a unique position to monitor communitywide trends regarding the prevalence of suicide, community education efforts, and specific suicide trends within the school over time as a function of unique local situations and events.

Example of an Adolescent Suicide Prevention Program

The Fairfax County Public Schools, the tenth largest local school district in the United States serving almost 124,000 students, developed The Adolescent Suicide Prevention Program in response to student suicides during the 1980–81 school year. The first step in designing the program was to review available research on the topic. The resulting bibliography provided publications for both faculty and laypeople. During this research phase, information about suicides in the community was gathered from school personnel and the police to build profiles of youth at risk and to dispel stereotypes about adolescent suicide. A second preliminary step involved the preparation of a list of all mental health agencies and practitioners in the community, public as well as private. The list was used to determine which agencies and professionals could be asked to assist in the development and implementation of the suicide prevention program. Following the review of research and assessment of community resources, an advisory committee was formed. The committee consisted of administrators, medical doctors, psychologists, social workers, school counselors, school nurses, police officers, parents, and department of social services staff.

The primary difficulty faced by the committee was to recommend a specific program of in-school activities for the prevention of suicide that would not impinge too much on an already crowded school day. Notwithstanding, the committee designed a series of awareness and prevention activities designed to reach teachers, parents, and students. A 2-day program was conducted for teachers in grades 7–12 because their students were considered more vulnerable than younger students. On the first day, the faculty presentation included a film, *Adolescent Suicide: A Matter of Life and Death,* and a 20-minute follow-up session led by a mental health specialist. As the program evolved, a concise lecture proved more effective because of time constraints. The pamphlet by Arthur Freese, *Adolescent Suicide: A Mental Health Challenge,* was also distributed. On the second day, a team consisting of the school's psychologist, social worker, counselor, and a community mental health specialist was present in the school throughout the day to talk informally during teacher planning periods. These follow-up sessions allowed teachers to ask questions and discuss issues that they were reluctant to raise in a group setting. The sessions, which allowed discussion of individual children in confidence with a trained professional, resulted in numerous referrals to mental health specialists.

Presentations on adolescent suicide were also held for parents throughout the school year in school buildings, county libraries, and community centers. These programs, which were held at various times during the day and evening to attract the widest audience possible, typically consisted of an appropriate film followed by an open discussion led by a mental health professional. All parent-teacher organizations were notified that a variety of information and prevention activities would be made available for their meetings.

The final part of the prevention program was devoted toward the students with the sensitive subject of suicide being discussed with all students, either in separate workshops or in a designated class. In addition to the use of appropriate films and speakers trained in mental health, the committee also supported the organizing of peer groups for discussion and counseling. The peer groups typically included a trained mental health specialist as a group leader and encouraged students to recognize students in need of help and dispelling the notion that it is disloyal to discuss a friend's need discreetly with potentially helpful adults. Because schools and student bodies were different, the programs varied somewhat across settings. The following four programs reflect the variability in the ways that schools dealt with the topic of student stress, a more comfortable and natural way to lead into the more sensitive topic of suicide.

First School—The school's psychologist, social worker, and guidance director trained a group of volunteer teachers in suicide awareness and formats for discussing the subjects of depression, stress, and problem solving. The teachers then went into classrooms on an established schedule and worked directly with students. At one school, this model was carried out by a group of physical education teachers using English classes to ensure that the prevention effort reached all students. An example of discussion materials is presented below in Madison High School.

Second School—A number of mental health professionals from the community were invited to speak to individual classes in the school. These sessions were conducted on the same day each week for 4 weeks, and each speaker conducted three or four presentations to different classes during each day. Enough speakers were used to ensure that no one speaker was burdened and that a large percentage of the student body heard a presentation.

Third School—Students who were enrolled in the peer counseling elective course in the school worked directly with other students after being given thorough training. A group of volunteer teachers were also trained to support the work of the students, and community mental health professionals were invited to be speakers to individual classes.

Fourth School—A staff psychologist, using a cognitive therapy model, prepared a workshop entitled "Dealing with Feelings of Hopelessness," based on the premise that thoughts cause feelings and there is a way to correct the process. She presented the workshop to the class of any teacher who requested it.

Madison High School

The Weekend Warriors are downstairs in the basement-turned-into-a-rec room. Susan is there, on a fluffy rug, next to the potted palm tree, sitting cross-legged with a beer. Up until the beer, she had been drinking New York ice teas and her head is spinning. The stereo is playing—Marvin Gaye—

something about sexual healing, very loud. Out in the center of the room, a handful of people are dancing. Paul is out there. Susan came to the party with him. This is their last night as steadies. Paul is dancing with another girl, Pam, and though Susan isn't supposed to mind that, she does. She also minds that someone in the bathroom is getting sick. Seems someone at these parties is always getting sick. It's part of being young. Susan feels there's a lot of wasted energy in being young, and she's tired of it. Maybe another beer. Then she remembers the one she has. It's cold and heavy because it's full and fresh from Jerry's fridge. She takes a sip.

To be fair to Susan on their last night of going steady, Paul didn't want to go out—not to this party anyway. He wanted to sit at Susan's home and watch TV with her mom. But ever since the divorce, Mom's been acting real distant. To sit there with her would have been like sitting at a funeral. Susan wanted to get out, so she talked Paul into coming here, to Jerry's. Once Paul got here and got a beer down, the macho man of Madison High took over and ever since Paul's been dancing and playing to the hilt the role of Joe Jock, throwing his muscles around on the dance floor. Maybe he's doing it to make her jealous. Susan can't tell. Paul keeps his eyes closed when he dances and this reminds Susan of her father. Why doesn't Dad just die, she wonders. It would settle things for Mom. It's killing Mom to have Dad away from the house, alive. She worries. All Mom does when she comes home from work is call her friend on the phone or cry. Parents—they're as screwed up as the kids.

People at the party keep touching Paul. This more than his dancing with Pam annoys Susan. Even the other guys, as if for luck. They slap Paul on the back and slide their hands over his shoulder, followed by "Good seeing ya, Paul," and "How goes it my man?" How is she to keep people from touching him? He is big, and she would look like a fool if she went over and tried to hold on.

A guy Susan knew 2 years ago comes and sits on the floor beside her. "Tee," he says, calling her by the letter she held up on the Madison High freshman cheerleading squad. She gave up cheerleading when she became a sophomore, preferring instead to spend time after school with this group. But the nickname "Tee" stuck and follows her around and into the second semester of her junior year. "How have you been?" he asks as if picking up a conversation begun 2 years ago. "How you doing in McKinley's college chem class?"

"I flunked the last two quizzes," she says, matter-of-factly. "If I'm lucky, I'll scrape through with a D."

"That's bad. It must be pretty rugged stuff." He says this in reference to Susan's being an honors student in science. Susan resents him bringing up the past like this. To change the subject, she asks back, "How are things with you?"

"Oh, up and down. I thought you really liked that chem stuff."

"I used to," she says. "I don't know. I've been really tired lately. Tough times with Paul and with my folks. McKinley asked me to stop by his office Monday before class. He thinks I'm cracking." But her friend is not listening. His eyes wander around the room.

"Don't you dance, Tee?"

"No." Paul has stopped dancing with Pam. They have gone over to the bar.

"I guess the people who want to dance are dancing. Except me, anyway."

"I should have such problems," says Susan. "Dance with Pam. She's free." He gets up and goes over and waits along the wall to make his move. Susan is proud of herself for this little maneuver. It deserves another beer. She heaves herself up, but she rises too quickly and stumbles against the potted palm tree. She feels like a fool and senses Paul is looking at her. But Paul is in the middle of chugging down a beer. Everyone watches him. When he finishes, the Weekend Warriors cheer. Paul turns not to Susan, who is stumbling, but to Pam. They get close and exchange a kiss. Susan sees the kiss and decides to abandon Paul at the party. She has the car. She decides to drive around for a while. Ahead, the road bends suddenly, the tires scream out. Everything closes in and she panics. "I'll show *you*," she says over and over while she turns the wheel. The car slips off the road and into a tree.

Note. From "A Guide to Adolescent Suicide Prevention Programs Within the Schools" (pp. 37–38) by Fairfax County Public Schools, Fairfax, Va.

SUMMARY

Suicide is not a syndrome but a multidetermined symptom. National statistics indicate that completed suicides are very rare in children under the age of 10 although clinical evidence suggests that preadolescents do manifest a variety of life-threatening behaviors designed to harm themselves. Successful suicides occur infrequently in the 10- to 14-year age group but increase dramatically in the 15- to 19-year age range. Successful suicides do not occur randomly. Rather they are associated with age, gender, and race, with White males in the late teenage years most at risk. Psychopathological conditions such as depression, conduct disorders, substance abuse, schizophrenia, and borderline personality increase the probability of completed suicide. Yet, one must know far more than an individual's diagnostic category to predict self-injury. The variability in findings about mood disorders and suicide suggests that adolescent mood disturbances may be more closely related to psychopathology than suicide. Indeed, many psychological problems previously associated with suicidal adolescents have little to do with suicide per se but rather are best regarded as indices of general psychological pathology (Smith, 1992).

Specific environmental crises, family history, alcohol and substance abuse, biological predispositions, social isolation, level of intelligence, and base rate should also be considered in the prediction process. In actual practice, short-term predictions may be the most common and pressing (e.g., "Can I send him home alone?").

Assessment, a process essential to development of an appropriate treatment plan, is often hindered by a lack of open communication by both parents and teenager. The factors to be assessed include events preceding the attempt, suicidal intent, motivations for the attempt, current concerns, psychological symptoms, family history, the youth's strengths, and his or her attitude toward treatment.

Treatment can be carried out in a variety of settings including outpatient clinics, pediatric hospital units, psychiatric day hospitals, residential treatment centers, and special schools. Given the taxing nature of the treatment process, the therapist may not handle more than one or two suicidal cases at a time. Individual therapy, family therapy, crisis intervention, and group therapy are among the treatment modalities. Unfortunately, treatment is the least studied aspect of suicidal behavior, with case reports of therapy constituting the major source of information. Prevention strategies may take many formats such as limiting lethal means, encouraging media responsibility, developing suicide prevention centers, increasing contact with community caregivers, and implementing programs in schools.

REFERENCES

Achenbach, I., & Edelbrock, C. (1979). The Child Behavior Checklist II: Boys aged 12–16 and girls aged 6–11 and 12–16. *Journal of Consulting and Clinical Psychology, 47,* 223–233.

Adelstein, A., & Mardon, C. (1975). Suicides 1961–1974. *Population trends* (No. 2). London: Her Majesty's Stationery Office.

Andrews, J., & Lewinsohn, P. (1992). Suicidal attempts among older adolescents: Prevalence and co-occurrence with psychiatric disorders. *Journal of the American Academy of Child and Adolescent Psychiatry, 31*, 655–662.

Beck, A., Schuyler, R., & Herman, J. (1974). Development of suicidal intent scales. In A. Beck, H. Resnick, & D. Lettieri (Eds.), *The prediction of suicide* (pp. 45–58). Glencoe, IL: Charles Press.

Berman, A., & Jobes, D. (1991). *Adolescent suicide: Assessment and intervention.* Washington, DC: American Psychological Association.

Blumenthal, S., & Hirschfeld, R. (1984). *Suicide among adolescents and young adults.* Washington, DC: National Institute of Mental Health.

Bollen, K., & Phillips, D. (1982). Imitative suicides: A national study of the effects of television news stories. *American Sociological Review, 47*, 802–809.

Brent, D. (1987). Correlates of medical lethality of suicide attempts in children and adolescents. *Journal of the American Academy of Child and Adolescent Psychiatry, 26*, 87–89.

Brent, D., Perper, J., & Allman, C. (1987). Alcohol, firearms and suicide among youth. *Journal of the American Medical Association, 257*, 3369–3372.

Brent, D., Perper, J., Moritz, G., Allman, C., Friend, A., Schweers, J., Roth, C., Balach, L., & Harrington, K. (1992). Psychiatric effects of exposure to suicide among friends and acquaintances of adolescent suicide victims. *Journal of the American Academy of Child and Adolescent Psychiatry, 31*, 629–640.

Carlson, G., Asarnow, J., & Orbach, I. (1987). Developmental aspects of suicidal behavior. *Journal of the American Academy of Child and Adolescent Psychiatry, 26*, 186–192.

Carlson, G., & Cantwell, D. (1982). Suicidal behavior and depression in children and adolescents. *Journal of the American Academy of Child Psychiatry, 21*, 361–368.

Children's suicide rate doubles. (1987, June 30). *Detroit News*, Section C, p. 1.

Choquet, M., Facy, F., & Davidson, F. (1980). Suicide and attempted suicide among adolescents in France. In R. Farmer & S. Hirsch (Eds.), *The suicide syndrome* (pp. 73–89) London: Cambridge University Press.

Clarizio, H. (1984). Childhood depression: Diagnostic considerations. *Psychology in the Schools, 21*, 181–197.

Cohen Sandler, R., Berman, A., & King, R. (1982). Life stress and symptomology: Determinants of suicidal behavior in children. *Journal of the American Academy of Child Psychiatry, 21*, 178–186.

Corder, B., & Haizlip, T. (1982, September). Recognizing suicidal behavior in children. *Medical Times*, pp. 255–305.

Cytryn, L., & McKnew, D., Jr. (1979). Affective disorders of childhood. In J. Nosphitz (Ed.) *Basic handbook of child psychiatry* (Vol. 2, pp. 321–340). New York: Basic Books.

Dabbagh, F. (1977). Family suicide. *British Journal of Psychiatry, 130*, 159–161.

Delisle, J. (1986). Death with honors: Suicide among gifted adolescents. *Journal of Counseling and Development, 64*, 558–560.

Delisle, J. (1992). *Guiding the social and emotional development of gifted youth.* New York: Longman.

Dew, M., Bromet, E., Brent, D., & Greenhouse, J. (1987). A quantitative literature review of the effectiveness of suicide prevention centers. *Journal of Consulting and Clinical Psychology, 55,* 239–244.

Drye, R., Goulding, R., & Goulding, M. (1973). No-suicide decisions: Patient monitoring of suicidal risk. *American Journal of Psychiatry, 130,* 171–174.

Eisenberg, L. (1980). Adolescent suicide: Or taking arms against a sea of troubles. *Pediatrics, 66,* 315–320.

Ettlinger, R. (1973). Evaluation of suicide prevention after attempted suicide. *Acta Psychiatrica Scandinavia 260* (Suppl.), 1-135.

Frederick, C. (1976). Trends in mental health. Self-destructive behavior among younger age groups. *Keynote, 4,* 3–5.

Frederick, C. (1978). Current trends in suicidal behavior in the United States. *American Journal of Psychotherapy, 32,* 172–200.

Frederick, C. (1985). An introduction and overview of youth suicide. In M. Peck, N. Farberow, & R. Litman (Eds.), *Youth suicide* (pp. 1–16). New York: Springer.

Garfield, B., Froese, A., & Hood, J. (1982). Suicide attempts in children and adolescents. *American Journal of Psychiatry, 139,* 1257–1261.

Garfinkel, B. (1986, June). *Major affective disorders in children and adolescents.* Paper presented at the conference on Suicide and Depression in Children and Adolescents: Assessment and Intervention Techniques. Minneapolis, MN.

Garfinkel, B., & Golembek, H. (1974). Suicide in depression in childhood and adolescence. *Canadian Medical Association Journal, 110,* 1278–1201.

Garfinkel, B., & Golembek, H. (1983). Suicidal behavior. In H. Golembek & B. Garfinkel (Eds.), *The adolescent and mood disturbance* (pp. 189–217). New York: International Universities Press.

Garland, A., & Zigler, E. (1993). Adolescent suicide prevention: Current research and social policy implications. *American Psychologist, 48,* 169–182.

Getz, W., Allen, D., Myers, R. & Lindner, K. (1983). *Brief counseling with suicidal persons.* Lexington, MA: DC Heath.

Glasser, K. (1965). Attempted suicide in children and adolescents. *American Journal of Psychotherapy, 19,* 220–227.

Goldacre, M., & Hawton, K. (1985). Repetition of self-poisoning and subsequent death in adolescents who take overdoses. *British Journal of Psychiatry, 146,* 395–398.

Gould, M., & Shaffer, D. (1986). The impact of suicide in television movies: Evidence of imitation. *New England Journal of Medicine, 315,* 690–694.

Grob, M., Klein, A., & Eisen, S. (1983). The role of the high school professional in identifying and managing adolescent suicidal behavior. *Journal of Youth and Adolescence, 12,* 163–173.

Haldane, J., & Haider, I. (1967). Attempted suicide in children and adolescents. *British Journal of Clinical Practice, 21,* 587–589.

Harras, A. (1987). *Issues in adolescent Indian health: Suicide.* Washington, DC: Department of Health and Human Services.

Hawton, K. (1986). *Suicide and attempted suicide among children and adolescents.* Beverly Hills, CA: Sage.

Hawton, K., & Catalan, J. (1982). *Attempted suicide: A practical guide to its nature and management.* Oxford: Oxford University Press.

Hawton, K., Cole, D., O'Grady, J., & Osborn, M. (1982). Motivational aspects of deliberate self-poisoning in adolescents. *British Journal of Psychiatry, 41,* 286-291.

Hawton, K., & Osborn, M. (1984). Suicide and attempted suicide in children and adolescents. In B. Lahey & A. Kazdin (Eds.), *Advances in clinical child psychology* (pp. 57-107). New York: Plenum.

Hunter, L., & Lloyd-Kolkin, D. (1985). *Teacher's Guide for Secondary School Unit on Youth Suicide.* Los Angeles, CA: Youth Suicide Prevention Program.

Husain, S., & Vandiver, T. (1984). *Suicide in children and adolescents.* Jamaica, NY: Spectrum.

Kashani, J., & Simonds, J. (1979). The incidence of depression in children. *American Journal of Psychiatry, 139,* 1203-1204.

Khuri, R., & Akiskal, H. (1983). Suicide prevention: The necessity of treating contributory psychiatric disorders. *Psychiatric Clinics of North America, 6,* 193-206.

Kovacs, M., Goldston, D., & Gatsonis, C. (1993). Suicidal behaviors and childhood-onset depressive disorders: A longitudinal investigation. *Journal of the American Academy of Child and Adolescent Psychiatry, 32,* 8-20.

Mattson, A., Seese, L., & Hawkins, J. (1969). Suicidal behavior as a child psychiatric emergency. *Archives of General Psychiatry, 20,* 100-109.

McBrien, R. (1983). Are you thinking of killing yourself? Confronting students' suicidal thoughts. *The School Counselor, 31,* 75-82.

McClure, G. (1984). Trends in suicide rate for England and Wales, 1975-1980. *British Journal of Psychiatry, 144,* 119-126.

McGuire, D. (1983). Teenage suicide: A search for sense. *International Journal of Offender Therapy and Comparative Criminology, 27,* 211-217.

Meehl, P., & Rosen, A. (1955). Antecedent probability and the efficiency of psychometric signs, patterns, or cutting scores. *Psychological Bulletin, 52,* 194-216.

Miller, H., Coombs, D., Leeper, J., & Barton, S. (1984). An analysis of the effects of suicide prevention facilities on suicide rates in the United States. *American Journal of Public Health, 74,* 340-343.

Motto, J. (1984). Treatment concerns in preventing youth suicide. In M. Peck, N. Farberow, & R. Litman (Eds.), *Youth suicide* (pp. 91-111). New York: Springer.

Myers, K., McCauley, E., Calderon, R., Mitchell, J., Burke, P., & Schloredt, K. (1991). Risks for suicidality in major depressive disorder. *Journal of the American Academy of Child and Adolescent Psychiatry, 30,* 86-94.

National Center for Health Statistics. (1980). *Youth suicide statistics.* Atlanta, GA: Author.
National Center for Health Statistics. (1986). *Youth suicide statistics.* Atlanta, GA: Author.
National Institute on Alcohol Abuse and Alcoholism. (1983). *Fifth special report to the U.S. Congress on alcohol and health.* Washington, DC: Author.
Neergaard, L. (1993). Suicide rate of youngsters rises. *Detroit Free Press,* p. 6A.
Offer, D., & Schonert-Reichl, A. (1992). Debunking the myths of adolescence: Findings from research. *Journal of the American Academy of Child and Adolescent Psychiatry, 31,* 1003–1014.
Opinion. (1987, March). *USA Today,* p. 12A.
Orbach, I. (1988). *Children who don't want to live.* San Francisco: Jossey-Bass.
Otto, U. (1966). Suicide attempts made by children. *Acta Psychiatrica Scandinavica, 55,* 64–72.
Otto, U. (1972). Suicidal behavior in childhood and adolescence. In J. Waldenstrom, T. Larsson, & N. Ljunstedt (Eds.), *Suicide and attempted suicide.* Stockholm: Nordiska Bokhand-elns Forlag.
Pettifor, J., Perry, D., Plowman, B., & Pitcher, S. (1983). Risk factors predicting childhood and adolescent suicides. *Journal of Child Care, 1,* 17–49.
Pfeffer, C. (1986). *The suicidal child.* New York: Guilford.
Pfeffer, C., Peskin, J., & Siefker, C. (1992). Suicidal children grown up: Psychiatric treatment during follow-up period. *Journal of the American Academy of Child and Adolescent Psychiatry, 31,* 679–685.
Pfeffer, C., Solomon, G., Plutchik, R., Mizruchi, M., & Weiner, A. (1982). Suicidal behavior in latency-age inpatients: A replication and cross-validation. *Journal of the American Academy of Child Psychiatry, 21,* 564–569.
Phillips, D., & Carstensen, L. (1986). Clustering of teenage suicides after television news stories about suicide. *New England Journal of Medicine, 315,* 685–689.
Rabkin, B. (1979). *Growing up dead.* Nashville, TN: Abingdon.
Ramon, S., Bancroft, J., & Skrimshire, A. (1975). Attitudes toward self-poisoning among physicians and nurses in a general hospital. *British Journal of Psychiatry, 127,* 257–264.
Reynolds, W. (1988). *Suicidal ideation questionnaire.* Odessa, FL: Psychological Assessment Resources.
Reynolds, W. (1991). A school-based procedure for the identification of adolescents at risk for suicidal behaviors. *Family Community Health, 14,* 64–75.
Reynolds, W. (1992). *Suicidal Behaviors Interview.* Odessa, FL: Psychological Assessment Resources.
Reynolds, W., & Mazza, J. (1992a, June). *Suicidal behavior in nonreferred adolescents: Results from a national sample.* Paper presented at the International Conference on Suicidal Behavior, Pittsburgh.
Reynolds, W., & Mazza, J. (1992b, June). *Psychosocial characteristics of adolescent suicide attempters.* Paper presented at the International Conference on Suicidal Behavior, Pittsburgh.
Richman, J. (1986). *Family therapy for suicidal people.* New York: Springer.

Robbins, D., & Conroy, R. (1983). A cluster of adolescent suicide attempts: Is suicide contagious? *Journal of Adolescent Health Care, 3,* 253–255.

Rosen, A. (1959). Detection of suicidal patients: An example of some limitations in the prediction of infrequent events. *Journal of Consulting Psychology, 18,* 397–405.

Rosenthal, P., & Rosenthal, S. (1984). Suicidal behavior by preschool children. *American Journal of Psychiatry, 141,* 520–525.

Ross, C. (1985). Teaching children the facts of life and death: Suicide prevention in the schools. In M. Peck, N. Farberow, & R. Litman (Eds.), *Youth suicide* (pp. 147–169). New York: Springer.

Sargent, M. (1984). Adolescent suicide: Studies reported. *Child and Adolescent Psychotherapy, 1,* 49–50.

Schneidman, E. (1971). Perturbation and lethality as precursors of suicide in a gifted group. *Life-threatening Behavior, 1,* 23–46.

Seiden, R. (1966). Campus tragedy: A study of student suicide. *Journal of Abnormal Psychology, 13,* 242–245.

Seiden, R. (1972). Why are suicides of young blacks increasing? *HSMHA Health Reports, 87,* 3–8.

Shaffer, D. (1974). Suicide in childhood and early adolescence. *Journal of Child Psychology and Psychiatry, 15,* 275–291.

Shaffer, D. (1986). Developmental factors in child and adolescent suicide. In M. Rutter, C. Izard, & P. Read (Eds.), *Depression in young people* (pp. 383–396). New York: Guilford.

Shaffer, D., Garland, A., Vieland, V., Underwood, M., & Busner, C. (1991). The impact of curriculum-based suicide prevention programs for teenagers. *Journal of the American Academy of Child and Adolescent Psychiatry, 30,* 588–596.

Shaffer, D., Vieland, V., Garland, A., Rojas, M., Underwood, M., & Busner, C. (1990). Adolescent suicide attempters: Response to suicide prevention programs. *Journal of the American Medical Association, 264,* 3151–3155.

Smith, K. (1992). Suicidal behavior in children and adolescents. In W. Reynolds (Ed.), *Internalizing disorders in children and adolescents* (pp. 255–282). New York: Wiley.

Swartz, J. (1987). Ontario gun law fails to reduce suicide rate. *APA Monitor, 18,* 22.

Taylor, E., & Stansfield, S. (1984). Children who poison themselves: I. Clinical comparison with psychiatric controls, and II. Prediction of attendance for treatment. *British Journal of Psychiatry, 145,* 127–135.

Tishler, C. (1983). Detection and prevention of suicidal behavior in adolescents. In L. Arnold (Ed.), *Preventing adolescent alienation* (pp. 97–104). Lexington, MA: Lexington.

Toolan, J. (1978). Therapy of depressed and suicidal children. *American Journal of Psychotherapy, 32,* 243–251.

Triolo, S., McKenry, P., Tishler, C., & Blyth, D. (1984). Social and psychological discriminants of adolescent suicide: Age and sex differences. *Journal of Early Adolescence, 4,* 239–251.

Twiname, B. (1981). No suicide contract for nurses. *Journal of Psychiatric Nursing and Mental Health Services, 19,* 11–12.
Webb, J., Meekstroth, E., & Tolon, S. (1982). *Guiding the gifted child.* Columbus, OH: Ohio Psychology Publishing Company.
West, D., & Farrington, D. (1977). *The delinquent way of life.* London: Heinemann.
White, H. (1974). Self-poisoning in adolescents. *British Journal of Psychiatry, 124,* 24–35.
Wilkins, J. (1970). Producing suicides. *American Behavioral Scientist, 14,* 185–201.

SUBJECT INDEX

Adjustment disorder with depressed mood (ADDM), 21, 72–73
Adolescent Activities Checklist, 142
Anaclitic depression, 55
Anhedonia, 10
Anorexia nervosa, 16
Antidepressant drugs, 170–176
 evaluation of, 175–176
 imipramine, 171–172
 lithium, 171, 174–175
 monoamine oxidase, 174
Anxiety disorder, 12–16
Assessment
 clinician-rated inventories, 99–111
 direct observation, 103–106
 guidelines for, 125–126
 multistage model, 117–119
 parent rating scales, 94–99
 peer ratings, 106–109
 psychiatric interviewing, 109–117
 reliability, 122–123
 self-report inventories, 87–94
 stability across raters and settings, 120–122
 symptom duration requirement, 120–125
 teacher-rated scales, 100–103
 validity, 123–125
Attempted suicide,
 characteristics of attempters, 202
 treatment of attempters, 213–223

Attention deficit disorder, 11
Attribution theory, 157

Beck Depression Inventory, 87
Behavior Evaluation Scale, 100–101
Behavior Rating Profile, 101–102
Bellevue Index of Depression, 99–100
Biochemical factors, 37
Biological rhythms, 37
Bipolar disorder, 17–18, 36
Body image, 58, 60

Catecholamines, 37–38
Child Behavior Checklist, 96–97
Childhood depression,
 adolescence, 58
 age of onset, 76
 depressive symptomology, 54–60
 developmental perspective, 49
 differentiation from normality, 7
 differentiation from related diagnoses, 8–16
 middle childhood, 57–58
 preschool period, 54–57
 schools of thought, 2–7
 subtypes, 26–28
Children's Affect Rating Scale, 99–100
Children's Depression Inventory, 87–90

Children's Depression Rating Scale—
    Revised, 99
Children's Depression Scale, 90–91
Children's Reinforcement Survey
    Schedule, 141
Classification systems, 16–28
    DSM-III-R, 16–22
    endogenous-reaction, 22–23
    for young people, 23–25
    organizational-developmental, 25–26
    subtypes, 26–28
    Weinberg criteria, 24
Cognitive therapies, 150–170
    Beck's views, 150–154
    Ellis's Rational Emotive Therapy,
        159–164
    Rehm's Self-Control, 166–170
    Seligman's Learned Helplessness,
        155–159
Cognitive triad, 151, 153–154
Competence, 50–51
Conduct disorders, 9, 11–12
Consultation in schools, 183–185
Continuity, 63–78
    early experience, 63–64
    follow-up studies, 65–75
    research designs, 64–65
    retrospective studies, 75–78
Cyclothymia, 17

Definition, 2–7
Demoralization, 7–8
Depressive equivalents, 3–4
Dexamethasone suppression test (DST), 38
Diagnosis,
    levels of, 85–86
Diagnostic and Statistical Manual
    (DSM-III-R), 6, 16–22
Drug therapy, 170–176
Dysthymia, 17–18, 20, 72–73

Emotional awareness, 53–54
Etiology, 31–39
    biological bases, 34–39
    psychosocial factors, 31–34
Extinction, 139

Family therapy, 176–179
    case study, 176–177
    depressogenic environment, 179
    parental depression, 176–179

Follow-up studies,
    of depression, 65–70
    of suicide attempters, 222–223

Gender differences, 60–65
Genetics, 204–205
Gifted youth, 205–209
Guilt, 53
Gun control, 223–224

Identification,
    multistage model, 117–119
    of suicidal youth, 206–211
Interviewing, 109–117

Kiddie-SADS, 109–111

Learned helplessness, 155–159
    attributional style, 157
    evaluation of, 156–159
Learning disabilities, 9–11
Longitudinal research, 65–75
    advantages, 65
    catch-up prospective study, 64–65
    disadvantages, 65
    prospective study, 64–65
    retrospective study, 75–78

Major depressive disorder (MDD), 19–20
Mania, 17–18
Masked depression, 3–5
Motivation, 58
Multistage screening, 117–119

Negative affectivity, 12–13
Neurotransmitters, 37–39
    catecholamines, 37–39
    dopamine, 37
    indolamines, 37
    norepinephrine, 37
    serotonin, 37
Normal grief, 8

Organizational-developmental approach, 25

Parent-child relations, 56, 64, 75, 176–179
Parent ratings, 94–99
    advantages, 94
    disadvantages, 94
Peer Nomination Inventory of Depression,
    107–109

Subject Index

Personality Inventory for Children, 95–96
Physical abuse, 55
Pleasant events, 141–142
Positive reinforcement, 138–144
Prediction of suicide, 200–210
  age, 198–199
  biological factors, 204–205
  cognitive factors, 205–207
  gender, 202
  psychiatric status, 201–204
Prevalence of depression, 28–31
  age trends, 58–60
  gender differences, 60–63
Prevalence of suicide, 197–200
  age, 198–199
  gender, 199
  race, 200
  underrating, 197–198
Prevention of suicide, 223–239
  caretakers, 228–230
  limiting means, 223–225
  media, 225–227
  peers, 230–232
  prevention centers, 227–228
  school measures, 232–239
Psychiatric interviewing, 109–117
  general demands on the child, 111–113
  specific demands on the child, 113
Punishment, 141

Rational Emotive Therapy, 159–166
  basic principles, 160–161
  evaluation of, 161–164
Reynolds Adolescent Depression Scale, 92–94
Reynolds Child Depression Scale, 91–92

School-based interventions,
  for depression, 146–148, 183–184
  for suicide, 232–239
School performance, 57–58
School refusal, 12
Schizophrenia, 16
Self-esteem, 57–58
Self-management, 166–170
  deficits in, 166
  evaluation of, 167–170
Self-report inventory, 87–94
Self-understanding, 51–53
  transitions from absolute to relative, 52
  transitions from action-based to competency-based, 52
  transitions from physicalistic to psychological, 51–52
Suicide, 185–246
  alcohol, 203–204
  assessment of, 211–213
  base rates, 210–211
  biological factors, 204–205
  definition, 196–197
  depression, 202–203
  genetic factors, 205
  gifted young, 205–209
  identification, 206–211
  media influence, 225–227
  prevalence, 197–200
  prevention, 223–239
  psychiatric factors, 201–204
  specific events, 209–210
  treatment, 213–223

Teacher Affect Rating Scale, 103
Treatment for suicide attempters, 213–223
  antidepressants, 215
  crisis intervention, 217–220
  family therapy, 215–217
  individual treatment, 217–221
  no-suicide contracts, 222
  outcomes, 222–223
Treatment of depression, 135–194
  behavioral approaches, 138–150
  cognitive approaches, 150–170
  drug therapy, 170–176
  family therapy, 176–179
  implications for practice, 181–184
  multimodal, 179–181
  psychoanalytic, 137–138
  rational emotive therapy, 159–164
  school-based, 146–148, 183–184

Validity
  content validity, 123–124
  convergent validity, 125
  criterion validity, 124–125
  discriminant validity, 125

Weinberg criteria, 23–25

AUTHOR INDEX

Aboud, F., 57
Abraham, K., 137
Abramson, L., 52, 157
Achenbach, T., 4, 29, 67, 86, 96, 98, 102, 121
Adelstein, A., 198
Adrian, C., 32
Ainsworth, M., 51
Akiskal, H., 224
Albert, N., 29, 60
Allen, D., 222
Allen, L., 67
Allen-Meares, P., 30
Alloy, L. B., 157
Altmann, E., 109
Ambrosini, P., 38, 110, 174
Andershof, A., 175
Anderson, J., 58–60
Andrews, J., 143, 145, 199
Anthony, J., 60, 138
Apter, A., 110
Arana, G., 38
Asarnow, J., 199, 200
Audette, D., 109

Bailey, A., 37
Baker, D., 113
Baker, L., 6, 54, 58, 85, 86, 170
Bandura, A., 138

Banegas, M., 99
Bargew, D., 32
Barkley, R., 94
Barnett, K., 113
Barrett, R., 106
Barton, S., 227
Beauchesne, H., 97, 98
Beck, A., 5, 29, 51, 60, 87, 111, 123, 125, 137, 150, 151
Bedrosian, R., 164, 169, 176
Behrens, J., 30
Belmont, B., 34
Bemporad, J., 51
Berman, A., 96, 201, 203, 204, 211, 226
Bernard, M., 136, 160, 161, 163, 164
Bernstein, G., 12
Beshai, J., 89
Bianchi, E., 58
Bibring, E., 137
Biederman, J., 170
Bifulco, A., 157
Billings, A., 32
Birmaher, B., 38
Blau, S., 6
Blechman, E., 109
Blehar, M., 51
Bleuler, E., 2
Blumenthal, S., 202, 203, 205
Blyth, D., 199, 209
Boag, L., 26

Bollen, K., 225
Bolton, P., 37
Bordoin, D., 32, 76
Bornstein, M., 181
Bowlby, J., 2, 55, 137
Bowring, M., 17, 61, 175
Boyd, J., 160
Boyle, M., 61, 74
Bradley, C., 10
Brennan-Quattrock, J., 32
Brent, D., 224
Brewin, C. R., 156, 158
Brookman, C., 146, 147, 148, 177
Brooks-Gunn, J., 60
Brown, G., 8, 157
Brown, L., 101
Brumbach, R., 10, 28, 57
Brumley, H., 33
Buchanan, M., 10
Buchsbaum, Y., 99
Bunney, W., 6, 36
Burbach, D., 32, 76
Burke, P., 37, 202
Burland, S., 160, 166
Burlingham, D., 2
Burney, E., 32
Burroughs, J., 16
Burton, N., 3, 67
Buss, R., 140, 143
Butler, L., 165, 183, 184, 185
Brumbach, R. A., 170

Calderon, R., 202
Calpin, J., 144
Cantwell, D., 6, 11, 15, 16, 23, 26, 27, 28, 29, 31, 54, 58, 65, 85, 86, 109, 117, 170, 176, 202, 203
Carella, E., 109
Carey, M., 140, 142, 143
Carlson, G., 2, 7, 11, 15, 17, 18, 22, 23, 26, 27, 28, 29, 31, 55, 57, 58, 60, 61, 65, 70, 75, 77, 117, 175
Caro, J., 178
Caron, C., 33
Carpentieri, S., 107
Carstensen, L., 226
Carter, A., 148
Casat, C., 38
Cast, C., 12, 15
Catalan, J., 220, 221, 233
Cautela, J., 140, 141
Chadwick, O., 29

Chambers, W., 6, 22, 109
Chandler, C., 158
Chess, S., 2, 21, 69
Choquet, M., 223
Chrousos, R., 59
Cichetti, D., 6, 50, 53, 54
Cimbolic, P., 38
Ciminero, A., 176
Cincirpini, P., 144
Clarizio, H., 10, 11, 76, 136, 146, 152, 203
Clark, E., 144
Clark, G., 143, 145, 186
Clark, L., 15
Clarkson, S. E., 60
Clayton, P., 8
Coates, K., 154, 167, 183
Coates, T., 170
Cohen, D., 61, 137, 138
Cohen, P., 111
Cohen-Sandler, R., 96, 201, 202, 203, 204
Cohler, B., 178
Colbus, D., 90, 98, 99, 100, 120
Cole, D., 107, 223
Cole, E., 165
Cole, P., 167
Collingwood, T. R., 149
Compas, B., 60
Conger, J., 149
Cone, T., 10
Conners, C., 111, 121, 181
Conroy, R., 210, 225
Cools, J., 111
Coombs, D., 227
Cooper, T., 174
Corder, B., 215
Cordes, C., 62, 159
Costello, G., 2, 140
Coyne, J., 32, 33, 60, 156
Craighead, L., 88, 89
Craighead, W., 88, 89, 157
Crockett, L., 10, 67
Crook, T., 32, 75, 151, 157
Crouse-Novak, M., 8, 11, 12, 72, 76, 77
Cytryn, L., 100, 106, 175, 176, 209

Dabbagh, F., 205
Dahl, R., 38
Dahl, V., 61, 68
Damon, W., 114
Darcie, G., 113
Davenport, Y., 75
Davidson, F., 223, 226
Davidson, W., 62

Author Index

Davies, M., 22, 30, 32, 59, 66, 111, 174
Davison, K., 61
Delamater, A., 181
Delisle, J., 206
DeLong, G., 175
Depue, R., 18
deSaussure, R., 2
Dietz, S., 23, 25, 28, 171
DiGiuseppe, R., 136, 161
DiMascio, A., 75
Dobson, K., 12
Dodge, K., 32, 34
Dohrenwend, B., 117
Doleys, D., 176
Domfeld, L., 38
Dorn, L., 59
Douglas, R., 28
Downey, G., 32, 33, 60
Drye, R., 220
Duchnowski, A., 157
Durlak, J., 182, 183
Dush, D., 170
Dweck, C., 62, 157, 160

Eastgate, J., 70, 72
Eaves, L., 13
Ebata, A., 157
Edelbrock, C., 4, 29, 67, 203
Edelsohn, G., 10, 67
Edelstein, C., 38
Edwards, G., 88
Efron, A., 36
Eischens, R., 149
Eisen, S., 210
Eisenberg, L., 175, 176, 224
Eliot, J., 32, 75, 151, 157
Elkins, R., 183
Ellis, A., 160–164
Emery, G., 150
Emery, S., 164, 169, 176
Endicott, J., 22
Enna, B., 62
Esveldt-Dawson, K., 98, 99, 120, 122, 152
Evert, T., 119
Ey, S., 60

Facy, F., 223
Farrington, D., 204
Farris, J., 149
Fasman, J., 75
Fawzy, A., 38
Feeman, M., 58

Feinberg, T., 8, 11, 12
Feinstein, C., 106
Fendrich, M., 32, 33, 34
Ferster, C., 139
Fetner, H., 174
Fialkor, M., 143
Finch, A., 12, 15, 88
Fine, S., 97, 120, 122, 145
Finkelstein, R., 8, 11, 12, 72, 76, 77
Fisher, P., 111
Fishman, R., 61
Fleming, J., 30, 74
Forehand, R., 89
Forness, S., 26, 173, 176
Forth, A., 145
Fox, M., 34
Frame, D., 143
Frazier, R., 146, 147, 148
Frederick, C., 196, 199, 230
Freeman, L., 99
Freeman, R., 171
French, N., 66, 99, 121, 122, 125, 152
Freud, A., 2
Fried, J., 174
Friedlander, M., 109
Friedman, R., 165
Froese, A., 198
Frommer, C., 27
Fudge, H., 4, 75
Fuhrman, T., 182, 183

Gadow, K., 171, 176
Gaensbauer, R., 55
Gallant, D., 178
Garber, J., 2, 7, 23, 28, 96, 100, 121, 125, 140, 164, 169, 176
Garfinkel, B., 3, 9, 10, 12, 22, 38, 197, 198, 200, 204, 205, 210, 217, 219, 232, 234
Garland, A., 200, 224
Garmezy, N., 157
Garvin, V., 88, 90
Gatsonis, C., 3, 202
Geller, G., 174
Gershon, E., 36
Getz, W., 222
Ghareeb, G., 89
Gibbons, R., 99
Gilbert, M., 145
Gilbert, P. 159–169
Gilmore, L., 70, 72
Gilpin, D., 138

AUTHOR INDEX

Girgus, J., 60
Gittelman, R., 7
Glasberg, R., 57
Glasser, K., 209
Goldacre, M., 223
Goldston, D., 202
Golembek, H., 197, 204, 205, 210
Goodman, S., 33
Goodwin, F., 34, 35, 37, 177
Gordon, N., 30, 107
Gorman, B., 115
Gotlib, B., 109
Gotlib, I. H., 156
Gould, M., 226
Goulding, R., 220
Goulding, M., 220
Goyette, C., 121
Graham, D., 174
Graham, P., 29, 30, 111, 121
Graham, S., 52, 158
Grant, K., 60
Grapentine, W., 97, 98
Green, B., 88, 89
Green, J., 16, 58
Greenhill, L., 6
Grieger, R., 160
Griest, J., 149
Grinker, R., 138
Grob, M., 210
Grossman, J., 99
Grunebaum, H., 178
Gutkin, T., 161

Haider, I., 223
Haizlip, T., 215
Haldane, J., 223
Haley, G., 97, 120, 122, 145
Hall, B., 89, 108
Hammen, C., 32
Hammill, D., 101
Hanna, G., 36
Harrington, R., 4, 37, 75
Harris, A., 200
Harris, P., 157
Harris, T., 8
Hart, D., 114
Hassanein, R., 171
Hassanyeh, G., 61
Hassibi, M., 2, 21, 69
Hawkins, J., 203
Hawton, K., 198, 201, 203, 211, 212, 213, 216, 220, 221, 222, 223, 228, 233

Heath, A., 13
Hendren, R., 28
Herjanic, B., 70, 111
Hersbacker, P., 176
Hill, A., 4
Hill, J., 75
Hirschfeld, R., 202, 203, 205
Hirt, M., 170
Hoberman, H., 141, 142, 151, 167
Hodges, K., 100, 111
Holland, C., 113
Holmgren, S., 157
Honzik, M., 67
Hood, J., 198
Hops, H., 143, 145, 186
Horney, K., 138
Howell, C., 98, 121
Hudson, J., 38
Hughes, C., 171
Hughes, J., 89, 108, 113
Hunter, L., 232
Husain, A., 100
Husain, S., 198, 200

Ialongo, N., 10, 67
Igel, G., 36
Inamdar, S., 58
Izard, C., 55

Jackoway, M., 10, 28
Jacobson, E., 137
Jacobson, S., 75
Jamison, K., 75
Jarman, B., 148
Javors, M., 38
Jefferson, J., 175
Jenson, W., 144
Jobes, D., 204, 211, 226
Johnson, N., 28
Jones, R., 29
Jorm, A., 40
Joyce, M., 163

Kahn, J., 144
Kalter, N., 88
Kaminer, Y., 106
Kandel, D., 30, 59, 66
Kashani, J., 29, 55, 57, 60, 100, 124, 209
Kaslow, N., 110, 119, 150, 152, 154, 157, 166, 167, 168, 169, 182

Author Index

Kaufman, C., 178
Kazdin, A., 66, 85, 87, 90, 91, 93, 98, 99, 100, 104, 120, 121, 122, 123, 125, 143, 152, 167, 168
Keane, S., 149
Kehle, T., 144
Kellam, S., 10, 67
Kelley, A., 119
Kelley, M., 140, 142, 143, 175
Keltner, N., 170, 174, 175
Kendall, P., 12, 14, 96, 100, 121, 125
Kendler, K., 13
Kennedy, R., 59
Kessler, R., 13
Khuri, R., 224
King, J., 174
King, R., 96, 201, 203, 204
Kleem, S., 39
Klein, A., 210
Klein, D., 7, 17
Klein, M., 149
Klein, R., 13
Klinedinst, J., 95, 123
Kobasigawa, A., 113
Kochanska, G., 33
Koizumi, S., 89
Kornblith, S., 144
Kovacs, M., 3, 5, 8, 11, 17, 53, 61, 72, 76, 77, 88, 89, 90, 93, 100, 109, 111, 113, 116, 119, 132, 137, 150, 151, 175, 202
Krahenbuhl, V., 68
Krupnick, J., 33
Kuyler, P., 36

Lababidi, A., 29
Lachar, D., 95, 123
Laffer, P., 38
Lampert, C., 74
Lampman, C., 182, 183
Landau, S., 14
Lang, M., 90, 97, 122, 123, 124
Larson, D., 151
Laseg, H., 110
Last, C., 13
Laurant, J., 14
Leber, D., 88
LeCouteur, A., 37
Ledwidge, B., 169
Lee, J., 110
Leenaars, A., 11
Leeper, J., 227
Lefkowitz, M., 3, 10, 30, 60, 66, 67, 107, 108, 120, 121

Leigh, J., 100, 102
Leon, G., 96, 100, 121, 125
Leonard, M. A., 35
Lewinsohn, P., 117, 140, 141, 142, 143, 145, 151, 167, 186, 199
Lindner, K., 222
Ling, W., 23
Lipovsky, J., 12, 15
Little, V., 89, 108
Livingston, R., 152, 154
Lloyd-Kolkin, D., 232
Lo, E., 38
Lovell, M., 96
Lowe, T., 60
Lukens, E., 32
Lupatkin, W., 35

Maag, J., 26, 30, 173, 176
Maas, J., 38
MacDonald, H., 37
Macedo, C., 38
Magnussen, M., 32, 34
Malmquist, C., 26
Mardon, C., 198
Marriage, K., 97, 120, 122
Marsteller, F., 174
Martinez, P., 34
Marx, J., 6
Masters, J., 53
Matson, J., 143, 144
Mattson, A., 203
Mazza, J., 199, 203
McCarney, S., 100, 102
McCauley, E., 202
McConaughy, S., 86, 98, 121
McConville, B., 26, 27
McCoy, G., 11, 76, 146
McCracken, J., 36
McCrary, M., 35
McDonald, H., 37
McEnroc, M., 109
McFarlane, J., 67
McGee, R., 58, 60, 67, 74
McGowan, R., 148
McGuire, D., 202
McKenry, P., 199, 209
McKnew, D., Jr., 6, 33, 36, 60, 100, 106, 176, 209
McNeal, E., 38
Meehl, P., 210
Meekstroth, E., 205
Meichenbaum, D., 160, 166

AUTHOR INDEX

Mendelson, W., 28
Metz, C., 110
Mezzich, A., 120, 124
Mezzich, J., 120, 124
Miezitis, S., 165, 183, 184, 185
Miller, H., 227
Miller, J., 138
Miller, N., 161
Minde, K., 28
Mitchell, J., 202
Mizruchi, M., 201, 203, 211
Molling, P., 175
Mooney, K., 96
Moos, R., 32
Moretti, M., 97, 120, 122
Morrell, W., 74
Morris-Yates, A., 39, 97
Moses, T., 110
Motto, J., 213, 217
Munoz, R., 151
Munro, A., 75
Myers, K., 202
Myers, R., 222

Neale, M., 13
Nelson, B., 38
Nelson, S., 62
Nelson, W., 117
Nemeth, E., 28
Niemark, E., 163
Nolen-Hoeksema, S., 60
Nottelmann, E., 34
Novaco, R., 160
Novacenko, H., 38
Nunn, R., 138
Nunnally, J., 138
Nurcombe, B., 97, 98

Ofer, D., 197
Offord, D., 30, 74
Oftedal, G., 23
O'Grady, J., 223
Orbach, I., 199, 200
O'Reilly, P., 176
Osborn, M., 198, 203, 223
Orvaschel, H., 110, 113, 125
Osborn, M., 58
Oster, G., 178
Otto, U., 210

Padian, N., 125
Parker, G., 8

Parker, J., 89
Pataki, C., 175
Paulauskos, S., 3, 8, 11, 12, 72, 76, 77
Pearce, J., 60, 68, 170
Pederson, D., 148
Penick, E., 23, 25, 28, 171
Perel, J., 35
Perris, C., 75, 157
Perris, H., 157
Perry, D., 204
Peskin, J., 222
Petersen, A., 59, 60, 157, 159
Peterson, C., 156, 157, 169
Petrinack, R., 90
Petti, T., 87, 93, 99, 100, 103, 106, 122, 123, 170, 179, 180, 181
Pettiform, J., 204
Pfeffer, C., 196, 201, 203, 211, 216, 217, 219, 222
Phillips, D., 225, 226
Phillips, S., 10
Piacentini, J., 111
Pickles, A., 4, 75
Pitcher, S., 204
Platt, J., 152
Pliszka, S., 171, 175
Plowman, B., 204
Plutchik, R., 201, 203, 211
Pollack, M., 72, 76, 77
Politano, P., 117
Pope, H., 38
Powell, K., 38
Poznanski, E., 29, 32, 68, 69, 99
Prabucki, K., 110
Preodor, D., 61
Preskorn, S., 171
Price, R., 3, 11, 15
Printz, B., 152, 154
Puig-Antich, J., 4, 6, 22, 32, 35, 37, 38, 109, 110, 174
Purohit, A., 26

Quinton, D., 177
Quitkin, F., 7

Rabinovich, A., 174
Rabinovich, H., 38
Rabkin, B., 209
Radke-Yarrow, M., 34
Radloff, L., 91
Rapoport, J., 183
Rapport, M., 175

Author Index

Raskin, A., 32, 75, 151
Ray-Burne, R., 38
Reese, J., 10
Regier, D., 111
Rehm, L., 148, 150, 166, 168, 169
Reich, W., 111
Reiss, D., 34
Rey, J., 39, 97
Reynolds, C., 96, 117
Reynolds, W., 10, 30, 67, 87, 91, 92, 110, 119, 122, 154, 161, 167, 183, 199, 202, 203, 233
Richards, C., 3
Richman, J., 215, 216, 217
Rickard, K., 89
Rie, H. E., 152
Rifkin, D., 7
Rigali, J., 171
Rizley, R., 155
Robbins, D., 210, 225
Robins, E., 22
Robins, L., 3, 11, 15, 61, 68
Rodgers, A., 90, 100
Rogeness, G., 38
Rosen, A., 210
Rosenstock, M., 31
Rosenthal, P., 197
Rosenthal, S., 197
Ross, C., 230
Rothermel, R., 96
Rourke, B., 11
Rush, J., 150, 154
Rutman, J. M., 23, 25, 28, 171
Rutter, M., 4, 6, 7, 8, 29, 33, 37, 51, 55, 58, 62, 63, 75, 111, 177
Ryan, N., 38, 174

Sabshin, M., 138
Salkin, B., 16
Sargent, M., 205
Sarigiani, P., 59
Saylor, C., 88
Schloredt, K., 202
Schmidt, S., 74
Schneider-Rosen, K., 6, 50, 53, 54
Schonert, Reichl, A., 197
Schwab-Stone, M., 111
Schwartz, G., 55
Schwartz, R., 53, 114
Scioli, A., 97, 98
Scott, P., 60
Scott, W., 140, 143

Schroeder, H., 170
Schwartz, M., 176
Seagull, E., 10
Seat, P., 95, 123
Seese, L., 203
Seiden, R., 200
Seifer, R., 97, 98, 106
Seligman, M., 52, 60, 155, 156, 157, 159, 168
Selman, R., 51
Shaffer, D., 111, 196, 198, 203, 204, 205
Shaw, B., 150
Shaw, D., 140
Shekim, W., 100
Sherick, R., 98, 99, 120, 152
Shrout, P., 117
Shure, M., 152, 160
Siefker, C., 222
Silver, H., 39
Silverman, W., 109
Simmons, J., 113
Simonds, J., 29, 124, 209
Siomopoulus, G., 58
Skinner, B. F., 139
Slater, J., 18
Smith, K., 206
Smucker, M., 88, 89, 157
Solomon, G., 201, 203, 211
Sonis, W., 143
Spitz, R., 2, 55, 137
Spitzer, R., 22
Spivak, G., 152, 160
Sroufe, A., 51
Stansfield, S., 222
Stanton, H., 89, 108
Stanton, S., 89, 108
Stark, K., 14, 93, 110, 119, 146, 147, 148, 152, 154, 167, 177, 183
Staton, R. D., 170
Stemmler, M., 60
Stevens, L., 106
Strober, M., 22, 36, 37, 58, 70, 74, 99, 171
Sturzenberger, S., 16
Sullivan, L., 23, 25, 28, 171
Susman, E., 59
Swartz, J., 10, 224
Swets, J., 97

Tabrizi, M., 22
Tannebaum, R. L., 157
Taylor, E., 222
Teasdale, J., 52, 155, 157

Teri, L., 4, 58, 117
Tesiny, E., 10, 30, 60, 66, 107, 108, 120, 121
Tharinger, D., 93
Thomas, A., 2, 21, 69
Thorensen, C., 170
Tisher, M., 90, 97, 122, 123, 124
Tishler, C., 199, 209, 210
Tizard, J., 4
Todak, G., 32
Tolon, S., 205
Toolan, J. M., 138, 204
Torres, D., 174
Trabasso, T., 53, 114
Trad, P., 183
Tramontana, M., 97, 98
Trexler, L., 161
Triolo, S., 199, 209
Trotter, R., 156
Tsai, S., 152, 154
Tucker, S., 171
Tuma, J., 96
Turkington, C., 58, 60
Twiname, B., 220
Tyano, S., 110

Ulrich, R., 121
Unis, A., 66, 99, 121, 122, 125, 152

Vandiver, T., 198, 200
Vincenzi, H., 10
Von Knorring, L., 157
Vosk, B., 89

Wadeson, H., 138
Wahler, R., 87,
Wall, S., 51
Walton, L. A., 60
Ward, L., 109
Warner, V., 32, 33, 34
Waters, E., 51, 161
Watson, B., 10
Watson, D., 12, 15
Webb, J., 205

Weinberg, W., 10, 23, 24, 25, 28, 30, 36, 39, 57, 171
Weiner, A., 202, 203, 211
Weiner, B., 52, 158
Weinshank, A., 10
Weise, C., 175
Weiss, G., 28
Weissman, M., 3, 32, 33, 34, 125
Weller, E., 171
Weller, R., 171
Wells, J., 174
Welner, A., 35, 61
Welner, Z., 61, 111
Werry, J., 28, 99
Werthamer-Larsson, L., 10, 67
Wessman, A., 115
West, D., 204
White, H., 210
Whitmore, K., 4
Wickramaratne, P., 32, 33, 34
Wierzbicki, M., 35
Wilkes, T., 154
Wilkins, J., 198
Willett, L., 149
Williams, J., 159, 169
Williams, S., 58, 60, 74
Williamson, D., 38
Wilson, A., 51
Wilson, H., 170
Wilson, L., 10
Wippman, J., 51
Wirt, R., 95, 123
Wolf, J., 10
Wolf, K., 137
Wolpert, E., 61
Worchel, F., 89, 108
Wright, F., 102
Wright-Strowederman, C., 10

Young, G., 11
Yule, W., 29

Zahn-Waxler, C., 33
Zeitlin, H., 68, 77
Zigler, E., 200, 224
Zoccolillo, M., 3, 11, 12, 15
Zrull, J., 29, 32, 687